THE MUSKERRY BOOK
OF HUNTING FICTION

THE MUSKERRY BOOK OF HUNTING FICTION

edited by
STEPHEN MAHONY

The Muskerry Hunt Club
1992

*FOR
LUCINDA*

ISBN 0 9519563 0 2
Preface and Selection © Stephen Mahony 1992
First published 1992

CONTENTS

PREFACE vii
SQUIRE WESTERN
Tom Jones (1749) Henry Fielding 1
HUNTING AT CHARLIE'S HOPE
Guy Mannering (1815) Sir Walter Scott 4
THE HUNT
Charles O'Malley, the Irish Dragoon (1840) Charles Lever 8
MR JORROCKS
Handley Cross (1843) R. S. Surtees 21
MR JORROCKS'S ORATION
Handley Cross (1843) R. S. Surtees 24
THE CAT AND CUSTARD POT DAY
Handley Cross (1843) R. S. Surtees 27
WRITING UP A HUNT
Mr Sponge's Sporting Tour (1853) R. S. Surtees 39
THE O'CONORS OF CASTLE CONOR
Tales of All Countries (1860) Anthony Trollope 46
MR JOB SLOPER
Market Harborough (1861) G. J. Whyte-Melville 61
THE DREAM OF AN OLD MELTONIAN (1864)
W. Davenport Bromley 68
LAURA HUNTINGCROP
Sketches in the Hunting Field (1880) Alfred E. T. Watson 71
PHILIPPA'S FOXHUNT
Some Experiences of an Irish RM (1890) E. Œ. Somerville and Martin Ross 79
THE POLICY OF THE CLOSED DOOR
Some Experiences of an Irish RM (1890) E. Œ. Somervile and Martin Ross 92
WARE HOLES (1898)
Sir Arthur Conan Doyle 103
HOW THE BRIGADIER SLEW THE FOX
Adventures of Gerard (1903) Sir Arthur Conan Doyle 105
THE FOX MEDITATES
Rudyard Kipling 116
THE BAG
Reginald in Russia (1910) 'Saki' (H. H. Munro) 118
MY FIRST DAY'S FOX-HUNTING
Memoirs of a Fox-hunting Man (1928) Siegfried Sassoon 122

CUBBING
Memoirs of a Fox-hunting Man (1928) Siegfried Sassoon 129
A HUNTING DAY
Foxiana (1929) Isaac Bell, MFH 131
MEDITATIONS OF MR BLOWHARD
Foxiana (1929) Isaac Bell, MFH 134
THE COCK-AND-PYE DAY
The Hawbucks (1929) John Masefield 138
THE RECTOR OF ST TIMOTHY'S
The Silver Horn (1934) Gordon Grand 149
THE MISTER
Sherston's Progress (1936) Siegfried Sassoon 157
LITTLE FUNKS
The Rising Tide (1937) M. J. Farrell (Molly Keane) 172
HOLIDAYS AT ALCONLEIGH
The Pursuit of Love (1945) Nancy Mitford 177
RUFUS
Wild Lone (1947) Denys Watkins-Pitchford 179
OUT WITH THE COOLMORE HARRIERS'
(1950) Major E. J. Tonson Rye 187
THE HUNT TO SLIEVEMORE
A Long Way to Go (1952) Marigold Armitage 191

LIST OF SUBSCRIBERS 213
ACKNOWLEDGEMENTS 218

PREFACE

This book is being published to celebrate the two hundred and fiftieth anniversary of the Muskerry Hunt in Ireland.

The Muskerry foxhounds were started by John Rye of Rye Court near the village of Farnanes in the west part of County Cork. The blue of the hunt collar is said to have been the favourite colour of his wife and it is the colour of the dress in which Mrs Rye sat for her portrait.

John Rye hunted hounds until 1758. A memorandum giving the breeding of the puppies sent out to walk in 1755 records that Venus had a litter by Bounder and that one of the puppies a 'tanned dog with white ring round its neck' was 'sent to the Priests' which suggests a measure of good humored toleration despite the Penal Laws.

John Rye was followed in the mastership by his son and great-grandson, and today, after several changes, the kennels are back at Rye Court. While this is not the place to write the history of the hunt, its character may be illustrated by two stories.

Among the leading figures of the hunt in the nineteenth century were the nine Hawkes brothers, sons of Mr Samuel Hawkes of Hawkemount who was Master from 1797 to 1815. A Mr John Courtenay wrote a challenge to *Bell's Life*, the leading sporting periodical of the day, offering to back the nine hard-riding Hawkes brothers for £1,000 against any nine brothers in the world, to ride their own horses over four miles of country. The prudent Mr Courtenay's challenge was never taken up.

A Victorian Master, Sir Augustus Warren (1866–7), had a huntsman named Coady who trained his hounds to open on reaching an earth regardless of whether the fox had gone in or not. One day Coady dismounted and made his way into a thick piece of gorse, with his hounds giving tongue, where a fox was supposed to have gone. After a long interval Sir Augustus, tired of waiting, pushed his way in to discover Coady sitting down eating his lunch with the hounds baying around him.

Hunting in Ireland has left a vivid impression on many people. Siegfried Sassoon wrote of the Muskerry country 'I thought what a haunted ancient sort of land it was. It seemed to go deep into my heart while I looked at it.' Anthony Trollope learnt to hunt in Ireland and afterwards said that he never allowed the writing of novels to stand in the way of hunting. His story 'The O'Conors of Castle Conor' is based on an adventure of his own in Ireland.

This anthology has not been chosen just from Irish hunting fiction but from a wider range of writing so as to include characters as different as Jorrocks and Brigadier Gerard.

Surtees said 'A book can last a hunting man a long time'. This book has been made with that in mind.

SQUIRE WESTERN

Tom Jones
Henry Fielding
1749

The reader may be pleased to remember that the said squire departed from the inn in great fury, and in that fury he pursued his daughter. The ostler having informed him that she had crossed the Severn, he likewise passed that river with his equipage, and rode full speed, vowing the utmost vengeance against poor Sophia, if he should but overtake her.

He had not gone far before he arrived at a cross-way. Here he called a short council of war, in which, after hearing different opinions, he at last gave the direction of his pursuit to Fortune, and struck directly into the Worcester road.

In this road he proceeded about two miles, when he began to bemoan himself most bitterly, frequently crying out, 'What a pity it is! Sure never was so unlucky a dog as myself!' And then burst forth a volley of oaths and execrations.

The parson attempted to adminster comfort to him on this occasion. 'Sorrow not, sir,' says he, 'like those without hope. Howbeit we have not yet been able to overtake young madam, we may account it some good fortune that we have hitherto traced her course aright. Peradventure she will soon be fatigued with her journey, and will tarry in some inn, in order to renovate her corporeal functions; and in that case, in all moral certainty, you will very briefly be "compos voti."'

'Pogh! d—n the slut!' answered the squire, 'I am lamenting the loss of so fine a morning for hunting. It is confounded hard to lose one of the best scenting days, in all appearance, which hath been this season, and especially after so long a frost.'

Whether Fortune, who now and then shows some compassion in her wantonest tricks, might not take pity of the squire, and, as she had determined not to let him overtake his daughter, might not resolve to make him amends some other way, I will not assert; but he had hardly uttered the words just before commemorated, and two or three oaths at their heels, when a pack of hounds began to open their melodious throats at a small distance from them, which the squire's horse and his rider both perceiving, both immediately pricked up their ears, and the squire, crying, 'She's gone, she's gone! Damn me if she is not gone!' instantly clapped spurs to the beast, who little needed it, having indeed the same inclination with his master; and now the whole company, crossing into a corn-field, rode directly towards the hounds, with much hallooing and whooping, while the poor parson, blessing himself, brought up the rear. ... The hounds ran very hard, as it is called, and the squire pursued over hedge and ditch, with all his usual vociferation and alacrity, and with all his usual pleasure; nor did the thoughts of Sophia ever once intrude themselves to allay the satisfaction he enjoyed in the chase, and which he said was one of the finest he ever saw, and which he swore was very well worth going fifty miles for. As the squire forgot his daughter, the servants, we may easily believe, forgot their mistress; and the parson, after having expressed much astonishment, in Latin, to himself, at length likewise abandoned all further thoughts of the young lady, and, jogging on at a distance behind, began to meditate a portion of doctrine for the ensuing Sunday.

The squire who owned the hounds was highly pleased with the arrival of his brother squire and sportsman; for all men approve merit in their own way, and no man was more expert in the field than Mr Western, nor did any other better know how to encourage the dogs with his voice, and to animate the hunt with his halloa.

Sportsmen, in the warmth of a chase, are too much engaged to attend to any manner of ceremony, nay even to the offices of humanity; for if any of them meet with an accident by tumbling into a ditch or into a river, the rest pass on regardless, and generally leave him to his fate. During this time, therefore, the two squires, though often close to each other, interchanged not a single word. The master of the hunt, however, often saw and approved the great judgment of the stranger in drawing the dogs when they were at a fault, and hence conceived a very high opinion of his understanding, as the number of his attendants inspired no small reverence to his quality. As soon, therefore, as the sport was ended by the death of the little animal which had occasioned it, the two squires met, and in all squire-like greeting saluted each other.

The conversation was entertaining enough, and what we may perhaps relate in an appendix or on some other occasion; but as it nowise concerns this history, we cannot prevail on ourselves to give it a place here. It concluded with a second chase, and that with an invitation to dinner. This being accepted, was followed by a hearty bout of drinking, which ended in as hearty a nap on the part of Squire Western.

Our squire was by no means a match either for his host or for Parson Supple at his cups that evening; for which the violent fatigue of mind as well as body that he had undergone may very well account, without the least derogation from his honour. He was indeed, according to the vulgar phrase, whistle-drunk; for before he had swallowed the third bottle he became so entirely overpowered, that though he was not carried off to bed till long after, the parson considered him as absent; and having acquainted the other squire with all relating to Sophia, he obtained his promise of seconding those arguments which he intended to urge the next morning for Mr Western's return.

No sooner, therefore, had the good squire shaken off his evening and began to call for his morning draught, and to summon his horses in order to renew his pursuit, than Mr Supple began his dissuasives, which the host so strongly seconded, that they at length prevailed, and Mr Western agreed to return home; being principally moved by one argument, viz that he knew not which way to go, and might probably be riding farther from his daughter instead of towards her. He then took leave of his brother sportsmen, and expressing great joy that the frost had broken (which might perhaps be no small motive to his hastening home), set forwards, or rather backwards, for Somersetshire; but not before he had first despatched part of his retinue in quest of his daughter, after whom he likewise sent a volley of the most bitter execrations which he could invent.

HUNTING AT CHARLIE'S HOPE

Guy Mannering
Sir Walter Scott
1815

Brown rose early in the morning and walked out to look at the establishment of his new friend. All was rough and neglected in the neighbourhood of the house;—a paltry garden, no pains taken to make the vicinity dry or comfortable, and a total absence of all those little neatnesses which give the eye so much pleasure in looking at an English farm-house. There were, notwithstanding, evident signs that this arose only from want of taste or ignorance, not from poverty or the negligence which attends it. On the contrary, a noble cow-house, well filled with good milk-cows, a feeding-house, with ten bullocks of the most approved breed, a stable, with two good teams of horses, the appearance of domestics active, industrious, and apparently contented with their lot; in a word, an air of liberal though sluttish plenty indicated the wealthy farmer. The situation of the house above the river formed a gentle declivity, which relieve the inhabitants of the nuisances that might otherwise have stagnated around it. At a little distance was the whole band of children playing and building houses with peats around a huge doddered oak-tree, which was called Charlie's Bush, from some tradition respecting an old freebooter who had once inhabited the spot. Between the farm-house and the hill-pasture was a deep morass, termed in that country a slack; it had once been the defence of a fortalice, of which no vestiges now remained, but which was said to have been inhabited by the same doughty hero we have now alluded to. Brown endeavoured to make some acquaintance with the children, but 'the rogues fled from him like quick-silver,' though the two eldest stood peeping when they had got to some distance. The traveller then turned his course towards the hill, crossing the foresaid swamp by a range of stepping-stones, neither the broadest nor steadiest that could be imagined. He had not climbed far up the hill when he met a man descending.

He soon recognised his worthy host, though a 'maud,' as it is called, or a grey shepherd's plaid, supplied his travelling jockey-coat, and a cap, faced with wild-cat's fur, more commodiously covered his bandaged head than a hat would have done. As he appeared through the morning mist, Brown, accustomed to judge of men by their thewes and sinews, could not help admiring his height, the breadth of his shoulders, and the steady firmness of his step. Dinmont internally paid the same compliment to Brown, whose athletic form he now perused somewhat more at leisure than he had done formerly. After the usual greetings of the morning, the guest inquired whether his host found any inconvenient consequences from the last night's affray.

'I had maist forgotten't,' said the hardy Borderer; 'but I think this morning, now that I am fresh and sober, if you and I were at the Withershins' Latch, wi' ilka ane a gude oak souple in his hand, we wadna turn back, no for half a dizzen o' yon scaff-raff.'

'But are you prudent, my good sir,' said Brown, 'not to take an hour or two's repose after receiving such severe contusions?'

'Confusions!' replied the farmer, laughing in derision. 'Lord, Captain, naething confuses my head. I ance jumped up and laid the dogs on the fox after I had tumbled from the tap o' Christenbury Craig, and that might have confused me to purpose. Na, naething confuses me, unless it be a screed o' drink at an orra time. Besides, I behooved to be round the hirsel this morning and see how the herds were coming on; they're apt to be negligent wi' their footballs, and fairs, and trysts, when ane's away. And there I met wi' Tam o'Todshaw, and a wheen o' the rest o' the billies on the water side; they're a' for a fox-hunt this morning,—ye'll gang? I'll gie ye Dumple, and take the brood mare mysell.'

'But I fear I must leave you this morning, Mr Dinmont,' replied Brown.

'The fient a bit o' that,' exclaimed the Borderer. 'I'll no part wi' ye at ony rate for a fortnight mair. Na, na; we dinna meet sic friends as you on a Bewcastle moss every night.'

Brown had not designed his journey should be a speedy one; he therefore readily compounded with this hearty invitation by agreeing to pass a week at Charlie's Hope.

On their return to the house, where the goodwife presided over an ample breakfast, she heard news of the proposed fox-hunt, not indeed with approbation, but without alarm or surprise. 'Dand! ye're the auld man yet; naething will make ye take warning till ye're brought hame some day wi' your feet foremost.'

'Tut, lass!' answered Dandie, 'ye ken yoursell I am never a prin the waur o' my rambles.'

So saying, he exhorted Brown to be hasty in despatching his breakfast, as, 'the frost having given way, the scent would lie this morning primely.'

Out they sallied accordingly for Otterscope Scaurs, the farmer leading the way. They soon quitted the little valley, and involved themselves among hills as steep as they could be without being precipitous. The sides often presented gullies, down which, in the winter season, or after heavy rain, the torrents descended with great fury. Some dappled mists still floated along the peaks of the hills, the remains of the morning clouds, for the frost had broken up with a smart shower. Through these fleecy screens were seen a hundred little temporary streamlets, or rills, descending the sides of the mountains like silver threads. By small sheep-tracks along these steeps, over which Dinmont trotted with the most fearless confidence, they at length drew near the scene of sport, and began to see other men, both on horse and foot, making toward the place of rendezvous. Brown was puzzling himself to conceive how a fox-chase could take place among hills, where it was barely possible for a pony, accustomed to the ground, to trot along, but where, quitting the track for half a yard's breadth, the rider might be either bogged or precipitated down the bank. This wonder was not diminished when he came to the place of action.

They had gradually ascended very high, and now found themselves on a mountain-ridge, overhanging a glen of great depth, but extremely narrow. Here the sportsmen had collected, with an apparatus which would have shocked a member of the Pytchley Hunt; for, the object being the removal of a noxious and destructive animal, as well as the pleasures of the chase, poor Reynard was allowed much less fair play than when pursued in form through an open country. The strength of his habitation, however, and the nature of the ground by which it was surrounded on all sides, supplied what was wanting in the courtesy of his pursuers. The sides of the glen were broken banks of earth and rocks of rotten stone, which sunk sheer down to the little winding stream below, affording here and there a tuft of scathed brushwood or a patch of furze. Along the edges of this ravine, which, as we have said, was very narrow, but of profound depth, the hunters on horse and foot ranged themselves; almost every farmer had with him at least a brace of large and fierce greyhounds, of the race of those deer-dogs which were formerly used in that country, but greatly lessened in size from being crossed with the common breed. The huntsman, a sort of provincial officer of the district, who receives a certain supply of meal, and a reward for every fox he destroys, was already at the bottom of the dell, whose echoes thundered to the chiding of two or three brace of fox-hounds. Terriers, including the whole generation of Pepper and Mustard, were also in attendance, having been sent forward under the care of a shepherd. Mongrel, whelp, and cur of low degree filled up the burden of the chorus. The spectators on the brink of the ravine, or glen, held their greyhounds in leash in readiness to slip them at the fox as soon as the activity of the party below should force him to abandon his cover.

The scene, though uncouth to the eye of a professed sportsman, had something in it wildly captivating. The shifting figures on the mountain ridge, having the sky for their background, appeared to move in the air. The dogs, impatient of their restraint, and maddened with the baying beneath, sprung here and there, and strained at the slips, which prevented them from joining their companions. Looking down, the view was equally striking. The thin mists were not totally dispersed in the glen, so that it was often through their gauzy medium that the eye strove to discover the motions of the hunters below. Sometimes a breath of wind made the scene visible, the blue rill glittering as it twined itself through its rude and solitary dell. They then could see the shepherds springing with fearless activity from one dangerous point to another, and cheering the dogs on the scent, the whole so diminished by depth and distance that they looked like pigmies. Again the mists close over them, and the only signs of their continued exertions are the halloos of the men and the clamours of the hounds, ascending as it were out of the bowels of the earth. When the fox, thus persecuted from one stronghold to another, was at length obliged to abandon his valley, and to break away for a more distant retreat, those who watched his motions from the top slipped their greyhounds, which, excelling the fox in swiftness, and equalling him in ferocity and spirit, soon brought the plunderer to his life's end.

In this way, without any attention to the ordinary rules and decorums of sport, but appparently as much to the gratification both of bipeds and quadrupeds as if all due ritual had been followed, four foxes were killed on this active morning; and even Brown himself, though he had seen the princely sports of India, and ridden a-tiger-hunting upon an elephant with the Nabob of Arcot, professed to have received an excellent morning's amusement. When the sport was given up for the day, most of the sportsmen, according to the established hospitality of the country, went to dine at Charlie's Hope.

THE HUNT

Charles O'Malley, The Irish Dragoon
Charles Lever
1840

It was upon a clear frosty morning, when a bright blue sky and a sharp but bracing air seem to exercise upon the feelings a sense no less pleasurable than the balmiest breeze and warmest sun of summer, that I whipped my leader short round, and entered the precincts of 'Gurt-na-Morra.' As I proceeded along the avenue, I was struck by the slight traces of repairs here and there evident; a gate or two that formerly had been parallel to the horizon, had been raised to the perpendicular; some ineffectual efforts at paint were also perceptible upon the palings, and, in short, every thing seemed to have undergone a kind of attempt at improvement.

When I reached the door, instead of being surrounded, as of old, by a tribe of menials frieze-coated, bare-headed, and bare-legged, my presence was announced by a tremendous ringing of bells, from the hands of an old functionary, in a very formidable livery, who peeped at me through the hall-window, and whom, with the greatest difficulty, I recognised as my quondam acquaintance, the butler. His wig alone would have graced a king's counsel, and the high collar of his coat, and the stiff pillory of his cravat, denoted an eternal adieu to so humble a vocation as drawing a cork. Before I had time for any conjecture as to the altered circumstances about, the activity of my friend at the bell had surrounded me with 'four others worse than himself,' at least, they were exactly similarly attired; and, probably, from the novelty of their costume, and the restraints of so unusual a thing as dress, were as perfectly unable to assist themselves or others, as the Court of Aldermen would be, were they to rig out in plate armour of the fourteenth century. How much longer I might have gone on conjecturing the reasons for the masquerade around, I cannot say; but my servant, an Irish disciple of my uncle's, whispered in my ear—'It's a red breeches day, Master Charles—they'll have the hoith of company in the house.' From the phrase, it needed little explanation to inform me, *that it was* one of the occasions on which Mr Blake attired all the hangers-on of his house in livery, and that great preparations were in progress for a more than usually splendid reception.

In the next moment I was ushered into the breakfast-room, where a party of above a dozen persons were most gaily enjoying all the good cheer for which the house had a well-deserved repute. After the usual shaking of hands, and hearty greetings were over, I was introduced in all form to Sir George Dashwood, a tall, and singularly handsome man of about fifty, with an undress military frock and ribbon. His reception of me was somewhat strange, for, as they mentioned my relationship to Godfrey O'Malley, he smiled lightly and whispered something to Mr Blake, who replied—'Oh! no, no, not the least, a mere boy—and, besides,'—what he added I lost, for at that moment Nora Blake was presenting me to Miss Dashwood.

If the sweetest blue eyes that ever beamed beneath a forehead of snowy whiteness, over which dark brown and waving hair fell, less in curls than masses of locky richness, could only have known what wild work they were making of my poor heart, Miss Dashwood, I trust, would have looked at her tea-cup or her muffin, rather than at me, as she actually did on that fatal morning. If I were to judge from her costume, she had only just arrived, and the morning air had left upon her cheek a bloom, that contributed greatly to the effect of her lovely countenance. Although very young, her form had all the roundness of womanhood; while her gay and sprightly manner indicated all the *sans géne*, which only very young girls possess, and which, when tempered with perfect good taste and accompanied by beauty and no small share of talent, form an irresistible power of attraction.

Beside her sat a tall handsome man of about five-and-thirty or perhaps forty years of age, with a most soldierly air, who, as I was presented to him, scarcely turned his head, and gave me a half-nod of very unequivocal coldness. There are moments in life, in which the heart is, as it were, laid bare to any chance or casual impression, with a wondrous sensibility of pleasure, or its opposite. This to me was one of those; and, as I turned from the lovely girl, who had received me with a marked courtesy, to the cold air, and repelling *hateur* of the dark-browed Captain, the blood rushed throbbing to my forehead; and, as I walked to my place at the table, I eagerly sought his eye, to return him a look of defiance and disdain, proud and contemptuous as his own. Captain Hammersley, however, never took further notice of me, but continued to recount, for the amusement of those about, several excellent stories of his military career, which, I confess, were heard with every test of delight by all, save me. One thing galled me particularly—and how easy is it, when you have begun by disliking a person, to supply food for your antipathy—all his allusions to his military life were coupled with half-hinted and ill-concealed sneers at civilians of every kind, as though every man not a soldier were absolutely unfit for common intercourse with the world—still more, for any favourable reception in ladies' society.

The young ladies of the family were a well-chosen auditory, for their admiration of the army extended from the Life Guards to the Veteran Battalion, the Sappers and Miners included; and, as Miss Dashwood was the daughter of a soldier, she, of course, coincided in many, if not all his opinions. I turned towards my neighbour, a Clare gentleman, and tried to engage him in conversation, but he was breathlessly attending to the Captain. On my left, sat Matthew Blake, whose eyes were firmly rivetted upon the same person, and heard his marvels with an interest scarcely inferior to that of his sisters. Annoyed, and in ill-temper, I eat my breakfast in silence, and resolved that, the first moment I could obtain a hearing from Mr Blake, I should open my negociation, and take my leave at once of 'Gurt-na-Morra.'

We all assembled in a large room, called, by courtesy, the library, when breakfast was over; and then it was that Mr Blake taking me aside, whispered, 'Charley, it's right I should inform you that Sir George Dashwood there is the Commander of the forces, and is come down here at this moment to—.' What for, or how it should concern me, I was not to learn; for at that critical instant, my informant's attention was called off by Captain Hammersly asking, if the hounds were to hunt that day.

'My friend Charley, here, is the best authority upon that matter,' said Mr Blake, turning towards me.

'They are to try the Priest's meadows,' said I, with an air of some importance; 'but, if your guests desire a day's sport, I'll send word over to Brackley to bring the dogs over here, and we are sure to find a fox in your cover.'

'Oh, then, by all means,' said the Captain, turning towards Mr Blake, and addressing himself to him—'by all means, and Miss Dashwood, I'm sure, would like to see the hounds throw off.'

Whatever chagrin the first part of his speech caused me, the latter set my heart a throbbing; and I hastened from the room to despatch a messenger to the huntsman, to come over to Gurt-na-Morre, and also, another to O'Malley Castle, to bring my best horse and my riding equipments, as quickly as possible.

'Matthew, who is this Captain?' said I, as young Blake met me in the hall.

'Oh! he is the aide-de-camp of General Dashwood. A nice fellow, isn't he?'

'I don't know what you may think,' said I, 'but I take him for the most impertinent, impudent, supercilious—'

'The rest of my civil speech was cut short by the appearance of the very individual in question, who with his hands in his pockets, and a cigar in his mouth, sauntered forth down the steps, taking no more notice of Matthew Blake and myself, than the two fox terriers that followed at his heels.

However anxious I might be to open negociations on the subject of my mission, for the present the thing was impossible; for I found that Sir George Dashwood was closeted closely with Mr Blake, and resolved to wait till evening, when chance might afford me the opportunity I desired.

As the ladies had entered to dress for the hunt, and, as I felt no peculiar desire to ally myself with the unsocial Captain, I accompanied Matthew to the stable to look after the cattle and make preparations for the coming sport.

'There's Captain Hammersly's horse,' said Matthew, as he pointed out a highly bred but powerful English hunter: 'she came last night, for, as he expected some sport he sent his horses from Dublin on purpose. The other will be here to-day.'

'What is his regiment:' said I, with an appearance of carelessness, but in reality feeling curious to know if the captain was a cavalry or infantry officer.

'The —th Light Dragoons,' said Matthew.

'You never saw him ride?' said I.

'Never; but his groom there says he leads the way in his own country.'

'And where may that be?'

'In Leicestershire, no less,' said Matthew.

'Does he know Galway?'

'Never was in it before; it's only this minute he asked Mosey Daly if the ox-fences were high here.'

'Ox-fences! then he does not know what a wall is.'

'Devil a bit; but we'll teach him.'

'That we will,' said I, with as bitter a resolution to impart the instruction, as ever schoolmaster did to whip Latin grammar into one of the great unbreeched.'

'But I had better send the horses down to the Mill,' said Matthew; 'we'll draw that cover first.'

So saying, he turned towards the stable, while I sauntered alone towards the road, by which I expected the huntsman. I had not walked half-a-mile before I heard the yelping of the dogs, and, a little farther on, I saw old Brackely coming along at a brisk trot, cutting the hounds on each side, and calling after the stragglers.

'Did you see my horse on the road, Brackely?' said I.

'I did, Misther Charles, and troth I'm sorry to see him; sure yerself knows better than to take out the Badger, the best steeple-chaser in Ireland, in such a country as this; nothing but awkward stone-fences, and not a foot of sure ground in the whole of it.'

'I know it well Brackely; but I have my reasons for it.'

'Well, maybe you have; what cover will your honour try first?'

'They talk of the Mill,' said I, 'but I'd much rather try 'Morran-a-Gowl.'

'Morran-a-Gowl! do you want to break your neck entirely?'

'No Brackely, not mine.'

'Whose then, alannah?'

'An English Captain's, the devil fly away with him; he's come down here to-day, and from all I can see is a most impudent fellow; so Brackely—.'

'I understand; well, leave it to me, and, though I don't like the ould deer-park wall on the hill, we'll try it this morning with the blessing; I'll take him down by Woodford, over the 'Devil's Mouth,'—it's eighteen feet wide this minute with the late rains; into the four callows, then over the stone walls, down to Dangan; then take a short cast up the hill, blow him a bit, and give him the park wall at the top. You must come in then fresh, and give him the whole run home over Sleibhmich—the Badger knows it all—and takes the road always in a fly; a mighty distressing thing for the horse that follows, more particularly if he does not understand a stony country. Well, if he lives through this, give him the sunk fence and the stone wall at Mr Blake's clover-field, for the hounds will run into the fox about there; and though we never ride that leap since Mr Malone broke his neck at it, last October, yet, upon an occasion like this, and for the honour of Galway—.'

'To be sure, Brackely, and here's a guinea for you, and now trot on towards the house, they must not see us together, or they might suspect something. But, Brackely,' said I calling out after him, 'if he rides at all fair, what's to be done?'

'Troth then myself doesn't know; there is nothing so bad west of Athlone; have ye a great spite again him?'

'I have,' said I fiercely.

'Could ye coax a fight out of him.'

'That's true,' said I, 'and now ride on as fast as you can.'

Brackely's last words imparted a lightness to my heart and my step, and I strode along a very different man from what I had left the house half an hour previously.

Although we had not the advantages of a 'southerly wind and clouded sky,' the day, towards noon, became strongly overcast, and promised to afford us good scenting weather, and as we assembled at the meet, mutual congratulations were exchanged upon the improved appearance of the day. Young Blake had provided Miss Dashwood with a quiet and well-trained horse, and his sisters were all mounted, as usual, upon their own animals, giving to our turn-out quite a gay and lively aspect. I myself came to cover upon a hackney, having sent Badger with a groom, and longed ardently for the moment when, casting the skin of my great-coat and overalls, I should appear before the world in my well-appointed 'cords and tops.' Captain Hammersly had not as yet made his appearance, and many conjectures were afloat as to whether 'he might have missed the road or changed his mind,' or forgot all about it, as Miss Dashwood hinted.

'Why, pray, pitched upon this cover?' said Caroline Blake, as she looked with a practised eye over the country, on either side.

'There is no chance of a fox, later in the day, at the mills,' said the huntsman, inventing a lie for the occasion.

'Then of course you never intend us to see much of the sport, for after you break cover, you are entirely lost to us.'

'I thought you always followed the hounds,' said Miss Dashwood, timidly.

'Oh, to be sure we do, in any common country; but here it is out of the question—the fences are too large for any one, and, if I am not mistaken, these gentlemen will not ride far over this; there, look yonder, where the river is rushing down the hill—that stream widening as it advances, crosses the cover nearly mid-way; well, they must clear that, and then you may see these walls of large loose stones, nearly five feet in height; that is the usual course the fox takes, unless he heads towards the hills, and goes towards Dangan, and then there's an end of it; for the deer park wall is usually a pull up to every one except, perhaps, to our friend Charley there, who has tried his fortune against drowning more than once there.'

'Look, here he comes,' said Matthew Blake, 'and looking splendidly too—a little too much in flesh, perhaps, if any thing.'

'Captain Hammersly!' said the four Miss Blakes in a breath, 'where is he?'

'No, it's the Badger I'm speaking of,' said Matthew laughing, and pointing with his finger towards a corner of the field where my servant was leisurely throwing down a wall about two feet high to let him pass.

'Oh, how handsome—what a charger for a dragoon,' said Miss Dashwood.

Any other mode of praising my steed, would have been much more acceptable. The word dragoon was a thorn in my tenderest part that rankled and lacerated at every stir. In a moment I was in the saddle, and scarely seated when at once all the *mauvaise honte* of boyhood left me, and I felt every inch a man. I often look back to that moment of my life, and, comparing it with many similar ones, cannot help acknowledging how purely is the self-possession which so often wins success, the result of some slight and trivial association. My confidence in my horsemanship suggested moral courage of a very different kind, and I felt that Charles O'Malley curveting upon a thorough-bred and the same man ambling upon a shelty were two and very dissimilar individuals.

'No chance of the Captain,' said Matthew, who had returned from a *reconnaissance* upon the road, 'and after all it's a pity, for the day is getting quite favourable.'

While the young ladies formed picquets to look out for the gallant *militaire*, I seized the opportunity of prosecuting my acquaintance with Miss Dashwood; and, even in the few and passing observations that fell from her, learned how very different an order of being she was from all I had hitherto seen of country belles. A mixture of courtesy with *naïveté*—a wish to please, with a certain feminine gentleness, that always flatters a man, and still more a boy that fain would be one—gained momentarily more and more upon me, and put me also on my mettle to prove to my fair companion that I was not altogether a mere uncultivated and unthinking creature like the remainder of those about me.

'Here he is, at last,' said Helen Blake, as she cantered across a field, waiving her handkerchief as a signal to the Captain, who was now seen approaching at a brisk trot.

As he came along, a small fence intervened; he pressed his horse a little, and, as he kissed hands to the fair Helen, cleared it in a bound, and was in an instant in the midst of us.

'He sits his horse like a man, Misther Charles,' said the old huntsman; 'troth we must give him the worst bit of it.'

Captain Hammersly, was, despite all the critical acumen with which I canvassed him, the very *beau idéal* of a gentleman rider; indeed although a very heavy man, his powerful English thorough-bred, showing not less bone than blood, took away all semblance of over weight; his saddle, well fitting and well placed; his large and broad-reined snaffle; his own costume of black coat, leathers, and tops, was in perfect keeping, and even to his heavy handled hunting-whip, I could find nothing to cavil at. As he rode up he paid his respects to the ladies, in his usual free and easy manner, expressed some surprise, but no regret, at hearing that he was late, and never deigning any notice of Matthew or myself, took his place beside Miss Dashwood, with whom he conversed in a low undertone.

'There they go,' said Matthew, as five or six dogs, with their heads up, ran yelping along a furrow, then stopped, howled again, and once more set off together. In an instant all was commotion in the little valley below us. The huntsman, with his hand to his mouth, was calling off the stragglers, and the whipper-in following up the leading dogs with the rest of the pack. 'They're found!—they're away!' said Matthew; and, as he spoke, a great yell burst from the valley, and in an instant the whole pack were off at speed. Rather more intent that moment upon showing off my horsmanship than anything else, I dashed spurs into Badger's sides, and turned him towards a rasping ditch before me; over we went, hurling down behind us a rotten bank of clay and small stones, showing how little safety there had been in topping instead of clearing it at a bound. Before I was well seated again, the Captain was beside me. 'Now, for it, then,' said I, and away we went. What might be the nature of his feelings I cannot pretend to state, but my own were a strange *mélange* of wild boyish enthusiasm, revenge and recklessness. For my own neck I cared little—nothing; and as I led the way by half a length, I muttered to myself, 'Let him follow me fairly this day, and I ask no more.'

The dogs had got somewhat the start of us, and, as they were in full cry, and going fast, we were a little behind. A thought therefore struck me that, by appearing to take a short cut upon the hounds, I should come along upon the river where its breadth was greatest and thus at one *coup* might try my friend's mettle and his horse's performance at the same time. On we went, our speed increasing, till the roar of the river we were now approaching was plainly audible. I looked half around, and now perceived that the Captain was standing in his stirrups, as if to obtain a view of what was before him; otherwise his countenance was calm and unmoved, and not a muscle betrayed that he was not cantering on a parade. I fixed myself firmly in my seat, shook my horse a little together, and, with a shout whose import every Galway hunter well knows, rushed him at the river. I saw the water dashing among the large stones, I heard its splash, I felt a bound like the *ricochet* of a shot, and we were over, but so narrowly, that the bank had yielded beneath his hind legs, and it needed a bold effort of the noble animal to regain his footing. Scarcely was he once more firm, when Hammersley flew by me, taking the lead, and sitting quietly in his saddle, as if racing. I know of nothing in all my after life like the agony of that moment; for, although I was far, very far, from wishing real ill to him, yet I would gladly have broken my leg or my arm if he could not have been able to follow me. And now there he was, actually a length and a half in advance; and, worse than all, Miss Dashwood must have witnessed the whole, and doubtless his leap over the river was better and bolder than mine. One consolation yet remained, and while I whispered it to myself I felt comforted again. 'His is an English mare—they understand these leaps—but what can he make of a Galway wall?' The question was soon to be solved. Before us, about three fields were the hounds still in full cry; a large stone wall lay between, and to it we both directed our course together. Ha! thought I, he is floored at last, as I perceived that the captain held his horse rather more in hand, and suffered me to lead. 'Now, then, for it!' so saying I rode at the largest part I could find, well knowing that Badger's powers were here in their element. One spring, one plunge, and away we were, galloping along at the other side. Not so the Captain: his horse had refused the fence, and he was now taking a circuit of the field for another trial of it.

'Pounded, by Jove,' said I, as I turned round in my saddle to observer him. Once more she came at it, and once more baulked, rearing up at the same time, almost so as to fall backward.

My triumph was complete, and I again was about to follow the hounds; when, throwing a look back, I saw Hammersly clearing the wall in a most splendid manner, and taking a stretch of at least thirteen feet beyond it. Once more he was on my flanks, and the contest renewed. Whatever might be the sentiments of the riders (mine I confess to,) between the horses it now became a tremendous struggle. The English mare, though evidently superior in stride and strength, was still overweighted, and had not besides that cat-like activity an Irish horse possesses; so that the advantages and disadvantages on either side were about equalized. For about half an hour now the pace was awful. We rode side by side, taking our leaps exactly at the same instant, and not four feet apart. The hounds were still considerably in advance, and were heading towards the Shannon, when suddenly the fox doubled, took the hill side, and made for Dangan. Now, then, comes the trial of strength, I said half aloud, as I threw my eye up a steep and rugged mountain, covered with wild furze and tall heath, around the crest of which ran in a zig-zag direction, a broken and dilapidated wall, once the enclosure of a deer-park. This wall, which varied from four to six feet in height, was of solid masonry, and would, in the most favorable ground, have been a bold leap. Here, at the summit of a mountain, with not a yard of footing, it was absolutely desperation.

By the time that we reached the foot of the hill, the fox, followed closely by the hounds, had passed through a breach in the wall, while Matthew Blake, with the huntsmen and whipper-in, were riding along in search of a gap to lead the horses through. Before I put spurs to Badger, to face the hill, I turned one look towards Hammersly. There was a slight curl, half-smile, half-sneer upon his lip, that actually maddened me, and had a precipice yawned beneath my feet, I should have dashed at it after that. The ascent was so steep that I was obliged to take the hill in a slanting direction, and even thus, the loose footing rendered it dangerous in the extreme. At length I reached the crest, where the wall, more than five feet in height, stood frowning above and seeming to defy me. I turned my horse full round, so that his very chest almost touched the stones, and, with a bold cut of the whip and a loud halloo, the gallant animal rose, as if rearing, pawed for an instant to regain his balance, and then with a frightful struggle fell backwards, and rolled from top to bottom of the hill, carrying me along with him; the last object that crossed my sight, as I lay bruised and motionless, being the captain as he took the wall in a flying leap, and disappeared at the other side. After a few scrambling efforts to rise, Badger regained his legs, and stood beside me; but such was the shock and concussion of my fall, that all the objects around me seemed wavering and floating before me, while showers of bright sparks fell in myriads before my eyes. I tried to rise, but fell back helpless. Cold perspiration broke over my forehead, and I fainted. From that moment I can remember nothing, till I felt myself galloping along at full speed upon a level table land, with the hounds about three fields in advance, Hammersly riding foremost, and taking all his leaps coolly as ever. As I swayed to either side upon my saddle, from weakness, I was lost to all thought or recollection, save a flickering memory of some plan of vengeance, which still urged me forward. The chase had now lasted above an hour, and both hounds and horses began to feel the peace at which they were going. As for me, I rode mechanically; I neither knew nor cared for the dangers before me. My eye rested on but one object; my whole being was concentrated upon one vague and undetermined sense of revenge. At this instant the huntsman came alongside of me.

'Are you hurted, Misther Charles? did you fall?—your cheek is all blood, and your coat is torn in two; and, Mother o' God his boot is ground to powder; he does not hear me. Oh, pull up—pull, for the love of the Virgin; there's the clover field, and the sunk fence before you, and you'll be killed on the spot.'

'Where?' cried I, with the cry of madman, 'where's the clover field?—where's the sunk fence? Ha! I see it—I see it now.'

So, saying, I dashed the rowels into my horse's flanks, and in an instant I was beyond the reach of the poor fellow's remonstrances. Another moment, I was beside the Captain. He turned round as I came up; the same smile was upon his mouth—I could have struck him. About three hundred yards before us lay the sunk fence; its breadth was about twenty feet, and a wall of close brickwork formed its face. Over this the hounds were now clambering; some succeeded in crossing, but by far the greater number fell back howling into the ditch.

I turned towards Hammersly.—He was standing high in his stirrups, and, as he looked towards the yawning fence, down which the dogs were tumbling in masses, I thought (perhaps it was but a thought) that his cheek was paler. I looked again, he was pulling at his horse; ha! it was true then, he would not face it. I turned round in my saddle—looked him full in the face, and, as I pointed with my whip to the leap, called out in a voice hoarse with passion, 'come on.' I saw no more. All objects were lost to me from that moment. When next my senses cleared I was standing amid the dogs, where they had just killed. Badger stood blown and trembling beside me, his head drooping, and his flanks gored with spur marks. I looked about, but all consciousness of the past had fled; the concussion of my fall had shaken my intellect, and I was like one but half awake. One glimpse, short and fleeing, of what was taking place, shot through my brain, as old Brackley whispered to me, 'By my soul ye did for the Captain there.' I turned a vague look upon him, and my eyes fell upon the figure of a man that lay stretched and bleeding upon a door before me. His pale face was crossed with a purple stream of blood, that trickled from a wound beside his eye-brow; his arms lay motionless and heavily at either side. I knew him not. A loud report of a pistol aroused me from my stupor; I looked back. I saw a crowd that broke suddenly asunder and fled right and left. I heard a heavy crash upon the ground, I pointed with my finger, for I could not utter a word.

'It is the English mare, yer honour; she was a beauty this morning, but she's broke her collar bone, and both her legs, and it was best to put her out of pain.'

* * *

On the fourth day following the adventure detailed in the last chapter I made my appearance in the drawing-room; my cheek well blanched by copious bleeding, and my step tottering and uncertain. On entering the room I looked about in vain for some one who might give me an insight into the occurrences of the four preceding days, but no one was to be met with. The ladies, I learned, were out riding; Matthew was buying a new setter; Mr. Blake was canvassing; and Captain Hammersly was in bed. Where was Miss Dashwood?—in her room; and Sir George? he was with Mr. Blake.

'What! canvassing too?'

'Troth that same was possible,' was the intelligent reply of the old butler, at which I could not help smiling. I sat down therefore in the easiest chair I could find, and, unfolding the county paper, resolved upon learning how matters were going on in the political world. But, somehow, whether the editor was not brilliant, or the fire was hot, or that my own dreams were pleasanter to indulge in than his fancies, I fell sound asleep.

How differently is the mind attuned to the active busy world of thought and action, when awakened from sleep by any sudden and rude summons to arise and be stirring, and when called into existence by the sweet and silvery notes of softest music, stealing over the senses, and while they impart awakening thoughts of bliss and beauty scarcely dissipating the dreary influence of slumber; such was my first thought as, with closed lids, the thrilling cords of a harp broke upon my sleep, and aroused me to a feeling of unutterable pleasure. I turned gently round in my chair, and beheld Miss Dashwood. She was seated in a recess of an old-fashioned window; the pale yellow glow of a wintry sun at evening fell upon her beautiful hair, and tinged it with such a light as I have often since then seen in Rembrandt's pictures; her head leaned upon the harp, and, as she struck its cords at random, I saw that her mind was far away from all around her; as I looked, she suddenly started from her leaning attitude, and parting back her curls from her brow, she preluded a few chords, and then sighed forth, rather than sang, that most beautiful of Moore's Melodies,—

She is far from the land where her young hero sleeps.'

Never before had such pathos, such deep utterance of feeling, met my astonished sense; I listened breathlessly as the tears fell one by one down my cheek; my bosom heaved and fell; and, when she ceased, I hid my head between my hands and sobbed aloud. In an instant she was beside me, and placing her hand upon my shoulder, said,

'Poor dear boy, I never suspected you of being there, or I should not have sung that mournful air.'

I started and looked up, and, from what I know not, but she suddenly crimsoned to her very forehead, while she added in a less assured tone,

'I hope, Mr. O'Malley, that you are much better, and I trust there is no imprudence in your being here.'

'For the latter I shall not answer,' said I, with a sickly smile; 'but already I feel your music has done me service.'

'Then let me sing more for you.'

'If I am to have a choice, I should say, sit down and let me hear you talk to me; my illness and the doctor together, have made wild work of my poor brain; but, if you will, talk to me.'

'Well then, what shall it be about?—Shall I tell you a fairy tale?'

'I need it not: I feel I am in one this instant.'

'Well, then, what say you to a legend, for I am rich in my stores of them?'

'The O'Malleys have their chronicles, wild and barbarous enough, without the aid of Thor and Woden.'

'Then, shall we chat of every-day matters?—Should you like to hear how the election and the canvass go on?'

'Yes; of all things.'

'Well, then, most favourably. Two baronies, with most unspeakable names, have declared for us, and confidence is rapidly increasing among our party. This I learned by chance yesterday—for Papa never permits us to know anything of these matters; not even the names of the candidates.'

'Well, that was the very point I was coming to, for the government were about to send down some one, just as I left home; and I am most anxious to learn who it is.'

'Then am I utterly valueless; for I really can't say what party the government exposes, and only know of our own.'

'Quite enough for me, that you wish it success,' said I, gallantly; 'perhaps, you can tell me if my uncle has heard of my accident?'

'Oh yes; but somehow he has not been here himself; but sent a friend, a Mr. Considine I think; a very strange person he seemed. He demanded to see papa, and, it seems, asked him if your misfortune had been a thing of his contrivance, and whether he was ready to explain his conduct about it; and in fact, I believe he is mad'—

'Heaven confound him', I muttered between my teeth.

'And then he wished to have an interview with Captain Hammersly, but he is too ill; but as the doctor hoped he might be down stairs in a week, Mr. Considine kindly hinted, that he should wait.'

'Oh then, do tell me how is the Captain?'

'Very much bruised, very much disfigured, they say', said she, half smiling; 'but not so much hurt in body as in mind.'

'As how, may I ask?' said I, with an appearance of innocence.

'I don't exactly understand it; but it would appear that there was something like rivalry among you gentlemen chasseurs on that luckless morning, and that, while you paid the penalty of a broken head, he was destined to lose his horse, and break his arm.'

'I certainly am sorry—most sincerely sorry, for any share I might have had in the catastrophe; and my greatest regret, I confess, arises from the fact, that I should cause *you* unhappiness.'

'*Me*—pray explain?'

'Why, as Captain Hammersly—'

'Mr. O'Malley, you are too young now, to make me suspect you have an intention to offend; but I caution you, never repeat this.'

I saw that I had transgressed, but how, I most honestly confess, I could not guess; for though I certainly was the senior of my fair companion in years, I was most lamentably her junior in tact and discretion.

The gray dusk of evening had long fallen as we continued to chat together beside the blazing wood embers—she evidently amusing herself with the original notions of an untutored unlettered boy; and I drinking deep those draughts of love that nerved my heart through many a breach and battle field.

Our colloquy was at length interrupted by the entrance of Sir George, who shook me most cordially by the hand, and made the kindest inquiries about my health.

'They tell me you are to be a lawyer Mr. O'Malley,' said he; 'and, if so, I must advise you to take better care of your head-piece.'

'A lawyer, papa; oh dear me! I should never have thought of his being anything so stupid.'

'Why, silly girl, what would you have a man be?'

'A dragoon, to be sure, papa,' said the fond girl, as she pressed her arm around his manly figure, and looked up in his face, with an expression of mingled pride and affection.

That word sealed my destiny.

MR JORROCKS
Handley Cross
R. S. Surtees
1843

Mr Jorrocks was a great city grocer of the old school, one who was neither ashamed of his trade, nor of carrying it on in a dingy warehouse that would shock the managers of the fine mahogany-countered, gilt-canistered, puffing, poet-keeping establishments of modern times. He had been in business long enough to remember each succeeding lord mayor before he was anybody—'reg'lar little tuppences in fact,' as he used to say. Not that Mr Jorrocks decried the dignity of civic honour, but his ambition took a different turn. He was for the field, not the forum.

As a merchant he stood high—country traders took his teas without tasting, and his bills were as good as bank-notes. Though an unlettered man, he had great powers of thought and expression in his peculiar way. He was 'highly respectable,' as they say on 'Change—that is to say, he was very rich, the result of prudence and economy—not that he was stingy, but his income outstripped his expenses, and money, like snow, rolls up amazingly fast.

A natural-born sportsman, his lot being cast behind a counter instead of in the country, is one of those frolics of fortune that there is no accounting for. To remedy the error of the blind goddess, Mr Jorrocks had taken to hunting as soon as he could keep a horse, and though his exploits were long confined to the suburban county of Surrey, he should rather be 'credited' for keenness in following the sport in so unpropitious a region, that 'debited' as a Cockney and laughed at for his pains. But here the old adage of 'where ignorance is bliss,' &c. came to his aid, for before he had seen any better country than Surrey, he was impressed with the conviction that it was the 'werry best,' and their hounds the finest in England.

'Doesn't the best of everything come to London?' he would ask, 'and doesn't it follow as a nattaral consequence, that the best 'unting is to be had from it?'

Moreover, Mr Jorrocks looked upon Surrey as the peculiar province of Cockneys—we beg pardon—Londoners. His earliest recollections carried him back to the days of Alderman Harley, and though his participation in the sport consisted in reading the meets in a boot-maker's window in the Borough, he could tell of all the succeeding masters, and criticize the establishments of Clayton, Snow, Maberly, and the renowned Daniel Haigh.

It was during the career of the latter great sportsman that Mr Jorrocks shone a brilliant meteor in the Surrey hunt—he was no rider, but with an almost intuitive knowledge of the run of a fox, would take off his hat to him several times in the course of a run. No Saturday seemed perfect unless Mr Jorrocks was there; and his great chestnut horse, with his master's coat-laps flying out beyond his tail, will long be remembered on the outline of the Surrey hills. These are recollections that many will enjoy, nor will their interest be diminished as time throws them back in the distance. Many bold sportsmen now laid on the shelf, and many a bold one still going, will glow with animation at the thoughts of the sport they shared in with him.

Of the start before day-break—the cries of the cads—the mirth of the lads—the breakfasts at Croydon—the dear 'Derby Arms'—the cheery Charley Morton; then the ride to the meet—the jovial greeting—the glorious find, and the exhilarating scrambles up and down the Surrey hills. Then if they killed!—O, joy! unutterable joy! How they holloaed! How they hooped! How they lugged out their half-crowns for Tom Hill, and returned to town flush with victory and 'eau-de-vie.'

But we wander—

When the gates of the world were opened by railways, our friend's active mind saw that business might be combined with pleasure, and as first one line opened and then another, he shot down into the different countries—bags and all—Beckford in one pocket—order-book in the other—hunting one day and selling teas another. Nay, he sometimes did both together, and they tell a story of him in Wiltshire, holloaing out to a man who had taken a fence to get rid of him. 'Did you say *two* chests o' black and *one* o' green?'

Then when the Great Northern opened he took a turn down to Peterborough, and emboldened by what he saw with Lord Fitzwilliam, he at length ventured right into the heaven of heavens—the grass—or what he calls the 'cut 'em down' countries. What a commotion he caused! Which is Jorrocks? Show me Jorrocks! Is that old Jorrocks? and men would ride to and fro eyeing him as if he were a wild beast. Gradually the bolder ventured a word at him—observed it was a fine day—asked him how he liked their country, or their hounds. Next, perhaps, the MFH would give him a friendly lift—say 'Good morning, Mr Jorrocks'—then some of what Jorrocks calls the 'hupper crusts' of the hunt would begin talking to him, until he got fairly launched among them—when he would out with his order-book and do no end of business in tea. None but Jorrocks & Co's tea goes down in the midland counties. Great, however, as he is in the country, he is equally famous in London, where his 'Readings in Beckford' and sporting lectures in Oxenden Street procured him the attentions of the police.

Mr Jorrocks had now passed the grand climacteric, and balancing his age with less accuracy than he balanced his books, called himself somewhere between fifty and sixty. He wouldn't own to three pund, as he called sixty, at any price. Neither could he ever be persuaded to get into the scales to see whether he was nearer eighteen 'stun' or twenty. He was always "ticlarly engaged' just at the time, either goin' to wet samples of tea with his traveller, or with some one to look at 'an 'oss,' or, if hard pressed, to take Mrs J out in the chay. 'He didn't ride stipple chases,' he would say, 'and wot matter did it make 'ow much he weighed? It was altogether 'twixt him and his 'oss, and weighin' wouldn't make him any lighter.' In person he was a stiff, square-built, middle-sized man, with a thick neck and a large round head. A woolly broad-brimmed lowish-crowned hat sat with a jaunty sidelong sort of air upon a bushy nut-brown wig, worn for comfort and not deception. Indeed his grey whiskers would have acted as a contradiction if he had, but deception formed no part of Mr Jorrocks's character. He had a fine open countenance, and though his turn-up nose, little grey eyes, and rather twisted mouth were not handsome, still there was a combination of fun and good humour in his looks that pleased at first sight, and made one forget all the rest. His dress was generally the same—a puddingey white neckcloth tied in a knot, capacious shirt frill (shirt made without collars), a single-breasted high-collared buff waistcoat with covered buttons, a blue coat with metal ones, dark blue stockingnet pantaloons, and hessian boots with large tassels, displaying the liberal dimensions of his full, well-turned limbs. The coat pockets were outside, and the back buttons far apart.

MR JORROCKS'S ORATION

Handley Cross
R. S. Surtees
1843

"Ow are ye all?' said Mr Jorrocks with the greatest familiarity, nodding round to the meeting, and kissing his hand. "Opes you are well. Now my frind, Miserrimus, having spun you a yarn about who I am, and all that sort of thing, I'll not run his foil, but get upon fresh ground, and say a few words about how matters are to be managed.

'You see I've come down to 'unt your country, to be master of your 'ounds, in fact—and first of all I'll explain to you what *I* means by the word master. Some people call a man a master of 'ounds wot sticks an 'orn in his saddle, and blows when he likes, but leaves everything else to the 'untsman. That's not the sort of master of 'ounds I mean to be. Others call a man a master of 'ounds wot puts in the paper Mr So-and-so's 'ounds meet on Monday, at the Loin o' Lamb; on Wednesday, at the Brisket o' Weal; and on Saturday, at the Frying-pan; and after that, jest goes out or not, as suits his conwenience—but *that's* not the sort of master o' hounds I means to be. Again, some call themselves masters of 'ounds when they pay the different atwixt the subscription and the cost, leaving the managements of matters, the receipt of money, payment of damage, and all them sort of partiklars, to the secretary. But that's not the sort of master o' 'ounds I means to be. Still, I means to ride with an 'orn in my saddle. Yonder it is, see,' said he, pointing to the package behind the carriage, 'a regler Percival, silver mouth-piece, deep cup'd—and I means to adwertise the 'ounds in the paper, and not go sneakin' about like some of them beggarly Cockney 'unts, wot look more as if they were goin' to rob a hen-roost than 'unt a fox, but havin' fixed the meets, I shall attend them most punctual and regler, and take off my cap to all payin' subscribers as they come up (cheers). This, I thinks, will be the best way of doin' business, for there are some men wot don't care a copper for owin' the master money, so long as the matter rests atwixt themselves, and yet who would not like to see me sittin' among my 'ounds with my cap slouched over my eyes, takin' no more notice of them than if they were as many pigs, as much as to say to all the gemmen round, 'These are the nasty, dirty, seedy screws wot don't pay their subscriptions.'

'In short I means to be an MFH in reality, and not in name. When I see young chaps careering o'er the country without lookin' at the 'ounds, and in all humane probability not knowin' or carin' a copper where they are, and I cries, "*old 'ard!*" I shall expect to see them pull up, and not wait till the next fence fatches them too.'

Here Mr Jorrocks made a considerable pause, whereupon the cheering and drumming was renewed, and as it died away, he went on as follows:

'Of all sitivations under the sun, none is more enviable more 'onerable than that of a master of fox-'ounds! Talk of a MP! vot's an MP compared to an MFH? Your MP lives in a tainted hatmosphere among other MPs and loses his consequence by the commonness of the office, and the scoldings he gets from those who sent him there, but an MFH holds his levee in the stable, his levee in the kennel, and his levee in the 'untin' field—is great and important everywhere—has no one to compete with him, no one to find fault, but all join in doing honour to him to whom honour is so greatly due (cheers). And oh, John Jorrocks! my good friend,' continued the worthy grocer, fumbling the silver in his small clothes with upturned eyes to heaven, 'to think that you, after all the hups and downs of life—the crossin's and jostlin's of merchandise and ungovernable trade—the sortin' of sugars—the mexin' of teas—the postin' of ledgers, and handlin' of inwoices, to think that you, my dear feller, should have arrived at this distinguished post, is most miraculously wonderful, most singularly queer. Gentlemen, *this* is the proudest moment of my life! (cheers). I've now reached the top rail in the ladder of my hambition! (renewed cheers). Binjimin!' he holloaed out to the boy below, 'Binjimin! I say, give an eye to them 'ere harticles behind the chay—the children are all among the Copenhagen brandy and Dundee marmeylad! Vy don't you vollop them? Vere's the use of furnishing you with a whip, I wonder?'

'To resume,' said he, after he had seen the back of the carriage cleared of the children, and the marmalade and things put straight. "Untin', as I have often said, is the sport of kings—the image of war without its guilt, and only five-and-twenty per cent of its danger. To me the clink of the couples from a vipper-in's saddle is more musical than any notes that ever came out of Greasey's mouth (cheers). I doesn't wish to disparage the walue of no man, but this I may say, that no Nabob that ever was foaled, loves 'untin' better than me (cheers). It's the werry breath of my body! The liver and bacon of my existence! I doesn't know what the crazeyologists may say, but this I believes that my 'ead is nothin' but one great bump of 'untin' (cheers). 'Untin' fills my thoughts by day, and many a good run I have in my sleep. Many a dig in the ribs I gives Mrs J when I think they're runnin' into the warmint (renewed cheers). No man is fit to be called a sportsman wot doesn't kick his wife out of bed on a haverage once in three weeks! (applause, mingled with roars of laughter). I'm none of your fine, dandified Rotten Row swells, that only ride out to ride 'ome again, but I loves the smell of the mornin' hair, and the werry mud on my tops when I comes home of an evenin' is dear to my 'eart (cheers). Oh, my friends! if I could but go to the kennel now, get out the 'ounds, find my fox, have a good chivey, and kill him, for no day is good to me without blood, I'd—I'd—I'd—drink three pints of port after dinner 'stead of two! (loud cheers). That's the way to show Diana your gratitude for favours past, and secure a continuance of her custom in future (cheers). But that we will soon do, for if you've—

""'Osses sound, and dogs 'calthy,
Earths well-stopped, and foxes plenty,"

no longer shall a master be wantin' to lead you to glory (loud cheers). I'll not only show you how to do the trick in the field, but a scientific course o' lectors shall train the young idea in the art at 'ome. I've no doubt we shall all get on capitally—fox-'unters are famous fellows—tell me a man's a fox-hunter, and I loves him at once. We'll soon get 'quainted, and then you'll say that John Jorrocks is the man for your money. At present I've done— hoping werry soon to meet you all in the field—I now says adieu.'

Hereupon, Mr Jorrocks bowed, and kissing his hand, backed out of the balcony, leaving his auditory to talk him over at their leisure.

THE CAT AND CUSTARD-POT DAY

Handley Cross
R. S. Surtees
1843

The above day deserves a more extended notice than it receives in Mr Jorrock's journal. He writes that 'somehow or other in shavin', he thought they'd 'ave mischief,' and he went into the garden as soon as he was dressed to consult the prophet, Gabriel Junks, so that he might take his pocket Siphonia in case it was likely to be wet, but the bird was not there. Then just as he had breakfasted and was about ready for a start, young May, the grocer, sent him a horse to look at, and as 'another gen'l'man' was waiting for the next offer of him, Charley and Mr Jorrocks stayed behind to try him, and after a hard deal, Mr Jorrocks bought him for £30—which he makes a mem: 'to call £50.'

Meanwhile Pigg and Ben trotted on with the hounds, and when they reached the meet—the sign of the 'Cat and Custard-pot,' on the Muswell Road, they found an immense assemblage, some of whom greeted Pigg with the familiar inquiry, 'what he'd have to drink?'

'Brandy!' replied Pigg, 'brandy!' and tossing off the glass with great gusto, a second horseman volunteered one, then a third, then a fourth, then a fifth; for it is observable that there are people in the world who will give away drink to any extent, who yet would be chary of offering either money or meat. Pigg, who, as Mr Jorrocks says in his journal, is only a *lusus naturæ*, or loose 'un by natur', tosses off glass after glass, smacking his lips and slapping his thigh, getting noisier and noisier with each succeeding potation. Now he would sing them a song, now he would take the odds ag'in Marley Hill, then he would tell them about Deavilboger's farm, and how, but for his fore elder John, John Pigg, ye see, willin' his brass to the Formary ye see, he'd ha' been a gen'l'man that day and huntin' his own hunds. Then as another glass made its appearance, he would take off his cap and halloo out at the top of his voice, making the hounds stare with astonishment, 'Keep the tambourine a-rowlin'!' adding as he tossed it off, 'Brandy and baccy 'ill gar a man live for iver!' And now when he was about at the noisiest, with his cap turned peak-backwards, and the tobacco juice simmering down the deeply indented furrows of his chin, our master and Charley appear in the distance, jogging on, not too quickly for consequence, but sufficiently fast to show they are aware they are keeping the field waiting.

'Here he comes! here's Jorrocks! here's the old boy! here's Jackey at last!' runs through the meeting, and horsemen begin to arrange themselves for the reception.

'A—a—a sink!' exclaims Pigg, shaking his head, blinking and staring that way, 'here's canny ard sweet-breeks hissel!' adding with a slap of his thigh as the roar of laughter the exclamation produced subsided, 'A—a—a, but ar de like to see his feulish 'ard feace a-grinnin' in onder his cap!'

How way, canny man; how way!' now shouts Pigg, waving his hand as his master approached. 'How way! canny man, how way! and give us a wag o' thy neif,' Pigg extending his hand as he spoke.

Mr Jorrocks drew up with great dignity, and placing his fist in his side, proceeded to reconnoitre the scene.

'Humph!' grunted he, 'wot's all this about?'

'Sink, but ar'll gi' thou a gob full o'baccy,' continued James, nothing daunted by his master's refusal of his hand. 'Sink, but ar'll gi' thou a gob full o' baccy,' repeated he, diving into his waistcoat pocket and producing a large steel tobacco box as he spoke.

Mr Jorrocks signified his dissent by a chuck of the chin, and an ominous shake of the head.

'A—a—a man!' exclaimed Pigg, now changing his tone, 'but ar'll tell thee of a lass well worth her licks!'

'You deserve your *own*, sir, for gettin' so drunk,' observed Mr Jorrocks haughtily.

Pigg.—'Ar's as sober as ye are, and a deal wizer!'

Jorrocks (angrily).—'I'll not condescend to compare notes with ye!'

Pigg (now flaring up).—'Sink; if anybody 'ill had mar huss, ar'll get off and fight him.'

Jorrocks (contemptuously).—'Better stick to the shopboard as long as you can.'

Pigg (furious).—'Gin ar warn't afeard o' boggin' mar neif, ard gi' thou a good crack i' thy kite!'

Jorrocks (with emphasis).—'*Haw—da—cious* feller. I'll 'unt the 'ounds myself aford I'll put hup with sich himperence!'

Pigg (throwing out his arms and grinning in ecstasies);—'Ar'll be death of a guinea but arl coom and see thee!'

Jorrocks (looking indignantly round on the now mirth-convulsed company).—'Who's made my Pigg so drunk?'

Nobody answered.

'Didn't leave his sty so,' muttered our master, lowering himself jockey ways from his horse.

''Old my quad,' said he to Charley, handing him Arterxerxes, 'while I go in and see.'

Our master then stumped in, and presently encountering the great attraction of the place—the beautiful Miss D'Oiley—asked her, with a smiling countenance and a hand in a pocket, as if about to pay. 'Wot his 'untsman 'ad 'ad?'

'Oh, sir, it is all paid,' replied Miss D'Oiley, smiling as sweetly upon Jorrocks as she did on the generality of her father's customers, for she had no more heart than a punch-bowl.

'Is all paid?' muttered our friend.

'Yes, sir; each gentleman paid as he sent out the glass.'

'Humph!' twigged Mr Jorrocks, adding, with a grunt, 'and that's wot these critters call sport!'

Our master then stumped out. 'Well, gen'l'men,' exclaimed he, at the top of his voice off the horse-block, 'I 'opes you're satisfied wi' your day's sport!—you've made my nasty Pigg as drunk as David's sow, so now you may all go 'ome, for I shalln't throw off; and as to you,' continued our indignant master, addressing the now somewhat crestfallen Pigg, 'you go 'ome too, and take off my garments, and take yourself off to your native mountains, for I'll see ye at Jericho ayont Jordan afore you shall 'unt my 'ounds,' giving his thigh a hearty slap as he spoke.

'Wy, wy, sir,' replied Pigg, turning his quid; 'wy, wy, sir, ye ken best, only dinna ye try to hont them thysel'—*that's arle!*'

'There are as good fish i' the sea as ever came out on't!' replied Mr Jorrocks, brandishing his big whip furiously; adding, 'I'll see ye leadin' an old ooman's lap-dog 'bout in a string afore *you* shall 'unt 'em.'

'No, ye won't!' responded Pigg. 'No, ye won't! Arve ne carle te de nothin' o' the sort! Arve ne carle te de nothin' o' the sort!—Arle gan back to mar coosin Deavilboger's.'

'You may gan to the devil himself,' retorted Mr Jorrocks vehemently—'you may gan to the devil himself—I'll see ye sellin' small coals from a donkey-cart out of a quart pot afore you shall stay wi' me.'

'Thou's a varra feulish, noisy, gobby, insufficient, 'ard man!' retorted Pigg, 'and ar doesn't regard thee! No; AR DOESN'T REGARD THEE!' roared he, with a defiant flourish of his fist.

'You're a hignorant, hawdacious, rebellious rascal, and I'll see ye frightenin' rats from a barn wi' the bagpipes at a 'alfpenny a day, and findin' yoursel', afore I'll 'ave anything more to say to ye,' rejoined Mr Jorrocks, gathering up his big whip as if for the fray.

'Sink, arle tak' and welt thee like an ard shoe, if thou gives me ony mair o' thy gob!' rejoined the now furious Pigg, ejecting his baccy and motioning as if about to dismount.

Jorrocks, thinking he had done enough, then took his horse from Charley Stobbs, and hoisting himself on like a great crate of earthenware, whistled his hounds away from the still stupefied Pigg, who sat blinking and staring and shaking his head, thinking there were two Jorrock's on two Arterxerxes', two Ben's, two Charley Stobbs's, and something like five-and-forty couple of hounds.

The field remained behind praising Pigg and abusing Jorrocks, and declaring they would withdraw their subscriptions to the hounds if Pigg 'got the sack.' None of them would see Pigg want; and Harry Capper, more vehement than the rest, proposed an immediate subscription, a suggestion that had the effect of dispersing the field, who slunk off different ways as soon as ever the allusion to the pocket was made.

Jorrocks was desperately angry, for he had had an expensive 'stop,' and came bent on mischief. His confusion of mind made him mistake the road home, and go by Rumfiddler Green instead of Muswell Hill. He spurred, and cropped, and jagged Arterxerxes—now vowing that he would send him to the tanners when he got 'ome—now that he would have him in the boiler afore night. He was very much out of sorts with himself and everybody else—even the hounds didn't please him—always getting in his way, hanging back looking for James Pigg, and Ben had fine fun cutting and flopping them forrard.

Charley, like a wise man, kept aloof.

In this unamiable mood our master progressed, until the horrible apparition of a great white turnpike-gate, staring out from the gable-end of a brick toll-house, startled his vision and caused him to turn short up a wide green lane to the left. 'Take care o' the pence and the punds 'ill take care o' theirsels,' muttered our master to himself, now sensible that he had mistaken his road, and looking around for some landmark to steer by. Just as he was identifying White Choker Church in the distance, a sudden something shot through the body of the late loitering, indifferent hounds, apparently influencing them with a sort of invisible agency. Another instant, and a wild snatch or two right and left ended in a whimper and a general shoot up the lane.

'A fox! for a 'underd!' muttered our master, drawing breath as he eyed them. 'A fox! for two-and-twenty 'underd!' continued he, as Priestess feathered but spoke not.

'A fox! for a million!' roared he, as old Ravager threw his tongue lightly but confidently, and Jorrocks cheered him to the echo.

'A fox! for 'alf the national debt!' roared he, looking round at Charley as he gathered himself together for a start.

Now as Jorrocks would say, Beckford would say, 'Where are all your sorrows and your cares, ye gloomy souls? or where your pains and aches, ye complaining ones? one whimper has dispelled them all.'

Mr Jorrocks takes off his cap and urges the tail-hounds on. A few more driving shoots and stops, producing increased velocity with each effort, and a few more quick snatchy whimpers, end in a unanimous outburst of downrightly determined melody.

Jorrocks, cocking his cap on his ear, seats himself plump in his great saddle, and, gathering his reins, gallops after them in the full grin of delight. Away they tear up the rutty, grassy ride, as if it was a railway.

'F-o-o-r-rard on! F-o-o-r-rard on!' is his cry.

'H-o-i-c cry! h-o-i-c cry! h-o-i-c!' squeaks Ben, wishing himself at home at the mutton, and delighted at having got rid of James Pigg, who always would have the first cut.

It is a long lane that never has a turn, and this one was no exception to the rule, for in due course it came to an abrupt angle. A convenient meuse, however, inviting the fox onward, he abandoned the line and pursued his course over some bare, badly fenced pastures, across which Mr Jorrocks cheered and rode with all the confidence of a man who sees his way out. The pace mended as they went, and Jorrocks hugged himself with the idea of killing a fox without Pigg. From the pastures they got upon Straggleford Moor, pretty much the same sort of ground as the fields but the fox brushing as he went, there was a still further improvement of scent. Jorrocks then began to bet himself hats that he'd kill him, and went vowing what he would offer to Diana if he did. There was scarcely any promise too wild for him to make at this moment. The fox, however, was not disposed to accommodate Jorrocks with much more plan sailing for the purpose, and seeing, by the scarlet coats, that he was not pursued by his old friends the Dotfield harriers, as at first he thought, and with whom he had had many a game at romps, he presently sunk the hill and made for the stiffly fenced vale below.

'Blow me tight!' exclaimed Jorrocks, shortening his hold of Arterxerxes, and putting his head straight as he used to do down the Surrey hills, 'Blow me tight! but I wish he mayn't be gettin' me into grief. This looks to me werry like the Ingerleigh Wale, and if it is, it's a bit of a nasty ridin' grund as ever mortal man got into—yawnin' ditches with himpracticable fences, posts with rails of the most formidable order, and that nasty long Tommy bruk, twistin' and twinin' about in all directions like a child's rattle-snake. 'Owever, thank goodness, 'ere's a gap and a gate beyond,' continued he, as his quick eye caught a gap at the corner of the stubble field he was now approaching, which getting through, he rose in his stirrups and cheered on the hounds in the line of the other convenience. 'For-a-r-d! For-r-a-r-d!' shrieked he, pointing the now racing hounds out to Charlie, who was a little behind; 'for-rard! for-rard!' continued Jorrocks, rib-roasting Arterxerxes. The gate was locked, but Jackey—we beg his pardon—Mr Jorrocks—was quickly off, and setting his great back against it, lifted it off the hinges. 'Go on! never mind me!' cried he to Charley, who had pulled up as Jorrocks was dancing about with one foot in the stirrup, trying to remount. 'Go on! never mind me!' repeated he, with desperate energy, as he made another assault at the saddle. 'Get on, Ben, you most useless appendage!' continued he, now lying across the saddle, like a miller's sack. A few flounders land him in the desired haven, and he trots on, playing at catch-stirrup with his right foot as he goes.

'Forrard on! forrard on!' still screamed he, cracking his ponderous whip, though the hounds were running away from him as it was, but he wanted to get Charley Stobbs to the front, as there was no one to break his fence for him but him.

The hounds, who had been running with a breast-high scent, get their noses to the ground as they come upon fallow, and a few kicks, jags, and objurgations on Jorrocks's part soon bring Arterxerxes and him into the field in which they are. The scent begins to fail.

'G—e-e-e-nt—ly there!' cries Jorrocks, holding up his hand and reining in his horse, inwardly hoping the fox might be on instead of off to the right, where he sees his shiny friend, long Tommy, meandering smoothly along.

'*Yo dote!* Ravager, good dog, *yo dote*, Ravager!' cheers Jorrocks, as the sage feathers and scuttles up the furrow. '*Yo-o dote!*' continued Mr Jorrocks, cheering the rest on—adding as he looks at them scoring to cry, 'wot a petty it is we can't put new legs to old noses!' The spurt, however, is of short duration, for the ground gets worse as it rises higher, until the tenderest-nosed hound can hardly own the scent. A heavy cloud too oppresses the atmosphere. Jorrocks sees if he doesn't look sharp he'll very soon be run out of scent, so getting hold of his hounds, he makes a rapid speculation in his mind as to which way he would go if he were the fox, and having decided that point, he loses no time in getting the pack to the place. Jorrocks is right!—Ravager's unerring nose proclaims the varmint across the green headland, and the next field being a clover ley, with a handy gate in, which indeed somewhat influenced Jorrocks in his cast, the hounds again settle to the scent, with Jorrocks rolling joyfully after them, declaring he'd be the best 'untsman under the sun if it warn't for the confounded lips. Away he now crams, up the field road, with the hounds chirping merrily along on his right, through turnips, oat stubble, winter beans, and plough. A white farm onstead, Buckwheat Grange, with its barking cur in a barrel, causes the fox to change his course and slip down a broken but grassy bank to the left. 'Dash his impittance, but he's taken us into a most unmanageable country,' observes Mr Jorrocks,, shading his eyes from the now outbursting sun with his hand as he trotted on, eyeing the oft occurring fences as he spoke. 'Lost all idee of where I ham, and where I'm a-goin',' continued he, looking about to see if he could recognize anything. Hills, dales, woods, water were equally new to him.

Crash! now go the hounds upon an old dead thornfence, stuck on a low sod-bank, making Jorrocks shudder at the sound. Over goes Stobbs without doing anything for his followers.

'Go on, Binjimin! go on! Now,' cries Jorrocks, cantering up, cracking his whip, as if he wanted to take it in stride, but in reality to frighten Ben over to break it. 'Go on, ye miserable man-monkey of a boy!' repeats he, as Xerxes now turned tail, nearly upsetting our master—'Oh, you epitome of a tailor!' groaned Jorrocks; 'you're of no more use wi' 'ounds than a lady's-maid—do believe I could make as good a wipper-in out of a carrot! See! you've set my quad a-refusing', and I'll bet a guinea 'at to a 'alf-crown wide-awake he'll not face another fence to-day. Come hup, I say, you hugly beast!' now roared Jorrocks, pretending to put Arterxerxes resolutely at it, but in reality holding him hard by the head—'Get off, ye useless apology of a hosier and pull it down, or I'll give you sich a wopping as 'ill send you to Blair Atholl for the rest of the day,' exclaimed our half-distracted master, brandishing his flail of a whip as he spoke.

Ben gladly alighted, and by dint of pulling away the dead thorns, and scratching like a rabbit at the bank, he succeeded in greatly reducing the obstacle.

'Now lead him over!' cried Mr Jorrocks, applying his whip freely to Xerxes, and giving Ben a sly, accidental cut. Xerxes floundered over, nearly crushing Ben, and making plain sailing for Jorrocks. Our master then followed and galloped away, leaving Ben writhing and crying, and vowing that he would 'take him and pull him off his 'oss.'

The hounds had now shot a few fields ahead, but a flashy catching scent diminishing their pace, Mr Jorrocks was soon back to them yoicking and holding them on. 'Yooi, over he goes!' cheered he, taking off his cap, as Priestess endorsed Ranger's promissory note on a very wet undrained fallow—'Yooi, over he goes!' repeated he, eyeing the fence into it, and calculating whether he could lead over or scuttle up to the white gate on the left in less time, and thinking the latter was safer, having got the hounds over, he rose in his stirrups, and pounded away while Charley took the fence in his stride. They were now upon sound old pasture, lying parallel with tortuous Tommy, and most musical were the hounds' notes as each in turn prevailed. Mr Jorrocks had lit on his legs in the way of gates, and holloaed and rode as if he didn't know what craning was.

'Forrard on, Priestess, old betch!' cheered he, addressing himself to the now leading hound, 'forrard on!—for-rard!' adding, 'I'll gie ye *sich* a plate o' bones if we do but kill.'

On the hounds went bustling, chirping, and whimpering, all anxious to fly, but still not able to accomplish it. The scent was shifty and bad, sometimes serving them, and then as quickly failing, as if the fox had been coursed by a dog. Jorrocks, though desperately anxious to get them on better terms with their fox, trots gently on, anxiously eyeing them, but restraining his ardour, by repeating the old couplet:

> "'As well as shape full well he knows,
> To *kill* their fox they must have nose.'"

'Aye, aye, but full well he knows also,' continued our master, after he had repeated the lines three or four times over, 'that to kill their fox they must press 'im, at some period or other o' the chase, which they don't seem at all inclined to do,' continued he, looking at their indifferent, slack mode of proceeding. 'Forrard on!' at length cries our master, cracking his whip at a group of dwellers, who seemed inclined to reassure every yard of the ground—'Forrard on!' repeated he, riding angrily at them, adding, 'cus your unbelievin' 'eads, can't you trust old Priestess and Ravager?'

To increase our worthy master's perplexities, a formidable flock of sheep now wheel semicircularly over the line, completely obliterating any little sent that remained, and though our finest huntsman under the sun, aided by Charley as whip, quickly got the hounds beyond their foil, he was not successful in touching upon the line of the fox again.

'Humph,' grunted our master, reviewing his cast, 'the ship must ha' heat 'im, or he's wanished into thin hair'; adding, 'jest put 'em on to me, Charley, whilst I makes one o' Mr Craven Smith's patent all-round-my-'at casts, for that beggar Binjimin's of no more use with a pack of 'ounds than a hopera-box would be to a cow, or a frilled shirt to a pig.' So saying, Mr Jorrocks out with his tootler, and giving a shrill blast, seconded by Charley's whip, proceeded to go down wind, and up wind, and round about wind, without, however, feeling a touch of his fox. At length scarce a hound would stoop, and old black Lucifer gave unmistakable evidence of his opinion of matters by rolling himself just under Jorrock's horse's nose, and uttering a long-drawn howl, as much as to say, 'Come, old boy! shut up! it's no use bothering: let's off to dinner!'

Rot ye! ye great lumberin' henterpriseless brute!' roared Jorrocks, cutting indignantly at him with his whip, 'rot ye! d'ye think I boards and lodges and pays tax 'pon you to 'ave ye settin' up your 'olesale himperance that way?—g-e-e-t-e away, ye disgraceful sleepin' partner o' the chase!' continued he, as the frightened hound scuttled away with his tail between his legs.

'Well, it's nine 'underd and fifty thousand petties,' muttered our master now that the last of the stoopers had got up their heads, 'it's nine 'underd and fifty thousand petties that I hadn't got close away at his brush, for I'd ha' killed 'im to a dead certainty. Never was a fox better 'unted than that! Science, patience, judgement, skill, everything that constitutes an 'untsman—Goodhall, himself, couldn't ha' done it better! But it's not for mortals to command success,' sighed our now greatly dejected master.

Just as Mr Jorrocks was reining in his horse to blow his hounds together, a wild, shrill, view holloo, just such a one as a screech-owl gives on a clear frosty night, sounded through the country, drawing all eyes to Camperdown Hill, where against the blue sky sat a Wellington-statue-like equestrian with his cap in the air, waving and shouting for hard life.

The late lethargic hounds pricked their ears, and before Mr Jorrocks could ejaculate the word 'Pigg!' the now excited pack had broke away, and were streaming full cry across country to where Pigg was perched.

'Get away hooic! Get away hooic!' holloaed our master, deluding himself with the idea that he was giving them leave. 'Get away h-o-o-ick! Get away h-o-o-ick!' repeated he, cracking his ponderous whip.

The hollooing still continued—louder if possible than before.

'Blow me tight!' observed Mr Jorrocks to himself, 'wot a pipe the feller 'as! a'most as good as Gabriel Junks's!' and returning his horn to his saddle, he took a quick glance at the country for a line to the point, instead of crashing after Charley Stobbs, who seemed by the undue elevation of his horse's tail on the far side of the fence, to be getting into grief already. 'there 'ill be a way out by those stacks,' said Mr Jorrocks to himself, eyeing a military-looking line of burly corn stacks drawn up on the high side of a field to the left: so saying he caught Arterxerxes short round by the head, and letting in the Latchfords, tore away in a desperate state of flutter and excitement, the keys and coppers in his pockets contributing to the commotion.

Mr J was right, for convenient gaps converged to these stacks, from whence a view of the farm-house (Barley Hall) further on was obtained. Away he next tore for it, dashing through the fold-yards, leaving the gates open as if they were his own, and catching Ben draining a pot of porter at the back-door. Here our fat friend had the misfortune to consult farmer Shortstubble, instead of trusting to his own natural instinct for gaps and gates, and Shortstubble put him on a line as wide of his own wheat as he could, which was anything but as direct a road as friend Jorrocks could have found for himself. However, Camperdown Hill was a good prominent feature in the country, and by dint of brisk riding, Jorrocks reached it in a much shorter time than the uninitiated would suppose he could. Now getting Arterxerxes by the mane, he rose in his stirrups, hugging and cramming him up the rugged ride to the top.

When he reached the summit, Pigg, whose sight was much improved, had hunted his fox with a very indifferent scent round the base of the hill, and having just got a view, was capping the hounds on as hard as ever his horse could lay legs to the ground, whooping and forcing the fox away into the open.

'Wot a man it is to ride!' ejaculated Jorrocks, eyeing Pigg, putting one of Duncan Nevin's nags that had never seen hounds before at a post and rail that almost made him rise perpendicularly to clear. 'Well done you!' continued Mr Jorrocks, as with a flounder and scramble James got his horse on his legs on the far side, and proceeded to scuttle away again as hard as before. 'Do believe he's got a view o' the varmint,' continued Mr Jorrocks, eyeing Pigg's cap-in-hand progress.

'Wot a chap it would be if it could only keep itself sober!' continued Mr Jorrocks, still eyeing James intently, and wishing he hadn't been too hard upon him. 'Of all 'bominable vices under the sun that of himtemperance is the most degradin' and disgustin',' continued our master emphatically, accompanying the assertion with a hearty crack of the whip down his leg.

Jorrocks now gets a view of the varmint stealing away over a stubble, and though he went stouter than our master would have liked if he had been hunting himself, he saw by Pigg's determined way that he was master of him, and had no doubt that he would have him in hand before long. Accordingly, our master got Arterxerxes by his great Roman-nosed head, and again letting the Latchfords freely into his sides, sent him scrambling down-hill at a pace that was perfectly appalling. Open went the gate at the bottom of the hill, down Jorrocks made for the Long

Tommy ford, splash he sent Arterxerxes in just like Johnny Gilpin in Edmondton Wash—

> '... throwing the water about,
> On both sides of the way,
> Just like a trundling mop,
> Or a wild goose at play.'

Then, having got through, he seized the horse by the mane, and rose the opposing bank, determined to be in at the death if he could. 'Blow me tight!' ejaculated he, 'do believe this hungry high-lander will grab him arter all!' And then rising in his stirrups and setting up his great shoulders, Jorrocks tore up the broken Muggercamp lane, sending the loose stones flying right and left as he went.

'If they can but pash him past Ravenswing-scar,' observed Mr Jorrocks, eyeing the leading hounds approaching it, 'they'll mop 'im to a certainty, for there's nothing' to save 'im arter it. Crikey! they're past! and its U.P. with old Pug! Well, if this doesn't bang Bannager, I doesn't know what does! If we do but kill 'un, I'll make sich a hofferin' to Bacchus as 'ill perfectly 'stonish 'im,' continued Mr Jorrocks, setting Arterxerxes a-going again. 'Gur-r-r along! you great 'airy 'eeled 'umbug!' groaned he, cropping and rib-roasting the horse with his whip.

Arterxerxes, whose pedigree, perhaps, hasn't been very minutely looked into, soon begins to give unmistakable evidence of satiety. He doesn't seem to care much about the whip, and no longer springs to the spur. He begins to play the castanets, too, in a way that is anything but musical to Mr Jorrocks's ear. Our master feels that it will very soon be U.P. with Arterxerxes too.

'Come hup, you snivellin', drivellin, son of a lucifer match-maker!' he roars out to Ben, who is coming lagging along in his master's wake. 'Come on!' roared he, waving his arm frantically, as, on reaching the top of Ravengswing-scar, he sees the hounds swinging down, like a bundle of clock pendulums, into the valley below. 'Come hup, I say, ye miserable, road-ridin', dish-lickin' cub! and give me that quad, for you're a disgrace to a saddle, and only fit to toast muffins for a young ladies' boarding school. Come hup, you preter-pluperfect tense of 'umbugs!' adding, 'I wouldn't give tuppence a dozen for such beggarly boys; no, not if they'd give me a paper bag to put them in.'

Mr Jorrocks, having established a comfortable landing-place on a grassy mound, proceeded to dismount from the nearly pumped-out Arterxerxes, and pile him self on to the much fresher Xerxes, who had been ridden more as a second horse than as a whipper-in's.

'Now go along!' cried our master, settling himself into his saddle, and giving Xerxes a hearty salute on the neck with his whip. 'Now go along!' repeated he, 'and lay yourself out as if you were in the cut-me-downs,' adding, 'there are twenty couple of 'ounds on the scent!

'By 'eavens, it's sublime!' exclaimed he, eyeing the hounds, streaming away over a hundred-acre pasture below. 'By 'eavens, it's sublime! 'ow they go, screechin' and towlin' along, jest like a pocket full o' marbles. 'Ow the old wood re-echoes their melody, and the old castle seemingly takes pleasure to repeat the sound. A Jullien concert's nothin' to it. No, not all the bands i' the country put together.'

'How I wish I was a heagle!' now exclaimed Mr Jorrocks, eyeing the wide stretching vale before him. 'How I wish I was a heagle, 'overin, over 'em, seein' which 'ound has the scent, which hasn't, and which are runnin' frantic for blood.'

'To guide a scent well over a country for a length of time, through all the changes and chances o' the chase, and among all difficulties usually encountered, requires the best and most experienced abilities,' added he, shortening his hold of his horse, as he now put his head down the steep part of the hill. Away Jorrocks went wobbling like a great shape of red Noyeau jelly.

An accommodating lane serves our master below, and taking the grassy side of it, he pounds along manfully, sometimes hearing the hounds, sometimes seeing Pigg's cap, sometimes Charley's hat, bobbing over the fences; and, at more favoured periods, getting a view of the whole panorama of the chase. Our master is in ecstacies! He whoops, and shouts, and grins, and rolls in his saddle, looking more like the drunken Huzzar at the circus, than the sober, well-conducted citizen.

'For-a-r-ard on!' is still his cry. Hark! They've turned and are coming towards him. Jorrocks hears them, and spurs on in hopes of a nick. Fortune favours him, as she generally does the brave and persevering, and a favourable fall of the land enables our friend to view the fox still travelling on at an even, stealthy sort of pace, though certainly slower than the still pressing, squeak, squeak, yap, yap, running pack. Pigg and Charley are in close attendance, and Jorrocks nerves himself for a grand effort to join them.

'I'll do it,' says he, putting Xerxes at a well-broken-down cattle-gap, into Wandermoor Common. This move lands him well inside the hounds, and getting upon turf, he hugs his horse, resolved to ride at whatever comes in his way. Another gap, not quite so well flatenned as the first, helps our friend on in his project, and emboldened by success, he rams manfully at a low stake and rice-bound gateway, and lands handsomely in the next field. He thus gains confidence.

'Come on, ye miserable, useless son of a lily-livered besom-maker,' he roars to Benjamin, who is craning and funking at the place his master has come so gallantly over. 'Rot ye,' adds Jorrocks, as the horse turns tail, 'I'll bind ye 'prentice to a salmon pickler.'

The next field is a fallow, but Jorrocks chooses a wet furrow, up which he spurts briskly, eyeing the country far and near, as well for the fox, as a way out. He sees both. The fox is skirting the brow of the opposite heathery hill, startling the tinkling belled sheep, while the friendly shepherd waves his cap, indicating an exit.

'Thank'ee,' cries Jorrocks, as he slips through the gate.

There is nothing now between him and the hounds, save a somewhat rough piece of moorland, but our master not being afraid of the pace so long as there is no leaping, sails away in the full glow of enthusiastic excitement. He is half frantic with joy!

The hounds now break from scent to view and chase the still flying fox along the hill-side—Duster, Vanquisher, and Hurricane have pitched their pipes up at the very top of their gamut, and the rest come shrieking and screaming as loudly as their nearly pumped-out wind will allow.

Dauntless is upon him, and now a snap, a turn, a roll, and it's all over with Reynard.

Now Pigg is off his horse and in the midst of the pack, now he's down, now he's up, and there's a pretty scramble going on!

'Leave him! leave him!' cries Charley, cracking his whip in aid of Pigg's efforts. A ring is quickly cleared, the extremities are whipped off, and behold, the fox is ready for eating.

'Oh, Pigg, you're a brick! a fire-brick!' gasps the heavily perspiring Mr Jorrocks, throwing himself exhausted from his horse, which he leaves outside the now riotous ring, and making up to the object of his adoration, he exclaimed, 'Oh, Pigg, let us fraternize!' Whereupon Jorrocks seized Pigg by the middle, and hugged him like a Polar bear, to the mutual astonishment of Pigg and the pack.

'A—a—a wuns, man, let's hev' him worried!' roared Pigg, still holding up the fox with both hands high above his head. 'A—a—a wuns, man, let's hev' him worried,' repeated James, as Jorrocks danced him about still harder than before.

'Team 'im and eat 'im!' roars Piggs, discharging himself of the fox, which has the effect of detaching Jorrocks, and sending him to help at the worry. Then the old boy takes a haunch, and tantalizes the first Brilliant, then Harmony, then Splendour, then Vengeance, all the eager young entry in short.

Great was Mr Jorrocks's joy and exultation. He stuck his cap on his whip and danced about on one leg. He forgot all about the Cat and Custard-Pot, and gob full of baccy, and crack in the kite, in his anxiety to make the most of the victory. Having adorned the head-stall of his own bridle with the brush, slung the head becomingly at Pigg's saddle side, and smeared Ben's face plentifully with blood, he got his cavalcade in marching order, and by dint of brisk trotting re-entered Handley Cross just at high change, when everybody was abusing him for his conduct to poor Pigg, and vowing that he didn't deserve so good a huntsman. Then when they saw what had happened, they changed their tunes, declaring it was a regular preconcerted do, abused both James and Jorrocks, and said they's withdraw their subscriptions from the hounds.

WRITING UP A HUNT

Mr Sponge's Sporting Tour
R. S. Surtees
1853

'Have you any 'baccy?' asked Jack, waddling in in his slippers, after having sucked off his tops without the aid of a boot-jack.

'There's some in my jacket-pocket,' replied Sponge, nodding to where it hung in the wardrobe; 'but it won't do to smoke here, will it?' asked he.

'Why not?' inquired Jack.

'Such a fine room,' replied Sponge, looking around.

'Oh, fine be hanged!' replied Jack; adding, as he made for the jacket, 'no place too fine for smokin' in.'

Having helped himself to one of the best cigars, and lighted it, Jack composed himself cross-legged in an easy, spring, stuffed chair, while Sponge fussed about among the writing implements, watering and stirring up the clotted ink, and denouncing each pen in succession, as he gave it the initiatory trial in writing the word 'Sponge.'

'Curse the pens!' exclaimed he, throwing the last bright crisp yellow thing from him in disgust. 'There's not one among 'em that can go!—all reg'larly stumped up.'

'Haven't you a penknife?' asked Jack, taking the cigar out of his mouth.

'Not I,' replied Sponge.

'Take a razor, then,' said Jack, who was good at an expedient.

'I'll take one of yours,' said Sponge, going into the dressing-room for one.

'Hang it, but you're rather too sharp,' exclaimed Jack, with a shake of his head.

'It's more than your razor 'll be when I'm done with it,' replied Sponge.

Having at length, with the aid of Jack's razor, succeeded in getting a pen that would write, Mr Sponge selected a sheet of best cream-laid satin paper, and taking a cane-bottomed chair, placed himself at the table in an attitude for writing. Dipping the fine yellow pen in the ink, he looked in Jack's face for an idea. Jack, who had now got well advanced in his cigar, sat squinting through his spectacles at our scribe, though apparently looking at the top of the bed.

'Well,' said Sponge, with a look of inquiry.

'Well,' replied Jack, in a tone of indifference.

'How shall I begin?' asked Sponge, twirling the pen between his fingers, and spluttering the ink over the paper.

'Begin!' replied Jack, 'begin, oh, begin, just as you usually begin.'

'As a letter?' asked Sponge.

'I'spose so,' replied Jack; 'how would you think?'

O, I don't know,' replied Sponge. 'Will *you* try your hand?' added he, holding out the pen.

'Why, I'm busy just now, you see,' said he, pointing to his cigar, 'and that horse of yours (Jack had ridden the redoubtable chestnut, Multum in Parvo, who had gone very well in the company of Hercules) pulled so confoundedly that I've almost lost the use of my fingers,' continued he, working away as if he had got the cramp in both hands; 'but I'll prompt you,' added he, 'I'll prompt you.'

'Why don't you begin, then?' asked Sponge.

'Begin!' exclaimed Jack, taking the cigar from his lips; 'begin!' repeated he, 'oh, I'll begin directly—didn't know you were ready.'

Jack then threw himself back in his chair, and sticking out his little bandy legs, turned the whites of his eyes up to the ceiling, as if lost in meditation.

'Begin,' said he, after a pause, 'begin, "This splendid pack had a stunning run."'

'But we must put *what* pack first,' observed Sponge, writing the words 'Mr Puffington's hounds' at the top of the paper. 'Well,' said he, writing on, 'this stunning pack had a splendid run.'

'No, not stunning *pack*,' growled Jack, '*splendid* pack—"this splendid pack had a stunning run."'

'Stop!' exclaimed Sponge writing it down; 'well,' said he, looking up, 'I've got it.'

'This stunning pack had a splendid run,' repeated Jack, squinting away at the ceiling.

'I though you said *splendid* pack,' observed Sponge.

'So I did,' replied Jack.

'You said stunning just now,' rejoined he.

'Ah, that was a slip of the tongue,' said Jack. 'This splendid pack had a stunning run,' repeated Jack, appealing again to his cigar for inspiration; 'well then,' said he, after a pause, 'you just go on as usual, you know,' continued he, with a flourish of his great red hand.

'As usual!' exclaimed Sponge, 'you don't s'pose one's pen goes of itself.'

'Why no,' replied Jack, knocking the ashes of his cigar on to the arabesque-patterned tapestry carpet—'why no, not exactly; but these things, you know, are a good deal matter of course; just describe what you saw, you know, and butter Puff well, that's the main point.'

'But you forget,' replied Sponge, 'I don't know the country, I don't know the people, I don't know anything at all about the run—I never once looked at the hounds.

'That's nothin',' replied Jack, 'there'd be plenty like you in that respect. However,' continued he, gathering himself up in his chair as if for an effort, 'you can say—let me see what you can say—you can say, "this splendid pack had a stunning run from Hollyburn Hanger, the property of its truly popular master, Mr Puffington," or—stop,' said Jack, checking himself, 'say, "the property of its truly popular and sporting master, Mr Puffington." The cover's just as much mine as it's his,' observed Jack; 'it belongs to old Sir Timothy Tensthemain, who's vegetating at Boulogne-sur-mer, but Puff says he'll buy in when it comes to the hammer, so we'll flatter him by considering it his already, just as we flatter him by calling him a sportsman—*sportsman* !' added Jack, with a sneer, 'he's just as much taste for the thing as a cow.'

'Well,' said Sponge, looking up, 'I've got "truly popular and sporting master, Mr Puffington,"' adding, 'hadn't we better say something about the meet and the grand spread here before we begin with the run?'

'True,' replied Jack, after a long-drawn whiff and another adjustment of the end of his cigar; 'say that "a splendid field of well-appointed sportsmen"—'

'A splendid field of well-appointed sportsmen,' wrote Sponge.

'"Among whom we recognised several distinguished strangers and members of Lord Scamperdale's hunt." That means you and I,' observed Jack.

'"Of Lord Scamperdale's hunt—that means you and I"'—read Sponge, as he wrote it.

'But you're not to put in that; you're not to write "that means you and I," my man,' observed Jack.

'Oh, I thought that was part of the sentence,' replied Sponge.

'No, no;' said Jack, 'I mean to say that you and I were the distinguished strangers and members of Lord Scamperdale's hunt; but that's between ourselves you know.'

'Good,' said Sponge; 'then I'll strike that out,' running his pen through the words 'that means you and I.' 'Now get on,' said he, appealing to Jack, adding, 'we've a deal to do yet.'

'Say,' said Jack, '"after partaking of the well-known profuse and splendid hospitality of Hanby House, they proceeded at once to Hollyburn Hanger, where a fine seasoned fox"—though some said he was a bag one—'

'Did they?' exclaimed Sponge, adding, 'well, I thought he went away rather queerly.'

'Oh, it was only old Bung the brewer, who runs down every run he doesn't ride.'

'Well, never mind,' replied Sponge, 'we'll make the best of it, whatever it was;' writing away as he spoke, and repeating the words 'bag one' as he penned them.

'"Broke away,"' continued Jack—

'"In view of the whole field,"' added Sponge.

'Just so,' assented Jack.

'"Every hound scoring to cry, and making the"—the—the—what d'ye call the thing?' asked Jack.

'Country,' suggested Sponge.

'No,' replied Jack, with a shake of the head.

'Hill and dale?' tried Sponge again.

'Welkin!' exclaimed Jack, hitting it off himself—'"makin' the welkin ring with their melody!" makin' the welkin *ring* with their melody,' repeated he, with exultation.

'Capital!' observed Sponge, as he wrote it.

'Equal to Littlelegs,'* said Jack, squinting his eyes inside out.

'We'll make a grand thing of it,' observed Sponge.

'So we will,' replied Jack, adding, 'if we had but a book of po'try we'd weave in some lines here. You haven't a book o' no sort with you that we could prig a little po'try from?' asked he.

'No,' replied Sponge, thoughtfully. 'I'm afraid not; indeed, I'm sure not. I've got nothin' but "Mogg's Cab Fares."'

'Ah, that won't do,' observed Jack, with a shake of the head. 'But stay,' said he, 'there are some books over yonder,' pointing to the top of an Indian cabinet, and squinting in a totally different direction. 'Let's see what they are,' added he, rising, and stumping away to where they stood. 'I Promessi Sposi,' read he off the back of one: 'what can that mean? Ah, its Latin,' said he, opening the volume. 'Contes à ma Filles,' read he off the back of another. 'That sounds like racin',' observed he, opening the volume: 'its Latin, too,' said he, returning it. 'However, never mind, we'll "sugar Puff's milk," as Mr Bragg would say, without po'try.' So saying, Mr Spraggon stumped back to his easy chair. 'Well, now,' said he seating himself comfortably in it, 'let's see, where did we go first? "He broke at the lower end of the cover, and crossing the brook, made straight for Fleeyhaugh, Water Meadows, over which," you may say, "there's always a ravishing scent."'

'Have you got that?' asked Jack, after what he thought a sufficient lapse of time for writing it.

'"Ravishing scent,"' repeated Sponge, as he wrote the words.

'Very good,' said Jack, smoking and considering. '"From there,"' continued he, '"he made a bit of a bend, as if inclining for the plantations at Winstead, but, changing his mind, he faced the rising ground, and crossing over nearly the highest part of Shillington Hill, made direct for the little village of Berrington Roothings below:"'

'Stop!' exclaimed Sponge, 'I haven't got half that; I've only got to "the plantations at Winstead."' Sponge made play with his pen, and presently held it up in token of being done.

'Well,' pondered Jack, 'there was a check there. Say', continued he, addressing himself to Sponge, '"Here the hounds came to a check."'

'Here the hounds came to a check," wrote Sponge. 'Shall we say anything about distance?' asked he.

---

* The Poetical Recorder of the Doings of the Dublin Garrison dogs, in *Bell's Life*.

'P'raps we may as well,' replied Jack. 'We shall have to stretch it though a bit.'

'Let's see,' continued he; 'from the cover to Berrington Roothings over by Shillington Hill and Fleecyhaugh Water Meadows will be—say, two miles and a half or three miles at the most,—call it four, well four miles,—say four miles in twelve minutes, twenty miles an hour,—too quick,—four miles in fifteen minutes, sixteen miles an hour; no—I think p'raps it'll be safer to lump the distance at the end, and put in a place or two that nobody knows the name of, for the convenience of those who were not out.'

'But those who *were* out will blab, won't they?' asked Sponge.

'Only to each other,' replied Jack. 'They'll all stand up for the truth of it as against strangers. You need never be afraid of over-eggin' the puddin' for those that were out.'

'Well, then,' observed Sponge, looking at his paper to report progress, 'we've got the hounds to a check. "Here the hounds came to a check,"' read he.

'Ah! now, then,' said Jack, in a tone of disgust, 'we must say summut handsome of Bragg; and of all conceited animals under the sun, he certainly is the most conceited. I never saw such a man! How that unfortunate, infatutated master of his keeps him, I can't for the life of me imagine. *Master!* faith, Bragg's the *master*,' continued Jack, who now began to foam at the mouth. 'He laughs at old Puff to his face; yet it's wonderful the influence Bragg has over him. I really believe he has talked Puff into believing that there's not such another huntsman under the sun, and really he's as great a muff as ever walked. He can just dress the character, and that's all.' So saying, Jack wiped his mouth on the sleeve of his red coat preparatory to displaying Mr Bragg upon paper.

'Well, now we are at fault,' said Jack, motioning Sponge to resume; 'we are at fault; now say,' but Mr. Bragg, who had ridden gallantly on his favourite bay, as fine an animal as ever went, though somewhat past mark of mouth—' He *is* a good horse, at least *was*,' observed Jack; adding, 'I sold Puff him, he was one of old Sugarlip's' meaning Lord Scamperdales.

'Sure to be a good'un then' replied Sponge, with a wink; adding, 'I wonder if he'd like to buy any more.'

'We'll talk about that after,' replied Jack, 'at present let us get on with our run.'

'Well,' said Sponge, 'I've got it: 'Mr Bragg, who had ridden gallantly on his favourite bay, as fine an animal as ever went, though somewhat past mark of mouth—"'

'"Was well up with his hounds,"' continued Jack, '"and with a *gently* Rantipole! and a single wave of his arm, proceeded to make one of those scientific casts for which this eminent huntsman is so justly celebrated." Justly *celebrated!*' repeated Jack, spitting on the carpet with a hawk of disgust; 'the conceited self-sufficient bantam-cock never made a cast worth a copper, or rode a yard but when he thought somebody was looking at him.'

'I've got it,' said Sponge, who had plied his pen to good purpose.

'Justly celebrated,' repeated Jack, with a snort. 'Well, then, say, "Hitting off the scent like a workman,"—big H, you know, for a fresh sentence,— "they went away again at score, and passing by Moorlinch farm-buildings, and threading the strip of plantation by Bexley Burn, he crossed Silverbury Green, leaving Longford Hutch to the right, and passing straight on by the gibbet at Harpen." Those are all bits of places,' observed Jack, 'that none but the country folks know; indeed, I shouldn't have known them but for shootin' over them when old Bloss lived at the Green. Well now, have you got all that?' asked he.

'"Gibbet at Harpen,"' read Sponge, as he wrote it.

'"Here, then, the gallant pack, breaking from scent to view,"' continued Jack, speaking slowly, '"run into their fox in the open close upon Mountnessing Wood, evidently his point from the first, and into which a few more strides would have carried him. It was as fine a run as ever was seen, and the hunting of the hounds was the admiration of all who saw it. The distance couldn't have been less than"—than—what shall we say?' asked Jack.

'Ten, twelve miles, as the crow flies,' suggested Sponge.

'No,' said Jack, 'that would be too much. Say ten; adding, 'that will be four more than it was.'

'Never mind,' said Sponge, as he wrote it; 'folks like good measure with runs as well as ribbons.'

'Now we must butter Old Puff,' observed Spraggon.

'What can we say for him?' asked Sponge; 'that he never went off the road?'

'No, by Jove!' said Jack; 'you'll spoil all if you do that: better leave it alone altogether than do that. Say, "the justly popular owner of this most celebrated pack, though riding good fourteen stone" (he rides far more,' observed Jack; 'at least *sixteen;* but it'll please him to make out that he *can* ride fourteen), "led the welters, on his famous chestnut horse, Tappey Lappey."'

'What shall we say about the rest?' asked Sponge; 'Lumpleg, Slapp, Guano, and all those?'

'Oh, say nothing"' replied Jack; 'we've nothin' to do with nobody but Puff; and we couldn't mention them without bringin' in our Flat Hat men too, Blossomnose, Fyle, Fossick, and so on. Besides, it would spoil all to say that Guano was up—people would say directly it couldn't have been much of a run if Guano was there. You might finish off,' observed Jack, after a pause, 'by saying that "after this truly brilliant affair, Mr Puffington, like a thorough sportsman, and one who never trashes his hounds un-necessarily—unlike some masters," you may say, "who never know when to leave off" (that will be a hit at Old Scamp,' observed Jack, with a frightful squint), '"returned to Hanby House, where a distinguished party of sportsmen—" or, say "a distinguished party of noblemen and gentlemen"—that'll please the ass more—"a large party of noblemen and gentlemen were partaking of his"—his—what shall we call it?

'Grub!' said Sponge.

'No, no—summut genteel—his—his—his—"*splendid hospitality!*"' concluded Jack waving his arm triumphantly over his head.

'Hard work, authorship!' exclaimed Sponge, as he finished writing, and threw down the pen.

'Oh, I don't know,' replied Jack; adding, 'I could go on for an hour.'

'Ah, *you*!—that's all very well,' replied Sponge, 'for you, squatting comfortably in your arm-chair: but consider me, toiling with my pen, bothered with the writing, and craning at the spelling.'

'Never mind, we've done it,' replied Jack; adding, 'Puff'll be as pleased as Punch. We've polished him off uncommon. That's just the sort of account to tickle the beggar. He'll go riding about the country, showing it to everybody, and wondering who wrote it.'

'And what shall we send it to?—the *Sporting Magazine*, or what?' asked Sponge.

'*Sporting Magazine!*—no,' replied Jack; 'wouldn't be out till next year—quick's the word in these railway times. Send it to a newspaper—*Bell's Life*, or one of the Swillingford papers. Either of them would be glad to put it in.'

'I hope they'll be able to read it,' observed Sponge, looking at the blotched and scrawled manuscript.

'Trust them for that,' replied Jack; adding 'If there's any word that bothers them, they've nothin' to do but look in the dictionary—these folks all have dictionaries, wonderful fellows for spellin".'

Just then a little buttony page, in green and gold, came in to ask if there were any letters for the post; and our friends hastily made up their packet, directing it to the editor of the Swillingford "GUIDE TO GLORY AND FREEMAN'S FRIEND;' words that in the hurried style of Mr Sponge's penmanship looked very like 'GUIDE TO GROG, AND FREE-MAN'S FRIEND.'

THE O'CONORS OF CASTLE CONOR, COUNTY MAYO

Tales of All Countries
Anthony Trollope
1860

I shall never forget my first introduction to country life in Ireland, my first day's hunting there, or the manner in which I passed the evening afterwards. Nor shall I ever cease to be grateful for the hospitality which I received from the O'Conors of Castle Conor. My acquaintance with the family was first made in the following manner. But before I begin my story, let me inform my reader that my name is Archibald Green.

I had been for a fortnight in Dublin, and was about to proceed into county Mayo on business which would occupy me there for some weeks. My head-quarters would, I found, be at the town of Ballyglass; and I soon learned that Ballyglass was not a place in which I should find hotel accommodation of a luxurious kind, or much congenial society indigenous to the place itself.

'But you are a hunting man, you say,' said old Sir P— C—; 'and in that case you will soon know Tom O'Conor. Tom won't let you be dull. I'd write you a letter to Tom, only he'll certainly make you out without my taking the trouble.'

I did think at the time that the old baronet might have written the letter for me, as he had been a friend of my father's in former days; but he did not, and I started for Ballyglass with no other introduction to any one in the country than that contained in Sir P—'s promise that I should soon know Mr Thomas O'Conor.

I had already provided myself with a horse, groom, saddle and bridle, and these I sent down, en avant, that the Ballyglassians might know that I was somebody. Perhaps, before I arrived, Tom O'Conor might learn that a hunting man was coming into the neighbourhood, and I might find at the inn a polite note intimating that a bed was at my service at Castle Conor. I had heard so much of the free hospitality of the Irish gentry as to imagine that such a thing might be possible.

But I found nothing of the kind. Hunting gentlemen in those days were very common in county Mayo, and one horse was no great evidence of a man's standing in the world. Men there, as I learnt afterwards, are sought for themselves quite as much as they are elsewhere; and though my groom's top-boots were neat, and my horse a very tidy animal, my entry into Ballyglass created no sensation whatever.

In about four days after my arrival, when I was already infinitely disgusted with the little pot-house in which I was forced to stay, and had made up my mind that the people in county Mayo were a churlish set, I sent my horse on to a meet of the fox-hounds, and followed after myself on an open car.

No one but an erratic fox-hunter such as I am,—a fox-hunter, I mean, whose lot has it been to wander about from one pack of hounds to another,—can understand the melancholy feeling which a man has when he first intrudes himself, unknown by any one, among an entirely new set of sportsmen. When a stranger falls thus as it were out of the moon into a hunt, it is impossible that men should not stare at him and ask who he is. And it is so disagreeable to be stared at, and to have such questions asked! This feeling does not come upon a man in Leicestershire or Gloucestershire, where the numbers are large, and a stranger or two will always be overlooked, but in small hunting fields it is so painful that a man has to pluck up much courage before he encounters it.

We met on the morning in question at Bingham's Grove. There were not above twelve or fifteen men out, all of whom, or nearly all, were cousins to each other. They seemed to be all Toms, and Pats, and Larrys, and Micks. I was done up very knowingly in pink, and thought that I looked quite the thing; but for two or three hours nobody noticed me.

I had my eyes about me, however, and soon found out which of them was Tom O'Conor. He was a fine-looking fellow, thin and tall, but not largely made, with a piercing gray eye, and a beautiful voice for speaking to a hound. He had two sons there also, short, slight fellows, but exquisite horsemen. I already felt that I had a kind of acquaintance with the father, but I hardly knew on what ground to put in my claim.

We had no sport early in the morning. It was a cold bleak February day, with occasional storms of sleet. We rode from cover to cover, but all in vain. 'I am sorry, sir, that we are to have such a bad day, as you are a stranger here,' said one gentlemen to me. This was Jack O'Conor, Tom's eldest son, my bosom friend for many a year after. Poor Jack! I fear that the Encumbered Estates Court sent him altogether adrift upon the world.

'We may still have a run from Poulnaroe, if the gentleman chooses to come on,' said a voice coming from behind with a sharp trot. It was Tom O'Conor.

'Wherever the hounds go, I'll follow,' said I.

'Then come on to Poulnaroe,' said Mr O'Conor. I trotted on quickly by his side, and before we reached the cover had managed to slip in something about Sir P. C.

'What the deuce!' said he. 'What! a friend of Sir P—'s? Why the deuce didn't you tell me so? What are you doing down here? Where are you staying?' &c &c &c.

'At Poulnaroe we found a fox, but before we did so Mr O'Conor had asked me over to Castle Conor. And this he did in such a way that there was no possibility of refusing him—or, I should rather say, of disobeying him. For his invitation came quite in the tone of a command.

'You'll come to us of course when the day is over—and let me see; we're near Ballyglass now, but the run will be right away in our direction. Just send word for them to send your things to Castle Conor.'

'But they're all about, and unpacked,' said I.

'Never mind. Write a note and say what you want now, and go and get the rest to-morrow yourself. Here, Patsey!—Patsey! run in to Ballyglass for this gentleman at once. Now don't be long, for the chances are we shall find here.' And then, after giving some further hurried instructions he left me to write a line in pencil to the innkeeper's wife on the back of a ditch.

This I accordingly did. 'Send my small portmanteau,' I said, 'and all my black dress clothes, and shirts, and socks, and all that, and above all my dressing things which are on the little table, and the satin neck-handkerchief, and whatever you do, mind you send my *pumps;*' and I underscored the latter word; for Jack O'Conor, when his father left me, went on pressing the invitation. 'My sisters are going to get up a dance,' said he; 'and if you are fond of that kind of things perhaps we can amuse you.' Now in those days I was very fond of dancing—and very fond of young ladies too, and therefore glad enough to learn that Tom O'Conor had daughters as well as sons. On this account I was very particular in underscoring the word pumps.

'And hurry, you young divil,' Jack O'Conor said to Patsey.

'I have told him to take the portmanteau over on a car,' said I.

'All right; then you'll find it there on our arrival.'

We had an excellent run, in which I may make bold to say that I did not acquit myself badly. I stuck very close to the hounds, as did the whole of the O'Conor brood; and when the fellow contrived to earth himself, as he did, I received those compliments on my horse, which is the most approved praise which one foxhunter ever gives to another.

'We'll buy that fellow of you before we let you go,' said Peter, the youngest son.

'I advise you to look sharp after your money if you sell him to my brother,' said Jack.

And then we trotted slowly off to Castle Conor, which, however, was by no means near to us. 'We have ten miles to go;—good Irish miles,' said the father. 'I don't know that I ever remember a fox from Poulnaroe taking that line before.'

'He wasn't a Poulnaroe fox,' said Peter.

'I don't know that,' said Jack; and then they debated that question hotly.

Our horses were very tired, and it was late before we reached Mr O'Conor's house. That getting home from hunting with a thoroughly weary animal, who has no longer sympathy or example to carry him on, is very tedious work. In the present instance I had company with me;

but when a man is alone, when his horse toes at every ten steps, when the night is dark and the rain pouring, and there are yet eight miles of road to be conquered,—at such times a man is almost apt to swear that he will give up hunting.

At last we were in the Castle Conor stable yard;—for we had approached the house by some back way; and as we entered the house by a door leading through a wilderness of back passages, Mr O'Conor said out loud, 'Now, boys, remember I sit down to dinner in twenty minutes.' And then turning expressly to me, he laid his hand kindly upon my shoulder and said, 'I hope you will make yourself quite at home at Castle Conor,—and whatever you do, don't keep us waiting for dinner. You can dress in twenty minutes, I suppose?'

'In ten!' said I, glibly.

'That's well. Jack and Peter will show you your room,' and so he turned away and left us.

My two young friends made their way into the great hall, and thence into the drawing-room, and I followed them. We were all dressed in pink, and had waded deep through bog and mud. I did not exactly know whither I was being led in this guise, but I soon found myself in the presence of two young ladies, and of a girl about thirteen years of age.

'My sisters,' said Jack, introducing me very laconically; 'Miss O'Conor, Miss Kate O'Conor, Miss Tizzy O'Conor.'

'My name is not Tizzy,' said the younger; 'it's Eliza. How do you do, sir? I hope you had a fine hunt! Was papa well up, Jack?'

Jack did not condescend to answer this question, but asked one of the elder girls whether anything had come, and whether a room had been made ready for me.

'Oh yes!' said Miss O'Conor; 'they came, I know, for I saw them brought into the house; and I hope Mr Green will find everything comfortable.' As she said this I thought I saw a slight smile steal across her remarkably pretty mouth.

They were both exceedingly pretty girls. Fanny the elder wore long glossy curls,—for I write, oh reader, of bygone days, as long ago as that, when ladies wore curls if it pleased them so to do, and gentlemen danced in pumps, with black handkerchiefs round their necks,—yes, long black, or nearly black silken curls; and then she had such eyes;—I never knew whether they were most wicked or most bright; and her face was all dimples, and each dimple was laden with laughter and laden with love. Kate was probably the prettier girl of the two, but on the whole not so attractive. She was fairer than her sister, and wore her hair in braids; and was also somewhat more demure in her manner.

In spite of the special injunctions of Mr O'Conor senior, it was impossible not to loiter for five minutes over the drawing-room fire talking to these houris—more especially as I seemed to know them intimately by intuition before half of the five minutes was over. They were so easy, so pretty, so graceful, so kind, they seemed to take it so much as a matter of course that I should stand there talking in my red coat and muddy boots.

'Well; do go and dress yourselves,' at last said Fanny, pretending to speak to her brothers but looking more especially at me. 'You know how mad papa will be. And remember, Mr Green, we expect great things from your dancing to-night. You coming just at this time is such a Godsend.' And again that soupçon of a smile passed over her face.

I hurried up to my room, Peter and Jack coming with me to the door. 'Is everything right?' said Peter, looking among the towels and water-jugs. 'They've given you a decent fire for a wonder,' said Jack, stirring up the red hot turf which blazed in the grate. 'All right as a trivet,' said I. 'And look alive like a good fellow,' said Jack. We had scowled at each other in the morning as very young men do when they are strangers; and now, after a few hours, we were intimate friends.

I immediately turned to my work, and was gratified to find that all my things were laid out ready for dressing; my portmanteau had of course come open, as my keys were in my pocket, and therefore some of the excellent servants of the house had been able to save me all the trouble of unpacking. There was my shirt hanging before the fire; my black clothes were spread upon the bed, my socks and collar and handkerchief beside them; my brushes were on the toilet table, and everything prepared exactly as though my own man had been there. How nice!

I immediately went to work at getting off my spurs and boots, and the proceeded to loosen the buttons at my knees. In doing this I sat down in the arm-chair which had been drawn up for me, opposite the fire. But what was the object on which my eyes then fell;—the objects I should rather say!

Immediately in front of my chair was placed, just ready for my feet, an enormous pair of shooting-boots—half-boots, made to lace up round the ankles, with thick double leather soles, and each bearing half a stone of iron in the shape of nails and heel-pieces. I had superintended the making of these shoes in Burlington Arcade with the greatest diligence. I was never a good shot; and, like some other sportsmen, intended to make up for my deficiency in performance by the excellence of my shooting apparel. 'Those nails are not large enough,' I had said; 'nor nearly large enough.' But when the boots came home they struck even me as being too heavy, too metalsome. 'He, he, he,' laughed the boot boy as he turned them up for me to look at. It may therefore be imagined of what nature were the articles which were thus set out for the evening's dancing.

And then the way in which they were placed! When I saw this the conviction flew across my mind like a flash of lightning that the preparation had been made under other eyes than those of the servant. The heavy big boots were placed so prettily before the chair, and the strings of each were made to dangle down at the sides, as though just ready for tying! They seemed to say, the boots did, 'Now, make haste.

We at any rate are ready—you cannot say that you were kept waiting for us.' No mere servant's hand had ever enabled a pair of boots to laugh at one so completely.

But what was I to do? I rushed at the small portmanteau, thinking that my pumps also might be there. The woman surely could not have been such a fool as to send me those tons of iron for my evening wear! But, alas, alas! no pumps were there. There was nothing else in the way of covering for my feet; not even a pair of slippers.

And now what was I to do? The absolute magnitude of my misfortune only loomed upon me by degrees. The twenty minutes allowed by that stern old paterfamilias were already gone and I had done nothing towards dressing. And indeed it was impossible that I should do anything that would be of avail. I could not go down to dinner in my stocking feet, nor could I put on my black dress trousers over a pair of mud-painted top-boots. As for those iron-soled horrors—; and then I gave one of them a kick with the side of my bare foot which sent it half way under the bed.

But what was I to do? I began washing myself and brushing my hair with this horried weight upon my mind. My first plan was to go to bed, and send down word that I had been taken suddenly ill in the stomach; then to rise early in the morning and get away unobserved. But by such a course of action I should lose all chance of any further acquaintance with those pretty girls! That they were already aware of the extent of my predicament, and were now enjoying it—of that I was quite sure.

What if I boldly put on the shooting-boots, and clattered down to dinner in them? What if I took the bull by the horns, and made, myself, the most of the joke? This might be very well for the dinner, but it would be a bad joke for me when the hour for dancing came. And, alas! I felt that I lacked the courage. It is not every man that can walk down to dinner, in a strange house full of ladies, wearing such boots as those I have described.

Should I not attempt to borrow a pair? This, all the world will say, should have been my first idea. But I have not yet mentioned that I am myself a large-boned man, and that my feet are especially well developed. I had never for a moment entertained a hope that I should find any one in that house whose boot I could wear. But at last I rang the bell. I would send for Jack, and if everything failed, I would communicate my grief to him.

I had to ring twice before anybody came. The servants, I well knew, were putting the dinner on the table. At last a man entered the room, dressed in rather shabby black, whom I afterwards learned to be the butler.

'What is your name, my friend?' said I, determined to make an ally of the man.

'My name? Why Larry sure, yer honer. And the masther is out of his sinses in a hurry, because yer honer don't come down.'

'Is he though? Well now, Larry; tell me this; which of all the gentlemen in the house has got the largest foot?'

'Is it the largest foot, yer honer?' said Larry, altogether surprised by my question.

'Yes; the largest foot,' and then I proceeded to explain to him my misfortune. He took up first my top-boot, and then the shooting-boot—in looking at which he gazed with wonder at the nails;—and then he glanced at my feet, measuring them with his eye; and after this he pronounced his opinion.

'Yer honer couldn't wear a morsel of leather belonging to ere a one of 'em, young or ould. There niver was a foot like that yet among the O'Conors.'

'But are there no strangers staying here?'

'There's three or four on 'em come in to dinner; but they'll be wanting their own boots I'm thinking. And there's young Misther Dillon; he's come to stay. But Lord love you—' and he again looked at the enormous extent which lay between the heel and the toe of the shooting apparatus which he still held in his hand. 'I niver see such a foot as that in the whole barony,' he said, 'barring my own.'

Now Larry was a large man, much larger altogether than myself, and as he said this I looked down involuntarily at his feet; or rather at his foot, for as he stood I could only see one. And then a sudden hope filled my heart. On that foot there glittered a shoe—not indeed such as were my own which were now resting ingloriously at Ballyglass while they were so sorely needed at Castle Conor; but one which I could wear before ladies, without shame—and in my present frame of mind with infinite contentment.

'Let me look at that one of your own,' said I to the man, as though it were merely a subject for experimental inquiry. Larry, accustomed to obedience, took off the shoe and handed it to me. My own foot was immediately in it, and I found that it fitted me like a glove.

'And now the other,' said I—not smiling, for a smile would have put him on his guard; but somewhat sternly, so that that habit of obedience should not desert him at this perilous moment. And then I stretched out my hand.

'But yer honer can't keep 'em, you know,' said he. 'I haven't the ghost of another shoe to my feet.' But I only looked more sternly than before, and still held out my hand. Custom prevailed. Larry stooped down slowly, looking at me the while, and pulling off the other slipper handed it to me with much hesitation. Alas! as I put it to my foot I found that it was old, and worn, and irredeemably down at heel;—that it was in fact no counterpart at all to that other one which was to do duty as its fellow. But nevertheless I put my foot into it, and felt that a descent to the drawing-room was now possible.

'But yer honer will give 'em back to a poor man?' said Larry almost crying. 'The masther's mad this minute becase the dinner's not up.

Glory to God, only listhen to that!' And as he spoke a tremendous peal rang out from some bell down stairs that had evidently been shaken by an angry hand.

'Larry,' said I—and I endeavoured to assume a look of very grave importance as I spoke—'I look to you to assist me in this matter.'

'Och—wirra sthrue then, and will you let me go? just listhen to that,' and another angry peal rang out, loud and repeated.

'If you do as I ask you,' I continued, 'you shall be well rewarded. Look here; look at these boots,' and I held up the shooting-shoes new from Burlington Arcade. 'They cost thirty shillings—thirty shillings! and I will give them to you for the loan of this pair of slippers.'

'They'd be no use at all to me, yer honer; not the laist use in life.'

'You could do with them very well for to-night, and then you could sell them. And here are ten shillings besides,' and I held out half a sovereign which the poor fellow took into his hand.

I waited no further parley but immediately walked out of the room. With one foot I was sufficiently pleased. As regarded that I felt that I had overcome my difficulty. But the other was not so satsifactory. Whenever I attempted to lift it from the ground the horrid slipper would fall off, or only just hang by the toe. As for dancing, that would be out of the question.

'Och, murther, murther,' sang out Larry, as he heard me going down stairs. 'What will I do at all? Tare and 'ounds; there, he's at it agin, as mad as blazes.' This last exclamation had reference to another peal which was evidently the work of the master's hand.

I confess I was not quite comfortable as I walked down stairs. In the first place I was nearly half an hour late, and I knew from the vigour of the peals that had sounded that my slowness had already been made the subject of strong remarks. And then my left shoe went flop, flop, on every alternate step of the stairs. By no exertion of my foot in the drawing up of my toe could I induce it to remain permanently fixed upon my foot. But over and above and worse than all this was the conviction strong upon my mind that I should become a subject of merriment to the girls as soon as I entered the room. They would understand the cause of my distress, and probably at this moment were expecting to hear me clatter through the stone hall with those odious metal boots.

However, I hurred down and entered the drawing-room, determined to keep my position near the door, so that I might have as little as possible to do on entering and as little as possible in going out. But I had other difficulties in store for me. I had not as yet been introduced to Mrs O'Conor; nor to Miss O'Conor, the squire's unmarried sister.

'Upon my word I thought you were never coming,' said Mr O'Conor as soon as he saw me. 'It is just one hour since we entered the house. Jack, I wish you would find out what has come to the that fellow Larry,' and again he rang the bell. He was too angry, or it might be too impatient to go through the ceremony of introducing me to anybody.

I saw that the two girls looked at me very sharply, but I stood at the back of an arm-chair so that no one could see my feet. But that little imp Tizzy walked round deliberately, looked at my heels, and then walked back again. It was clear that she was in the secret.

There were eight or ten people in the room, but I was too much fluttered to notice well who they were.

'Mamma,' said Miss O'Conor, 'let me introduce Mr Green to you.'

It luckily happened that Mrs O'Conor was on the same side of the fire as myself, and I was able to take the hand which she offered me without coming round into the middle of the circle. Mrs O'Conor was a little woman, apparently not of much importance in the world, but, if one might judge from first appearance, very good-natured.

'And my aunt Die, Mr Green,' said Kate, pointing to a very straight-backed, grim-looking lady, who occupied a corner of a sofa, on the opposite side of the hearth. I knew that politeness required that I should walk across the room and make acquaintance with her. But under the existing circumstances how was I to obey the dictates of politeness? I was determined therefore to stand my ground, and merely bowed across the room at Miss O'Conor. In so doing I made a enemy who never deserted me during the whole of my intercourse with the family. But for her, who knows who might have been sitting opposite to me as I now write?

'Upon my word, Mr Green, the ladies will expect much from an Adonis who takes so long over his toilet,' said Tom O'Conor in that cruel tone of banter which he knew so well how to use.

'You forget, father, that men in London can't jump in and out of their clothes as quick as we wild Irishmen,' said Jack.

'Mr Green knows that we expect a great deal from him this evening. I hope you polk well, Mr Green,' said Kate.

I muttered something about never dancing, but I knew that that which I said was inaudible.

'I don't think Mr Green will dance,' said Tizzy; 'at least not much.' The impudence of that child was, I think, unparalleled by any that I have ever witnessed.

'But in the name of all that's holy, why don't we have dinner?' And Mr O'Conor thundered at the door. 'Larry, Larry, Larry!' he screamed.

'Yes, yer honer, it'll be all right in two seconds,' answered Larry, from some bottomless abyss. 'Tare an' ages; what'll I do at all,' I heard him continuing, as he made his way into the hall. Oh what a clatter he made upon the pavement,—for it was all stone! And how the drops of perspiration stood upon my brow as I listened to him!

And then there was a pause, for the man had gone into the dining-room. I could see now that Mr O'Conor was becoming very angry, and Jack the eldest son—oh, how often he and I have laughed over all this since—left the drawing-room for the second time. Immediately afterwards Larry's footsteps were again heard, hurrying across the hall, and then there was a great slither, and an exclamation, and the noise of a fall—and I could plainly hear poor Larry's head strike against the stone floor.

'Ochone, ochone!' he cried at the top of his voice—'I'm murthered with 'em now intirely; and d—'em for boots—St Peter be good to me.'

There was a general rush into the hall, and I was carried with the stream. The poor fellow who had broken his head would be sure to tell how I had robbed him of his shoes. The coachman was already helping him up, and Peter good-naturedly lent a hand.

'What on earth is the matter?' said Mr O'Conor.

'He must be tipsy,' whispered Miss O'Conor, the maiden sister.

'I aint tipsy at all thin,' said Larry, getting up and rubbing the back of his head, and sundry other parts of his body. 'Tipsy indeed!' And then he added when he was quite upright, 'The dinner is sarved—at last.'

And he bore it all without telling! 'I'll give that fellow a guinea tomorrow morning,' said I to myself—'if it's the last that I have in the world.'

I shall never forget the countenance of the Miss O'Conors as Larry scrambled up cursing the unfortunate boots—'What on earth has he got on?' said Mr O'Conor.

'Sorrow take 'em for shoes,' ejaculated Larry. But his spirit was good and he said not a word to betray me.

We all then went in to dinner how we best could. It was useless for us to go back into the drawing-room, that each might seek his own partner. Mr O'Conor 'the masther', not caring much for the girls who were around him, and being already half beside himself with the confusion and delay, led the way by himself. I as a stranger should have given my arm to Mrs O'Conor; but as it was I took her eldest daughter instead, and contrived to shuffle along into the dining-room without exciting much attention, and when there I found myself happily placed between Kate and Fanny.

'I never knew anything so awkward,' said Fanny; 'I declare I can't conceive what has come to our old servant Larry. He's generally the most precise person in the world, and now he is nearly an hour late—and then he tumbles down in the hall.'

'I am afraid I am responsible for the delay,' said I.

'But not for the tumble I suppose,' said Kate from the other side. I felt that I blushed up to the eyes, but I did not dare to enter into explanations.

'Tom,' said Tizzy, addressing her father across the table, 'I hope you had a good run to-day,' It did seem odd to me that a young lady should call her father Tom, but such was the fact.

'Well; pretty well,' said Mr O'Conor.

'And I hope you were up with the hounds.'

'You may ask Mr Green that. He at any rate was with them, and therefore he can tell you.'

'Oh, he wasn't before you, I know. No Englishman could get before you;—I am quite sure of that.'

'Don't you be impertinent, miss,' said Kate. 'You can easily see, Mr Green, that papa spoils my sister Eliza.'

'Do you hunt in top-boots, Mr Green?' said Tizzy.

To this I made no answer. She would have drawn me into a conversation about my feet in half a minute, and the slightest allusion to the subject threw me into a fit of perspiration.

'Are you fond of hunting, Miss O'Conor?' asked I, blindly hurrying into any other subject of conversation.

Miss O'Conor owned that she was fond of hunting—just a little; only papa would not allow it. When the hounds met anywhere within reach of Castle Conor, she and Kate would ride out to look at them; and if papa was not there that day,—an omission of rare occurrence,—they would ride a few fields with the hounds.

'But he lets Tizzy keep with them the whole day,' said she, whispering.

'And has Tizzy a pony of her own?'

'Oh yes, Tizzy has everything. She's papa's pet, you know.'

'And whose pet are you?' I asked.

'Oh—I am nobody's pet, unless sometimes Jack makes a pet of me when he's in a good humour. Do you make pets of your sisters, Mr Green?'

'I have none. But if I had I should not make pets of them.'

'Not of your own sisters?'

No. As for myself, I'd sooner make a pet of my friend's sister; a great deal.'

'How very unnatural,' said Miss O'Conor, with the prettiest look of surprise imaginable.

'Not at all unnatural I think,' said I, looking tenderly and lovingly into her face. Where does one find girls so pretty, so easy, so sweet, so talkative as the Irish girls? And then with all their talking and all their ease who ever hears of their misbehaving? They certainly love flirting as they also love dancing. But they flirt without mischief and without malice.

I had now quite forgotten my misfortune, and was beginning to think how well I should like to have Fanny O'Conor for my wife. In this frame of mind I was bending over towards her as a servant took away a plate from the other side, when a sepulchral note sounded in my ear. It was like the memento mori of the old Roman;—as though some one pointed in the midst of my bliss to the sword hung over my head by a thread. It was the voice of Larry, whispering in his agony just above my head—

'They're disthroying my poor feet intirely, intirely; so they is! I can't bear it much longer, yer honer.' I had committed murder like Macbeth; and now my Banquo had come to disturb me at my feast.

'What is it he says to you?' asked Fanny.

'Oh nothing,' I answered, once more in my misery.

'There seems to be some point of confidence between you and our Larry,' she remarked.

'Oh no,' said I, quite confused; 'not at all.'

'You need not be ashamed of it. Half the gentlemen in the county have their confidences with Larry;—and some of the ladies too, I can tell you. He was born in this house, and never lived anywhere else; and I am sure he has a larger circle of acquaintance than any one else in it.'

I could not recover my self-possession for the next ten minutes. Whenever Larry was on our side of the table I was afraid he was coming to me with another agonised whisper. When he was opposite, I could not but watch him as he hobbled in his misery. It was evident that the boots were too tight for him, and had they been made throughout of iron they could not have been less capable of yielding to the feet. I pitied him from the bottom of my heart. And I pitied myself also, wishing that I was well in bed upstairs with some feigned malady, so that Larry might have had his own again.

And then for a moment I missed him from the room. He had doubtless gone to relieve his tortured feet in the servants' hall, and as he did so was cursing my cruelty. But what mattered it? Let him curse. If he would only stay away and do that, I would appease his wrath when we were alone together with pecuniary satisfaction.

But there was no such rest in store for me. 'Larry, Larry,' shouted Mr O'Conor, 'where on earth has the fellow gone to?' They were all cousins at the table except myself, and Mr O'Conor was not therefore restrained by any feeling of ceremony. 'There is something wrong with that fellow to-day; what is it, Jack?'

'Upon my word, sir, I don't know,' said Jack.

'I think he must be tipsy', whispered Miss O'Conor, the maiden sister, who always sat at her brother's left hand. But a whisper though it was, it was audible all down the table.

'No, ma'am; it aint drink at all,' said the coachman. 'It is his feet as does it.'

'His feet!' shouted Tom O'Conor.

'Yes; I know it's his feet,' said that horrid Tizzy. 'He's got on great thick nailed shoes. It was that that made him tumble down in the hall.'

I glanced at each side of me, and could see that there was a certain consciousness expressed in the face of each of my two neighbours;—on Kate's mouth there was decidedly a smile, or rather, perhaps, the slightest possible inclination that way; whereas on Fanny's part I though I saw something like a rising sorrow at my distress. So at least I flattered myself.

'Send him back into the room immediately,' said Tom, who looked at me as though he had some consciousness that I had introduced all this confusion into his household. What should I do? Would it not be best for me to make a clean breast of it before them all? But alas! I lacked the courage.

The coachman went out, and we were left for five minutes without any servant, and Mr O'Conor the while became more and more savage. I attempted to say a word to Fanny, but failed. Vox faucibus hæsit.

'I don't think he has got any others,' said Tizzy—'at least none others left.'

On the whole I am glad I did not marry into the family, as I could not have endured that girl to stay in my house as a sister-in-law.

'Where the d— has that other fellow gone to?' said Tom. 'Jack, do go out and see what is the matter. If anybody is drunk send for me.'

'Oh, there is nobody drunk,' said Tizzy.

Jack went out, and the coachman returned; but what was done and said I hardly remember. The whole room seemed to swim round and round, and as far as I can recollect the company sat mute, neither eating nor drinking. Presently Jack returned.

'It's all right,' said he. I always liked Jack. At the present moment he just looked towards me and laughed slightly.

'All right?' said Tom. 'but is the fellow coming?'

'We can do with Richard, I suppose,' said Jack.

'No—I can't do with Richard,' said the father. 'And I will know what it all means. Where is that fellow Larry?'

Larry had been standing just outside the door, and now he entered gently as a mouse. No sound came from his footfall, nor was there in his face that look of pain which it had worn for the last fifteen minutes. But he was not the less abashed, frightened, and unhappy.

'What is all this about, Larry?' said his master, turning to him. 'I insist upon knowing.'

'Och thin, Mr Green, yer honer, I wouldn't be afther telling agin yer honer; indeed I wouldn't thin, av' the masther would only let me hould my tongue.' And he looked across at me, deprecating my anger.

'Mr Green!' said Mr O'Conor.

'Yes, yer honer. It's all along of his honer's thick shoes;' and Larry, stepping backwards towards the door, lifted them up from some corner, and coming well forward, exposed them with the soles uppermost to the whole table.

'And that's not all, yer honer; but they've squoze the very toes of me into a jelly.'

There was now a loud laugh, in which Jack and Peter and Fanny and Kate and Tizzy all joined; as too did Mr O'Conor—and I also myself after a while.

'Whose boots are they?' demanded Miss O'Conor senior, with her severest tone and grimmest accent.

''Deed then and the divil may have them for me, Miss,' answered Larry. 'They war Mr Green's, but the likes of him won't wear them agin afther the likes of me—barring he wanted them very particular,' added he, remembering his own pumps.

I began muttering something, feeling that the time had come when I must tell the tale. But Jack with great good nature, took up the story and told it so well, that I hardly suffered in the telling.

'And that's it,' said Tom O'Conor, laughing till I thought he would have fallen from his chair. 'So you've got Larry's shoes on—'

'And very well he fills them,' said Jack.

'And it's his honer that's welcome to 'em,' said Larry, grinning from ear to ear now that he saw that 'the masther' was once more in a good humour.

'I hope they'll be nice shoes for dancing,' said Kate.

'Only there's one down at the heel I know,' said Tizzy.

'The servant's shoes!' This was an exclamation made by the maiden lady, and intended apparently only for her brother's ear. But it was clearly audible by all the party.

'Better that than no dinner,' said Peter.

'But what are you to do about the dancing?' said Fanny, with an air of dismay on her face which flattered me with an idea that she did care whether I danced or not.

In the mean time Larry, now as happy as an emperor, was tripping round the room without any shoes to encumber him as he withdrew the plates from the table.

'And it's his honer that's welcome to 'em,' said he again, as he pulled off the table-cloth with a flourish. 'And why wouldn't he, and he able to folly the hounds better nor any Englishman that iver war in these parts before,—anyways so Mick says!'

Now Mick was the huntsman, and this little tale of eulogy from Larry went far towards easing my grief. I had ridden well to the hounds that day, and I knew it.

There was nothing more said about the shoes, and I was soon again at my ease, although Miss O'Conor did say something about the impropriety of Larry walking about in his stocking feet. The ladies however soon withdrew,—to my sorrow, for I was getting on swimmingly with Fanny; and then we gentlemen gathered round the fire and filled our glasses.

In about ten minutes a very light tap was heard, the door was opened to the extent of three inches, and a female voice which I readily recognised called to Jack.

Jack went out, and in a second or two put his head back into the room and called to me—'Green,' he said, 'just step here a moment, there's a good fellow.' I went out, and there I found Fanny standing with her brother.

'Here are the girls at their wits' ends,' said he, 'about your dancing. So Fanny has put a boy upon one of the horses, and proposes that you should send another line to Mrs Meehan at Ballyglass. It's only ten miles, and he'll be back in two hours.'

I need hardly say that I acted in conformity with this advice. I went into Mr O'Conor's book room, with Jack and his sister, and there scribbled a note. It was delightful to feel how intimate I was with them, and how anxious they were to make me happy.

'And we won't begin till they come,' said Fanny.

'Oh, Miss O'Conor, pray don't wait,' said I.

Oh, but we will will,' she answered. 'You have your wine to drink, and then there's the tea; and then we'll have a song or two. I'll spin it out; see if I don't.' And so we went to the front door where the boy was already on his horse—her own nag as I afterwards found.

'And Patsey,' said she, 'ride for your life; and Patsey, whatever you do, don't come back without Mr Green's pumps—his dancing-shoes you know.'

And in about two hours the pumps did arrive; and I don't think I ever spent a pleasanter evening or got more satisfaction out of a pair of shoes. They had not been two minutes on my feet before Larry was carrying a tray of negus across the room in those which I had worn at dinner.

'The Dillon girls are going to stay here,' said Fanny as I wished her good night at two o'clock. 'And we'll have dancing every evening as long as you remain.'

'But I shall leave to-morrow,' said I.

'Indeed you won't. Papa will take care of that.'

And so he did. 'You had better go over to Ballyglass yourself to-morrow,' said he, 'and collect your own things. There's no knowing else what you may have to borrow of Larry.'

I stayed there three weeks, and in the middle of the third I thought that everything would be arranged between me and Fanny. But the aunt interfered; and in about a twelvemonth after my adventures she consented to make a more fortunate man happy for his life.

MR JOB SLOPER

Market Harborough
G. J. Whyte-Melville
1861

Mr Sawyer found himself entering a dilapidated farmyard, of which three sides consisted of tumble-down sheds and out-houses; while the fourth, in somewhat better repair, denoted by its ventilating windows, latched doors, and occasional stable-buckets, that its inmates were of the equine race. Stamping up a bricked passage, on either side of which sundry plants were dying in about three inches of mould, our friend wisely entered the open door of the kitchen, preferring that easy ingress to the adjacent portal, of which a low scraper and rusty knocker seemed to point out that it was chiefly intended for visits of ceremony. Here he encountered nothing more formidable than a white cat sleeping by the fire, and a Dutch clock, with an enormous countenance, ticking drowsily in the warmest corner of the apartment.

Coughing loudly, and shuffling his feet against the sanded floor, he soon succeeded in summoning a bare-armed maid-of-all-work, with a dirty face and flaunting ribbons in her cap, who, to his inquiries whether 'Mr Sloper was at home,' answered, as maids-of-all-work invariably do, that 'Master had just stepped out for a minute, but left word he would be back directly; would you please to take a seat?'

This interval, our friend, who, as he often remarked, 'wasn't born yesterday,' determined to spend in a private visit to the stables, and left the kitchen accordingly for that purpose. It is needless to observe that he had barely coasted a third of the ocean of muck which constituted the centre of the yard, ere he encountered the proprietor himself coming leisurely to greet him, with a welcome on his ruddy face and a straw in his mouth.

Mr Sloper was a hale hearty man of some three-score years or so, who must have been very good-looking in his prime; but whose countenance, from the combined effects of good-living and hard weather, had acquired that mottled crimson tinge which, according to Dickens, is seldom observed except in underdone boiled beef and the faces of old mail coachmen and guards. It would have puzzled a physiognomist to say whether good-humour or cunning prevailed in the twinkle of his bright little blue eye; but the way in which he wore his shaved hat, and stuck his hands into the pockets of his wide-skirted grey riding-coat, would have warned any observer of human nature that he was skilled in horseflesh and versed in all the secrets that lend their interest to that fascinating animal. Somehow Honesty seems to go faster on horseback than afoot.

Not that a man of Mr Sloper's years and weight ever got upon the backs of his purchases, save perhaps in very extreme cases, and where 'the lie with circumstances' was as indispensable as 'the lie direct.' No, he confined himself to dealing for them over dark-coloured glasses of brandy and water, puffing them unconscionably in the stable, and pretending to ignore them completely when he met his own property out of doors. 'His eyesight,' he said, 'was failing him; positively he didn't know his own nags now when he met them in his neighbour's field!'

Tradition asserted, however, that Job Sloper, when a younger man, had been one of the best and boldest riders in the Old Country. The limp which affected his walk had been earned in a rattling fall over a turnpike-gate for a wager of a new hat, and Fiction herself panted in detailing his many exploits by flood and field when he first went into the trade. These had lost nothing by time and repetition, but even now, in those exceptional cases where he condescended to get into the saddle, there was no question that the old man could put them along still, for as lusty and heavy as he'd grown. 'I'm a sad cripple now, sir,' he'd say, in a mild reflective voice; 'and they wants to be very quiet and gentle for me. I never had not what I call good nerve in the best of times, though I liked to see the hounds run a bit too. I was always fond of the sport, you see; and even now it does me good to watch a gent like yourself in the saddle. What I calls a *reel* 'orseman—as can give-an'-take, and bend his back like old Sir 'Arry; him as kept our hounds for so long. If it ain't taking too great a liberty, perhaps you're related to Sir 'Arry; you puts me in mind of him so much, the way you carries your 'ands!'

The old hypocrite! Ingenuous youth was pretty sure to 'stop and have a bit of lunch' after that, and after lunch was it not human nature that it should buy?

'Mornin', sir,' says Mr Sloper, scenting a customer as he accosts his guest. 'Oh, it's you, is it, Mr Sawyer? Won't ye step in and set down after your walk? Take a glass of mild ale and a crust of bread and cheese, or a drop of sherry or anything?'

'No hunting to-day, Job,' answers the visitor, declining the refreshment; 'so I just toddled over to see how you're getting on, and have a look round the stables; no harm in looking, you know.'

Mr Sloper's face assumes an expression of profound mystery.

'I'm glad you come over to-day, sir,' he says, in a tone of confidential frankness, 'of all days in the year. I've a 'orse here, as I should like to ast your opinion about—a gent like *you* as knows what a 'unter really is. And so you should, Mr Sawyer, for there's no man alive takes greater liberties with 'em when they *can* go and do it. And I've got one in that box, as I think, just is more than curious.'

'Would he carry me?' asks Mr Sawyer, with well-affected indifference, as if he had not come over expressly to find one that would. 'Not that I want a horse, you know; but if I saw one I liked very much, and you didn't price him too high, why, I *might* be induced to buy against next season, perhaps.'

Job took his hands out of his coat-pockets, and spread them abroad, as it were to dry. The action denoted extreme purity and candour.

'No; I don't think as he ought to carry you, sir,' was the unexpected reply. 'Now, I ain't a-going to tell you a lie, Mr Sawyer. This horse didn't ought to be ridden, not the way *you* take and ride them, Mr Sawyer; leastways not over such a blind heart-breaking country as this here. He's too good, he is, for that kind of work; he ought to be in Leicestershire, he ought; the Harborough country, that's the country for him. He's too fast for us, and that's the truth. Only, to be sure, we have a vast of plough hereabout, and *I* never see such a sticker through dirt. It makes no odds to him, pasture *or* plough, and the sweetest hack ever I clapped eyes on besides. However, you shall judge for yourself, Mr Sawyer. I won't ask you to believe me. You've a quicker eye to a horse than I have, by a long chalk, and I'd sooner have your opinion than my own. I would now, and that's the truth!'

Our purchaser began to think he might possibly have hit upon *the* animal at last. Often as he had been at the game, and often as he had been disappointed, he was still sanguine enough to believe he might draw the prize-ticket in the lottery at any time. As I imagine every man who pulls on his boots to go out hunting has a sort of vague hope that to-day may be his day of triumph with the hounds, so the oldest and wariest of us cannot go into a dealer's yard without a sort of half-conscious idea that there must be a trump card somewhere in the pack, and it may be our luck to hold it as well as another's.

But Sloper, like the rest of his trade, was not going to show his game first. It seems to be a maximum with all salesmen to prove their customers with inferior articles before they come to the real thing. Mr Sawyer had to walk through a four-stall stable, and inspect, preparatory to declining, a mealy bay cob, a lame grey, a broken-winded chestnut, and an enormous brown animal, very tall, very narrow, very ugly, with extremely upright forelegs and shoulders to match. The latter his owner affirmed to be 'an extraordinary shaped 'un,' as no doubt he was. A little playful *badinage* on the merits of this last enlivened the visit.

'What will you take for the brown, Sloper, if I buy him at so much the foot?' said the customer, as they emerged into the fresh air.

'Say ten pound a foot, sir!' answered Job, with the utmost gravity, 'and ten over, because *he always has a foot to spare*. Come now, Mr Sawyer, I can afford to let a good customer like you have that horse for *fefty*. *Fefty* guineas, or even pounds, sir, to you. I got him in a bad debt, you see, sir;—it's Bible truth I'm telling ye;—and he only stood me in forty-seven pounds ten, and a sov. I gave the man as brought him over. He's not everybody's horse, Mr Sawyer, that isn't; but I think he'll carry you remarkably well.'

'I don't think I'll ever give him a chance,' was the rejoinder. 'Come,

Job, we're burning daylight; let's go and have a look at the crack.'

One individual had been listening to the above conversation with thrilling interest. This was no less a personage than Barney, Mr Sloper's head groom, general factotum, and rough-rider in ordinary—an official whose business it was to ride anything *at* anything, for anybody who asked him. He was a little old man, with one eye, a red handkerchief, and the general appearance of a postboy on half-pay; a sober fellow, too and as brave as King Richard; yet had he expressed himself strongly about this said brown horse, the previous evening, to the maid-of-all-work.

'He's the wussest we've had yet,' was his fiat. 'It's nateral for 'em to fall; but when *he* falls, he's all over a chap till he's crumpled him.'

So his heroic heart beat more freely when they adjourned to the neighbouring box. Mr Sloper threw the door open with an air. It must be confessed he seldom had one that would bear, without preparation, a minute inspection from the eye of a sportsman; but he knew *this* was a sound one, and made the most of it. Clothed and hooded, littered to the hocks, and sheeted to the tail, there was yet something about his general appearance that fascinated Mr Sawyer at once. Job saw the spell was working, and abstained from disturbing it. As far as could be seen, the animal was a long, low, wellbred-looking roan, with short flat legs, large clean hocks, and swelling muscular thighs. His supple skin threw off a bloom, as if he was in first-rate condition; and when, laying his ears back and biting the manger, he lifted a foreleg, as it were, to expostulate with his visitors, the hoof was round, open, and well-developed, as blue, and to all appearance as hard, as a flint.

'Has he fashion enough, think ye, sir?' asked Job at length, breaking the silence. 'Strip him, Barney,' he added, taking the straw from his mouth.

The roan winced, and stamped, and whisked his tail, and set his back up during the process; but when it was concluded Mr Sawyer could not but confess to himself that if he was only as good as he looked he would do.

'Feel his legs, Mr Sawyer!' observed the dealer, turning away to conceal the triumph that would ooze out. 'There's some legs—there's some hocks and thighs! Talk of loins, and look where his tail's set on. Carries his own head, too; and if you could see his manners! I never saw such manners in the hunting-field. Six-year-old—not a speck or blemish; bold as a bull, and gentle as a lady; he can go as fast as you can clap your hands, and stay till the middle of the week after next—jump a town, too, and never turn his head from the place you put him at. As handy as a fiddle, as neat as a pink, and worth all the money to carry in your eye when you go out to buy hunters. But what's the use of talking about it to a judge like you? Lay your leg over him—only just lay your leg over him, Mr Sawyer. I don't want you to buy him! but get on him and feel his action, just as a favour to me.'

Our friend had made up his mind he would do so from the first. There was no mistaking the appearance of the animal; so good was it, that he had but two misgivings—some rank unsoundness to account for its being there, or so high a price as to be beyond his means; for Mr Sawyer was too fond of the sport to give a sum that he could not replace for so perishable an article as a hunter.

He was no mean equestrian, our friend, and quite at home on a strange horse. As he drew the curb-rein gently through his fingers, the roan dropped his long lean head, and champed the bit playfully, tossing a speck of froth back on his rider's boots.

'You've got a mouth, at anyrate,' quoth Mr Sawyer, and trotted him gently down the hard road, the animal stepping freely and gaily under him, full of life and spirits. The customer liked his mount, and couldn't help showing it. 'May I lark him?' said he, pulling up after a short canter to and fro on the turf by the wayside; during which Job Sloper had been exercising his mental arithmetic in what we may term a sum of problematical addition.

'Take him into the close, sir,' was the generous reply; 'put him at anything you like. If you can get him into one of these fences, I'll give him to you!'

So Mr Sawyer sat down to jump a low hedge and ditch, then stood up, and caught hold of the roan's head, and sent him a cracker through the adjoining plough, and across a larger fence into a pasture, and back again over a fair flight of rails, and lost his flat shooting-hat, and rucked his plaid trousers up to his knees; and Sloper marked his kindling eye and glowing cheek, and knew that he had landed him.

'Walk him about for ten minutes before you do him over,' said that worthy to Barney, as Mr Sawyer dismounted, and the latter brought him his hat. 'And now, sir,' added the hospitable dealer, 'you can't go away without tasting my cheese—the same you liked last time, if *you* please.'

So speaking, Mr Sloper ushered his guest into a neat little parlour with a strong odour of preserved tobacco-smoke, where a clean cloth set off a nice luncheon of bread and cheese, flanked by a foaming jug of strong ale and a decanter of oily-brown sherry. And herein the dealer showed his knowledge of human nature, and his discrimination in the different characteristics of the species. Had his guest been some generous scion of the aristocracy, with more money than nerves, he would have *primed* him first, and put him up to ride afterwards. But he knew his man. He was well aware that Mr Sawyer required no stimulant to make him jump, but a strong one to induce him to part with his money; so he proposed the luncheon after he was satisfied that his customer was pleased with his mount.

Neither of them touched on business during the meal, the conversation consisting chiefly of the runs that had lately taken place in the Old Country, with many an inferred compliment to the good riding of the possible purchaser. Then Mr Sawyer produced the Laranagas and offered one to Job, who bit it, and wet it, and smoked it, as men do who are more used to clay pipes, and then they went back to the stable to see the roan done up.

The gallop and the ale were working in Mr Sawyer's brain, but he didn't see his way into the roan at a hundred; so he obstinately held his tongue. The dealer was obliged to break the ice.

'I'd take it very friendly of you, sir, if you'd give me your honest opinion of that horse,' said he, waving the Laranaga towards the animal. 'I fancy he's too good for our country; and I've a brother-in-law down in Rutland as wants to have him very bad. He's just the cut, so he says, for these Melton gents; and he's a good judge, is my brother-in-law, and a pretty rider to boot. He'd give me my price, too; but then, you know, sir, askin' your pardon, it isn't always ready money between relations; and that cuts the other way again, as a man may say. What do *you* think, Mr Sawyer?'

'I'll find out what he wants for him, at any rate,' thought the customer. 'What's his figure?' was the abrupt rejoinder.

Mr Sloper hesitated.

'A hundred and'—eighty, he was going to say; but seeing his customer's eye resting on the roan's back-ribs—a point in which the horse was somewhat deficient—he dropped at once to seventy, and regretted it the next moment when he caught the expression of the listener's face.

'It isn't *even* money,' answered Mr Sawyer, without, however, making the same sort of face he had done several times before, when he had refused to give double the sum at which he had eventually purchased. 'I should say you might get a hundred and twenty for him down there, if you'd luck. But it's a great risk—a great risk—and a long distance; and perhaps have him sent back to you in the spring. If I wanted a horse, *I'd* give you a hundred for him, though he isn't exactly my sort. A hundred!—I'll tell you what, Sloper, I'll be hanged if I won't chance it—I'll give you a hundred— guineas—come! Money down, and no questions asked.'

'I can warrant him sound,' answered Mr Sloper; 'and I'd rather you had him than anybody. But it's childish talking of a hundred guineas and that horse on the same afternoon. However, I thank you kindly all the same, Mr Sawyer. Barney, shut the box up! Come in, sir, and have one glass of sherry before you start. The evenings get chill at this time of year, and that's old sherry, and won't hurt you no more than milk. He *is* a nice horse, Mr Sawyer, I think—a very nice horse, and I'm glad you're pleased with him.'

So they returned into the little parlour, and stirred up the fire, and finished the bottle of old sherry; nor is it necessary to remark that, with the concluding glass of that generous fluid, the roan became the property of John Standish Sawyer, under the following somewhat complicated agreement:—That he was to give an immediate cheque for a hundred and forty pounds, and ten pounds more at the end of the season; which latter donation was to be increased to twenty if he should sell him for anything over two hundred—a contingency which the dealer was pleased to observe amounted to what he called 'a moral.'

The new owner went to look at him once more in the stable, and thought him the nicest horse he ever saw in his life. The walk home, too, was delightful, till the sherry had evaporated, when it became rather tedious; and at dinner-time Mr Sawyer was naturally less hungry than thirsty. All the evening, however, he congratulated himself on having done a good day's work. All night, too, he dreamed of the roan; and on waking resolved to call him Hotspur.

When the horse came home next day, he certainly looked rather smaller than is new owner had fancied. Old Isaac, too, growled out his untoward opinion that he 'looked a sort as would work very light.' But then Isaac always grumbled—it was the old groom's way of enjoying himself.

THE DREAM OF AN OLD MELTONIAN
W. Davenport Bromley
1864

I am old, I am old, and my eyes are grown weaker,
    My beard is as white as the foam on the sea,
Yet pass me the bottle and fill me a beaker,
    A bright brimming toast in a bumper for me!
Back, back through long vistas of years I am wafted,
    But the glow at my heart's undiminished in force;
Deep, deep in that heart has fond memory engrafted
    Those quick thirty minutes from Ranksboro' Gorse.

What is time? The effluxion of life zoophitic
    In dreary pursuit of position or gain.
What is life? The absorption of vapours mephitic,
    And the burning of sunlight on senses and brain!
Such a life have I lived—though so speedily over,
    Condensing the joys of a century's course,
From the find till we eat him near Woodwellhead Cover,
    In thirty bright minutes from Ranksboro' Gorse.

Last night in St Stephen's so wearily sitting
    (The member for Boreham sustained the debate),
Some pitying spirit that round me was flitting
    Vouchsafed a sweet vision my pains to abate.
The Mace, and the Speaker, and House disappearing,
    The leather-clad bench is a thoroughbred horse;
'Tis the whimpering cry of the foxhound I'm hearing,
    And my 'seat' is a pigskin at Ranksboro' Gorse.

He's away! I can hear the identical holloa!
    I can feel my young thoroughbred strain down the ride,
I can hear the dull thunder of hundreds that follow,
    I can see my old comrades in life by my side.
Do I dream? All around me I see the dead riding,
    And voices long silent re-echo with glee;
I can hear the far wail of the Master's vain chiding,
    As vain as the Norseman's reproof to the sea.

Vain, indeed! for the bitches are racing before us—
    Not a nose to the earth—not a stern in the air;
And we know by the notes of that modified chorus
    How straight we must ride if we wish to be there!
With a crash o'er the turnpike, and onward I'm sailing,

    Released from the throes of the blundering mass,
Which dispersed right and left as I topped the high railing,
    And shape my own course o'er the billowy grass.

Select is the circle in which I am moving,
    Yet open and free the admission to all;
Still, still more select is that company proving,
    Weeded out by the funker, and thinned by the fall:
Yet here all are equal—no class legislation,
    No privilege hinders, no family pride:
    In the 'image of war' show the pluck of the nation;
    Ride, ancient patrician! democracy, ride!

Oh! gently, my young one; the fence we are nearing
    Is leaning towards us—'tis hairy and black,
The binders are strong, and necessitate clearing,
    Or the wide ditch beyond will find room for your back.
Well saved! we are over! now far down the pastures
    Of Ashwell the willows betoken the line
Of the dull-flowing stream of historic disasters;
    We must face, my bold young one, the dread Whissendine.

No shallow-dug pan with a hurdle to screen it,
    That cocktail imposture, the steeplechase brook:
But the steep broken banks tell us plain, if we mean it,
    The less we shall like it the longer we look.
Then steady, my young one, my place I've selected,
    Above the dwarf willow 'tis sound I'll be bail,
    With your muscular quarters beneath you collected,
    Prepare for a rush like the 'limited mail.'

Oh! now let me know the full worth of your breeding;
    Brave son of Belzoni, be true to your sires;
Sustain old traditions—remember you're leading
    The cream of the cream in the shire of the shires!
With a quick, shortened stride as the distance you measure
    With a crack of the nostril and cock of the ear,
And a rocketing bound, and we're over, my treasure,
    Twice nine feet of water, and landed all clear!

What! four of us only? Are these the survivors
    Of all that rode gaily from Ranksboro' ridge?
I hear the faint splash of a few hardy divers,
    The rest are in hopeless research of a bridge;
Væ Victis! the way of the world and the winners!
    Do we ne'er ride away from a friend in distress?
Alas! we are anti-Samaritan sinners,
    And streaming past Stapleford, onward we press.

Ah! don't they mean mischief, the merciless ladies?
    What fox can escape such implacable foes?
Of the sex cruel slaughter for ever the trade is,
    Whether human or animal—YONDER HE GOES!
Never more for the woodland! his purpose has failed him,
    Though to gain the old shelter he gallantly tries;
In vain the last double, for Jezebel's nailed him!
    WHO-WHOOP! in the open the veteran dies!

Yes, four of us only! But is it a vision?
    Dear lost ones, how come ye with mortals to mix?
Methought that ye hunted the pastures Elysian,
    And between us there rolled the unjumpable Styx!
Stay, stay but a moment! the grass fields are fading,
    And heavy obscurity palsies my brain:
Through what country, what ploughs and what sloughs am I wading?
    Alas! 'tis the member for Boreham again!

Oh, glory of youth! consolation of age!
    Sublimest of escstasies under the sun;
Though the veteran may linger too long on the stage,
    Yet he'll drink a last toast to a fox-hunting run.
And, oh! young descendants of ancient top-sawyers!
    By your lives to the world their example enforce;
Whether landlords, or parsons, or statesmen, or lawyers,
    Ride straight as they rode it from Ranksboro' Gorse.

Though a rough-riding world may bespatter your breeches,
    Though sorrow may cross you, or slander revile,
Though you plunge overhead in misfortune's blind ditches,
    Shun the gap of deception, the handgate of guile:
Oh, avoid them! for there see the crowd is contending,
    Ignoble the object—ill-mannered the throng;
Shun the miry lane, falsehood, with turns never ending,
    Ride straight for truth's timber, no matter how strong.

I'll pound you safe over! sit steady and quiet;
    Along the sound headland of honesty steer;
Beware of false holloas and juvenile riot;
    Though the oxer of duty be wide, never fear!
And when the run's over of earthly existence,
    And you get safe to ground, you will feel no remorse,
If you ride it—no matter what line or what distance,
    As straight as your fathers from Ranksboro' Gorse.

LAURA HUNTINGCROP

Sketches in the Hunting Field
Alfred E. T. Watson
1880

When, last November, I was seated before a blazing fire in Major Huntingcrop's town house, and his too charming daughter, Laura, expressed her enthusiastic admiration for hunting and everything connected with it—mildly at the same time hinting her contempt for those who were unskilled in the accomplishment—could I possibly admit that I was among the despised class? Was it not rather a favourable opportunity for showing our community of sentiment by vowing that the sport was the delight of my life, and firing off a few sentences laden with such sporting phraseology as I had happened to pick up in the course of desultory reading?

Laura listened with evident admiration. I waxed eloquent. My armchair would not take the bit between its teeth and run away; no hounds were in the neighbourhood to test my prowess; and I am grieved to admit that for an exciting ten minutes the 'father of—stories' (what a family he must have!) had it all his own way with me.

'*Altra cura sedit post equitem* indeed!' I concluded. 'You may depend upon it, Miss Huntingcrop, that man was mounted on a screw! Black Care would never dare to intrude his unwelcome presence on a galloper. Besides, why didn't the fellow put his horse at a hurdle? Probably Black Care wouldn't have been able to sit a fence. But I quite agree with you that it is the duty of a gentleman to hunt; and I only wish that the performance of some of my other duties gave me half as much pleasure!'

Where I should have ended it is impossible to say; but here our *tête-à-tête* was interrupted by the advent of the Major, who heard the tag end of my panegyric with manifest delight.

'Huntingcrop is the place for you, Mr Smoothley,' said he, with enthusiasm, 'and I shall be more than pleased to see you there. I think, too, we shall be able to show you some of your favourite sport this season. We meet four days a week, and you may reckon on at least one day with the Grassmere. It is always a sincere pleasure to me to find a young fellow whose heart is in it.'

As regards my heart, it was in my boots at the prospect; and, despite the great temptation of Laura's presence, I paused, carefully to consider the pros and cons before accepting.

How pleasant to see her fresh face every morning at the breakfast-table! How unpleasant to see a horse, most likely painfully fresh also, waiting to bear me on a fearsome journey as soon as the meal was concluded! How delightful to feel the soft pressure of her fingers as she gave me morning greeting! How awful to feel my own fingers numbed and stiff with tugging at the bridle of a wild, tearing, unmanageable steed! How enjoyable to—

'Are you engaged for Christmas, Mr Smoothley?' Laura inquired, and that query settled me. It might freeze; I could sprain my ankle, or knock up an excuse of some sort. Yes, I would go; and might good luck go with me.

For the next few days I unceasingly studied the works of Major Whyte-Melville, and others who have most to say on what they term sport, and endeavoured to get up a little enthusiasm. I did get up a little—*very* little; but when the desired quality had made its appearance, attracted by my authors' wizard-like power, it was of an extremely spurious character, and entirely evaporated when I had reached the little railway-station nearest to the Hall. A particularly neat groom, whom I recognised as having been in town with the Huntingcrops, was awaiting me in a dog-cart, and the conveyance was just starting when we met a string of horses, hooded and sheeted, passing along the road: in training, if I might be permitted to judge from their actions, for the wildest scenes in 'Mazeppa,' 'Dick Turpin,' or some other exciting equestrian drama. I did not want the man to tell me that they were his master's; I knew it at once; and the answers he made to my questions as to their usual demeanour in the field plunged me into an abyss of despair.

The hearty greeting of the Major, the more subdued but equally inspiring welcome of his daughter, and the contagious cheerfulness of a house full of pleasant people, in some measure restored me; but it was not until the soothing influence of dinner had taken possession of my bosom, and a whisper had run through the establishment that it was beginning to freeze, that I thoroughly recovered my equanimity, and was able to retire to rest with some small hope that my bed next night would not be one of pain and suffering.

Alas for my anticipations! I was awakened from slumber by a knock at the door, and the man entered my rooms with a can of hot water in one hand and a pair of tops in the other; whilst over his arm were slung my—in point of fact, my breeches; a costume which I had never worn except on the day it came home, when I spent the greater portion of the evening sportingly arrayed astride of a chair, to see how it all felt.

'Breakfast at nine, sir. Hounds meet at Blackbrook at half-past ten; and it's a good way to ride,' said the servant.

'The frost's all gone, I fea— I hope?' I said inquiringly.

'Yes, sir. Lovely morning!' he answered, drawing up the blinds.

In his opinion a lovely morning was characterised by slightly damp, muggy weather; in mine it would have been a daybreak of ultra-Siberian intensity.

I ruefully dressed, lamenting that my will was not a little stronger (nor were thoughts of my other will—and testament—entirely absent), that I might have fled from the trial or done something to rescue myself from the exposure which I felt must shortly overwhelm me. The levity of the men in the breakfast-room was a source of suffering to me, and even Laura's voice jarred on my ears as she petitioned her father to let her follow 'just a little way'—she was going to ride and see the hounds 'throw off,' a ceremony which I devoutly hoped would be confined to those animals—'because it was too hard to turn back when the real enjoyment commenced; and she would be good in the pony-carriage for the rest of the week.'

'No, no, my dear,' replied the Major, 'women are out of place in the hunting field. Don't you think so, Mr Smoothley?'

'I do indeed, Major,' I answered, giving Laura's little dog under the table a fearful kick, as I threw out my foot violently to straighten a crease which was severely galling the inside of my left knee. 'You had far better go for a quiet ride, Miss Huntingcrop, and'—how sincerely I added—'I shall be delighted to accompany you; there will be plenty of days for me to hunt when you drive to the meet.'

'No, no, Smoothley. It's very kind of you to propose it, but I won't have you sacrificing your day's pleasure,' the Major made answer, dashing the crumbs of hope from my hungering lips. 'You may go a little way, Laura, if you'll promise to stay with Sir William, and do all that he tells you. You won't mind looking after her, Heathertopper?'

Old Sir William's build would have forbidden the supposition that he was in any way given to activity, even if the stolidity of his countenance had not assured you that caution was in the habit of marking his guarded way; and he made suitable response. I was just debating internally as to the least circuitous mode by which I could send myself a telegram, requiring my immediate presence in town, when a sound of hoofs informed us that the horses were approaching; and gazing anxiously from the window before me, which overlooked the drive in front of the house, I noted their arrival.

Now the horse is an animal which I have always been taught to admire. A 'noble animal' he is termed by zoologists, and I am perfectly willing to admit his nobility when he conducts himself with reticence and moderation; but when he gyrates like a teetotum on his hind-legs, and wildly spars at the groom he ought to respect, I cease to recognise any qualities in him but the lowest and most degrading.

Laura hastened to the window, and I rose from the table and followed her.

'You pretty darlings!' she rapturously exclaimed. 'Oh! are you going to ride The Sultan, Mr Smoothley? How nice! I do so want to, but papa won't let me.'

'No, my dear, he's not the sort of horse for little girls to ride; but he'll suit you, Smoothley; he'll suit you, I know.'

Without expressing a like confidence, I asked, 'Is that The Sultan?'

pointing to a large chestnut animal at that moment in the attitude which, in a dog, is termed 'begging.'

'Yes; a picture, isn't he? Look at his legs. Clean as a foal's! Good quarters—well ribbed up—not like one of the waspy greyhounds they call thoroughbred horses nowadays. Look at his condition, too; I've kept that up pretty well, though he's been out of training for some time,' cried the Major.

'He's not a racehorse, is he?' I nervously asked.

'He's done a good deal of steeplechasing, and ran once or twice in the early part of this season. It makes a horse rush his fences rather, perhaps; but you young fellows like that, I know.'

'His—eye appears slightly bloodshot, doesn't it?' I hazarded; for he was exhibiting a large amount of what I imagine should have been white, in an unsuccessful attempt to look at his tail without turning his head round. 'Is he quiet with hounds?'

'Playful—a little playful,' was his unassuring reply.

'But we must be off, gentlemen. It's three miles to Blackbrook, and it won't do to be late!' And he led the way to the Hall, where I selected my virgin whip from the rack, and swallowing a nip of orange-brandy, which a servant providentially handed to me at that moment, went forth to meet my fate.

Laura, declining offers of assistance from the crowd of pink-coated young gentlemen who were sucking cigars in the porch, was put into the saddle by her own groom. I think she looked to me for aid, but I was constrained to stare studiously in the opposite direction, having a very vague idea of the method by which young ladies are placed in their saddles. Then I commenced, and ultimately effected, the ascent of The Sultan; a process which appeared to me precisely identical with climbing to the deck of a man-of-war.

'Stirrups all right, sir?' asked the groom.

'This one's rather too long. No, it's the other one, I think.' One of them didn't seem right, but it was impossible to say which in the agony of the moment.

He surveyed me critically from the front, and then took up one stirrup to a degree that brought my knee into close proximity with my waistcoat, The Sultan meanwhile exhibiting an uncertainty of temperament which caused me very considerable anxiety. Luckily I had presence of mind to say that he had shortened the leather too much, and there was not much difference between the two when, with Laura and some seven companions, I started down the avenue in front of the house.

The fundamental principles of horsemanship are three: keep your heels down; stick in your knees; and try to look as if you liked it. So I am informed, and I am at a loss to say which of the three is the most difficult of execution. The fact that The Sultan started jerkily some little time before I was ready to begin, thereby considerably deranging such plans as I was forming for guidance, is to be deplored; for my hat was not on very firmly, and it was just beginning to think that hunting was not so many degrees worse than the treadmill when we approached the scene of action.

Before us, as we rounded a turning in the road, a group of some thirty horsemen, to which fresh accessions were constantly being made, chatted together and watched a hilly descent to the right, down which the pack of hounds, escorted by several officials, was approaching. The Major and his party were cordially greeted, and no doubt like civilities would have been extended to me had I been in a position to receive them; but, unfortunately, I was not; for, on seeing the hounds, the 'playfulness' of The Sultan vigorously manifested itself, and he commenced a series of gymnastic exercises to which his previous performances had been a mere farce. I lost my head, but mysteriously kept what was more important—my seat, until the tempest of his playfulness had in some measure abated; and then he stood still, shaking with excitement. I sat still, shaking—from other causes.

'Keep your horse's head to the hounds, will you, sir?' was the salutation which the Master bestowed on me, cantering up as the pack defiled through a gate; and indeed The Sultan seemed anxious to kill a hound or two to begin with. 'Infernal Cockney!' was, I fancy, the term of endearment he used as he rode on; but I don't think Laura caught any of this short but forcible utterance, for just at this moment a cry was raised in the wood to the left, and the men charged through the gate and along the narrow cart-track with a wild rush. Again The Sultan urged on his wild career, half-breaking my leg against the gate-post, as I was very courteously endeavouring to get out of the way of an irascible gentleman behind me who appeared to be in a hurry, and then plunging me into the midst of a struggling, pushing throng of men and horses.

If the other noble sportsmen were not enjoying themselves more than I, it was certainly a pity that they had not stayed at home. Where was this going to end? and—but what was the matter in front? They paused, and then suddenly all turned round and charged back along the narrow path. I was taken by surprise, and got out of the way as best I could, pulling my horse back amongst the trees, and the whole cavalcade rushed past me. Out of the wood, across the road, over the opposite hedge, most of them; some turn off towards a gate to the right and away up the rise beyond, passing over which they were soon out of sight.

That The Sultan's efforts to follow them had been vigorous I need not say; but I felt that it was a moment for action, and pulled and tugged and sawed at his mouth to make him keep his head turned away from temptation. He struggled about amongst the trees, and I felt that, under the circumstances, I should be justified in hitting him on the head. I did so; and shortly afterwards—it was not exactly that I was thrown, but circumstances induced me to get off rather suddenly.

My foot was on my native heath. I was alone, appreciating the charms of solitude in a degree I had never before experienced; but after a few minutes of thankfulness, the necessity of action forced itself on my mind. Clearly, I must not be seen standing at my horse's head gazing smilingly at the prospect—that would never do, for the whole hunt might reappear as quickly as they had gone; so, smoothing out the most troublesome creases in my nether garments, I proceeded to mount. I say 'proceeded,' for it was a difficult and very gradual operation, but was eventually managed through the instrumentality of a little boy, who held The Sultan's head, and addressed him in a series of forcible epithets that I should never have dared to use: language, however, which, though reprehensible from a moral point of view, seemed to appeal to the animal's feelings, and was at any rate successful.

He danced a good deal when I was once more on his back, and seemed to like going in a series of small bounds, which were peculiarly irritating to sit. But I did not so much mind now, for no critical eye was near to watch my hand wandering to the convenient pommel or to note my taking such other little precautions as the exigencies of the situation, and the necessity for carrying out the first law of nature, seemed to suggest.

Hunting, in this way, wasn't really so very bad. There did not appear to be so very much danger, the morning air was refreshing and pleasant, and the country looked bright. There always seemed to be a gate to each field, which, though troublesome to open at first, ultimately yielded to patience and perseverance and the handle of my whip. I might get home safely after all; and as for my desertion, where everyone was looking after himself, it was scarcely likely they could have observed my defection. No; this was not altogether bad fun. I could say with truth for the rest of my life that I 'had hunted.' It would add a zest to the perusal of sporting literature, and, above all, extend the range of my charity by making me sincerely appreciate men who really rode.

But alas! though clear of the trees practically, I was, metaphorically, very far from being out of the wood. When just endeavouring to make up my mind to come out again some day I heard a noise, and, looking behind me, saw the whole fearful concourse, rapidly approaching the hedge which led into the ploughed field next to me on the right. Helter-skelter, on they came. Hounds popping through, and scrambling over. Then a man in pink topping the fence, and on again over the plough; then one in black over with a rush; two, three, four more in different places. Another by himself who came up rapidly, and, parting company with his horse, shot over like a rocket!

All this I noted in a second. There was no time to watch, for The Sultan had seen the opportunity of making up for his lost day, and started off with the rush of an express train. We flew over the field; neared the fence. I was shot into the air like a shuttlecock from a battledore—a moment of dread—then, a fearful shock which landed me lopsidedly somewhere on the animal's neck. He gives a spring which shakes me into the saddle again, and is tearing over the grass field beyond. I am conscious that I am in the same field as the Major, and some three or four other men. We fly on a frightful speed; there is a line of willows in front of us which we are rapidly nearing. It means water, I know. We get—or rather it comes nearer— nearer—nearer—ah-h-h! An agony of semi-unconsciousness—a splash, a fearful splash, a struggle . . .

I am on his back, somewhere in the neighbourhood of the saddle: without stirrups, but grimly clutching a confused mass of reins as The Sultan gently canters up the ascent to where the hounds are howling and barking round a man in pink, who waves something brown in the air before throwing it to them. I have no sooner reached the group than the Master arrives, followed by some four or five men, conspicuous among whom is the Major.

He hastens to me. To denounce me as an impostor? Have I done anything wrong, or injured the horse?

'I congratulate you, Smoothley, I congratulate you! I promised you a run, and you've had one, and, by Jove! taken the shine out of some of us. My Lord,' to the Master, 'let me present my friend, Mr Smoothley, to you. Did you see him take the water? You and I made for the Narrows, but he didn't turn away, and went at it as if Sousemere were a puddle. Eighteen feet of water if it's an inch, and with such a take-off and such a landing, there's not a man in the hunt who'd attempt it! Well, Heathertopper! Laura, my dear,' for she and the bulky Baronet at this moment arrived at the head of a straggling detachment of followers, 'you missed a treat in not seeing Smoothley charge the brook:

> 'The Swirl is in front, and of it I'm no lover;
> There's one way to do it, and that's at a dash;
> But Christian is leading, and lightly pops over,
> I follow—we rise—down!—No! done with a splash!

Isn't that it? It was beautiful!'

It might have been in his opinion; in mine it was simply an act of unconsciousness insanity, which I had rather die than intentionally repeat.

'I didn't see you all the time, Mr Smoothley; where were you?' Laura asked.

'Where was he?' cried the Major. 'Not following you, my dear. He took his own line, and, by Jove! it was a right one!'

It was not in these terms that I had expected to hear the Major addressing me, and it was rather bewildering. Still, I trust that I was not puffed up with an unseemly vanity as Laura rode back by my side. She looked lovely with the flush of exercise in her cheek, and the sparkle of excitement in her eyes; and as we passed homewards through the quiet country lanes I forgot the painful creases that were afflicting me, and with as much eloquence as was compatible with the motion of my steed—I ventured!

The blushes deepen on her cheek. She consents on one condition: I must give up hunting.

'You are so rash and daring,' she says, softly—very softly, 'that I should never be happy when you were out.'

Can I refuse her anything—even this? Impossible!

I promise: vowing fervently to myself to keep my word; and on no account do anything to increase the reputation I made at Huntingcrop Hall.

PHILIPPA'S FOXHUNT

Some Experiences of an Irish RM
E. Œ. Somerville and Martin Ross
1890

No one can accuse Philippa and me of having married in haste. As a matter of fact, it was but little under five years from that autumn evening on the river when I had said what is called in Ireland 'the hard word,' to the day in August when I was led to the altar by my best man, and was subsequently led away from it by Mrs Sinclar Yeates. About two years out of the five had been spent by me at Shreelane in ceaseless warfare with drains, eaveshoots, chimneys, pumps; all those fundamentals, in short, that the ingenuous and improving tenant expects to find established as a basis from which to rise to higher things. As far as rising to higher things went, frequent ascents to the roof to search for leaks summed up my achievements; in fact, I suffered so general a shrinkage of my ideals that the triumph of making the hall-door bell ring blinded me to the fact that the rat-holes in the hall floor were nailed up with pieces of tin biscuit boxes, and that the casual visitor could, instead of leaving a card, have easily written his name in the damp on the walls.

Philippa, however, proved adorably callous to these and similar shortcomings. She regarded Shreelane and its floundering, foundering ménage of incapables in the light of a gigantic picnic in a foreign land; she held long conversations daily with Mrs Cadogan, in order, as she informed me, to acquire the language; without any ulterior domestic intention she engaged kitchen-maids because of the beauty of their eyes, and housemaids because they had such delightfully picturesque old mothers, and she declined to correct the phraseology of the parlour-maid, whose painful habit it was to whisper 'Do ye choose cherry or clarry?' when proffering the wine. Fast-days, perhaps, afforded my wife her first insight into the sterner realities of Irish housekeeping. Philippa had what are known as High Church proclivities, and took the matter seriously.

'I don't know how we are to manage for the servants' dinner to-morrow, Sinclair,' she said coming in to my office one Thursday morning; 'Julia says she "promised God this long time that she wouldn't eat an egg on a fast-day," and the kitchen-maid says she won't eat herrings "without they're fried with onions," and Mrs Cadogan says she will "not go to them extremes for servants."'

'I should let Mrs Cadogan settle the menu herself,' I suggested.

'I asked her to do that,' replied Philippa, 'and she only said she "thanked God *she* had no appetite!"'

The lady of the house here fell away into unseasonable laughter.

I made the demoralising suggestion that, as we were going away for a couple of nights, we might safely leave them to fight it out, and the problem was abandoned.

Philippa had been much called on by the neighbourhood in all its shades and grades, and daily she and her trousseau frocks presented themselves at hall-doors of varying dimensions in due acknowledgment of civilities. In Ireland, it may be noted, the process known in England as 'summering and wintering' a newcomer does not obtain; sociability and curiousity alike forbid delay. The visit to which we owed our escape from the intricacies of the fast-day was to the Knoxes of Castle Knox, relations in some remote and tribal way of my landlord, Mr Flurry of that ilk. It involved a short journey by train, and my wife's longest basket-trunk; it also, which was more serious, involved my being lent a horse to go out cubbing the following morning.

At Castle Knox we sank into an almost forgotten environment of draught-proof windows and doors, of deep carpets, of silent servants instead of clattering belligerents. Philippa told me afterwards that it had only been by an effort that she had restrained herself from snatching up the train of her wedding-gown as she paced across the wide hall on little Sir Valentine's arm. After three weeks at Shreelane she found it difficult to remember that the floor was neither damp nor dusty.

I had the good fortune to be of the limited number of those who got on with Lady Knox, chiefly, I imagine, because I was a worm before her, and thankfully permitted her to do all the talking.

'Your wife is extremely pretty,' she pronounced autocratically, surveying Philippa between the candle-shades; 'does she ride?'

Lady Knox was a short square lady, with a weather-beaten face, and an eye decisive from long habit of taking her own line across country and elsewhere. She would have made a very imposing little coachman, and would have caused her stable helpers to rue the day they had the presumption to be born; it struck me that Sir Valentine sometimes did so.

'I'm glad you like her looks,' I replied, 'as I fear you will find her thoroughly despicable otherwise; for one thing, she not only can't ride, but she believes that I can!'

'Oh come, you're not as bad as all that!' my hostess was good enough to say; 'I'm going to put you up on Sorcerer to-morrow, and we'll see you at the top of the hunt—if there is one. That young Knox hasn't a notion how to draw these woods.'

'Well, the best run we had last year out of this place was with Flurry's hounds,' struck in Miss Sally, sole daughter of Sir Valentine's house and home, from her place half-way down the table. It was not difficult to see that she and her mother held different views on the subject of Mr Flurry Knox.

'I call it a criminal thing in any one's great-great-grandfather to rear up a preposterous troop of sons and plant them all out in his own country,' Lady Knox said to me with apparent irrelevance. 'I detest collaterals. Blood may be thicker than water, but it is also a great deal nastier. In this country I find that fifteenth cousins consider themselves near relations if they live within twenty miles of one!'

Having before now taken in the position with regard to Flurry Knox, I took care to accept these remarks as generalities, and turned the conversation to other themes.

'I see Mrs Yeates is doing wonders with Mr Hamilton,' said Lady Knox presently, following the direction of my eyes, which had strayed away to where Philippa was beaming upon her left-hand neighbour, a mildewed-looking old clergyman, who was delivering a long dissertation, the purport of which we were happily unable to catch.

'She has always had a gift for the Church,' I said.

'Not curates?' said Lady Knox, in her deep voice.

I made haste to reply that it was the elders of the Church who were venerated by my wife.

'Well, she has her fancy in old Eustace Hamilton; he's elderly enough!' said Lady Knox. 'I wonder if she'd venerate him as much if she knew that he had fought with his sister-in-law, and they haven't spoken for thirty years! though for the matter of that,' she added, 'I think it shows his good sense!'

'Mrs Knox is rather a friend of mine,' I ventured.

'Is she? H'm! Well, she's not one of mine!' replied my hostess, with her usual definiteness. 'I'll say on thing for her, I believe she's always been a sportswoman. She's very rich, you know, and they say she only married old Badger Knox to save his hounds from being sold to pay his debts, and then she took the horn from him and hunted them herself. Has she been rude to your wife yet? No? Oh, well, she will. It's a mere question of time. She hates all English people. You know the story they tell of her? She was coming home from London, and when she was getting her ticket the man asked if she had said a ticket for York. 'No, thank God, Cork!' says Mrs. Knox.'

'Well, I rather agree with her!' said I; 'but why did she fight with Mr Hamilton?'

'Oh, nobody knows. I don't believe they know themselves! Whatever it was, the old lady drives five miles to Fortwilliam every Sunday, rather than go to his church, just outside her own back gates,' Lady Knox said with a laugh like a terrier's bark. 'I wish I'd fought with him myself,' she said; 'he gives us forty minutes every Sunday.'

As I struggled into my boots the following morning, I felt that Sir Valentine's acid confidences on cub-hunting, bestowed on me at midnight, did credit to his judgment. 'A very moderate amusement, my dear Major,' he had said, in his dry little voice; 'you should stick to shooting. No one expects you to shoot before daybreak.'

It was six o'clock as I crept downstairs, and found Lady Knox and Miss Sally at breakfast, with two lamps on the table, and a foggy daylight oozing in from under the half-raised blinds. Philippa was already in the hall, pumping up her bicycle, in a state of excitement at the prospect of her first experience of hunting that would have been more comprehensible to me had she been going to ride a strange horse, as I was. As I bolted my food I saw the horses being led past the windows, and a faint twang of a horn told that Flurry Knox and his hounds were not far off.

Miss Sally jumped up.

'If I'm not on the Cockatoo before the hounds come up, I shall never get there!' she said, hobbling out of the room in the toils of her safety habit. Her small, alert face looked very childish under her riding-hat; the lamp-light struck sparks out of her thick coil of golden-red hair: I wondered how I had ever thought her like her prim little father.

She was already on her white cob when I got to the hall-door, and Flurry Knox was riding over the glistening wet grass with his hounds, while his whip, Dr Jerome Hickey, was having a stirring time with the young entry and the rabbit-holes. They moved on without stopping, up a back avenue, under tall and dripping trees, to a thick laurel covert, at some little distance from the house. Into this the hounds were thrown, and the usual period of fidgety inaction set in for the riders, of whom, all told, there were about half-a-dozen. Lady Knox, square and solid, on her big, confidential iron-grey, was near me, and her eyes were on me and my mount; with her rubicund face and white collar she was more than ever like a coachman.

'Sorcerer looks as if he suited you well,' she said, after a few minutes of silence, during which the hounds rustled and crackled steadily through the laurels; 'he's a little high on the leg, and so are you, you know, so you show each other off.'

Sorcerer was standing like a rock, with his good-looking head in the air and his eyes fastened on the covert. His manners, so far, had been those of a perfect gentleman, and were in marked contrast to those of Miss Sally's cob, who was sidling, hopping, and snatching unappeasably at his bit. Philippa had disappeared from view down the avenue ahead. The fog was melting, and the sun threw long blades of light through the trees; everything was quiet, and in the distance the curtained windows of the house marked the warm repose of Sir Valentine, and those of the party who shared his opinion of cubbing.

'Hark! hark to cry there!'

It was Flurry's voice, away at the other side of the covert. The rustling and brushing through the laurels became more vehement, then passed out of hearing.

'He never will leave his hounds alone,' said Lady Knox disapprovingly.

Miss Sally and the Cockatoo moved away in a series of heraldic capers towards the end of the laurel plantation, and at the same moment I saw Philippa on her bicycle shoot into view on the drive ahead of us.

'I've seen a fox!' she screamed, white with what I believe to have been personal terror, though she says it was excitement; 'it passed quite close to me!'

'What way did he go?' bellowed a voice which I recognised as Dr Hickey's, somewhere in the deep of the laurels.

'Down the drive!' returned Philippa, with a pea-hen quality in her tones with which I was quite unacquainted.

An electrifying screech of 'Gone away!' was projected from the laurels by Dr Hickey.

'Gone away!' chanted Flurry's horn at the top of the covert.

'This is what he calls cubbing!' said Lady Knox, 'a mere farce!' but none the less she loosed her sedate monster into a canter.

Sorcerer got his hind-legs under him, and hardened his crest against the bit, as we all hustled along the drive after the flying figure of my wife. I knew very little about horses, but I realised that even with the hounds tumbling hysterically out of the covert, and the Cockatoo kicking the gravel into his face, Sorcerer comported himself with the manners of the best society. Up a side road I saw Flurry Knox opening half of a gate and cramming through it; in a moment we also had crammed through, and the turf of a pasture field was under our feet. Dr Hickey leaned forward and took hold of his horse; I did likewise, with the trifling difference that my horse took hold of me, and I steered for Flurry Knox with single-hearted purpose, the hounds, already a field ahead, being merely an exciting and noisy accompaniment of this endeavour. A heavy stone wall was the first occurrence of note. Flurry chose a place where the top was loose, and his clumsy-looking brown mare changed feet on the rattling stones like a fairy. Sorcerer came at it, tense and collected as a bow at full stretch, and sailed steeply into the air; I saw the wall far beneath me, with an unsuspected ditch on the far side, and I felt my hat following me at the full stretch of its guard as we swept over it, then, with a long slant, we descended to earth some sixteen feet from where we had left it, and I was possessor of the gratifying fact that I had achieved a good-sized 'fly', and had not perceptibly moved in my saddle. Subsequent disillusioning experience has taught me that but few horses jump like Sorcerer, so gallantly, so sympathetically, and with such supreme mastery of the subject; but none the less the enthusiasm that he imparted to me has never been extinguished, and that October morning ride revealed to me the unsuspected intoxication of fox-hunting.

Behind me I heard the scrabbling of the Cockatoo's little hoofs among the loose stones, and Lady Knox, galloping on my left, jerked a maternal chin over her shoulder to mark her daughter's progress. For my part, had there been an entire circus behind me, I was far too much occupied with ramming on my hat and trying to hold Sorcerer, to have looked round, and all my spare faculties were devoted to steering for Flurry, who had taken a right-handed turn, and was at that moment surmounting a bank of uncertain and briary aspect. I surmounted it also, with the swiftness and simplicity for which the Quaker's methods of bank jumping had not prepared me, and two or three fields, traversed at the same steeplechase pace, brought us to a road and to an abrupt check. There, suddenly, were the hounds, scrambling in baffled silence down into the road from the opposite bank, to look for the line they had overrun, and there, amazingly, was Philippa, engaged in excited converse with several men with spades over their shoulders.

'Did ye see the fox, boys?' shouted Flurry, addressing the group.

'We did! we did!' cried my wife and her friends in chorus! 'he ran up the road!'

'We'd be badly off without Mrs Yeates!' said Flurry, as he whirled his mare round and clattered up the road with a hustle of hounds after him.

It occurred to me as forcibly as any mere earthly thing can occur to those who are wrapped in the sublimities of a run, that, for a young woman who had never before seen a fox out of a cage at the Zoo, Philippa was taking to hunting very kindly. Her cheeks were a most brilliant pink, her blue eyes shone.

'Oh, Sinclair!' she exclaimed, 'they say he's going for Aussolas, and there's a road I can ride all the way!

'Ye can, Miss! Sure we'll show you'! chorussed her *cortège*.

Her foot was on the pedal ready to mount. Decidedly my wife was in no need of assistance from me.

Up the road a hound gave a yelp of discovery, and flung himself over a stile into the fields; the rest of the pack went squealing and jostling after him, and I followed Flurry over one of those infinitely varied erections, pleasantly termed 'gaps' in Ireland. On this occasion the gap was made of three razor-edged slabs of slate learning against an iron bar, and Sorcerer conveyed to me his thorough knowledge of the matter by a lift of his hind-quarters that made me feel as if I were being skilfully kicked downstairs. To what extent I looked it, I cannot say, nor providentially can Philippa, as she had already started. I only know that undeserved good luck restored to me my stirrup before Sorcerer got away with me in the next field.

What followed was, I am told, a very fast fifteen minutes; for me time was not; the empty fields rushed past uncounted, fences came and went in a flash, while the wind sang in my ears, and the dazzle of the early sun was in my eyes. I saw the hounds occasionally, sometimes pouring over a green bank, as the charging breaker lifts and flings itself, sometimes driving across a field, as the white tongues of foam slide racing over the sand; and always ahead of me was Flurry Knox, going as a man goes who knows his country, who knows his horse, and whose heart is wholly and absolutely in the right place.

Do what I would, Sorcerer's implacable stride carried me closer and closer to the brown mare, till, as I thundered down the slope of a long field, I was not twenty yards behind Flurry. Sorcerer had stiffened his neck to iron, and to slow him down was beyond me; but I fought his head away to the right, and found myself coming hard and steady at a stonefaced bank with broken ground in front of it. Flurry bore away to the left, shouting something that I did not understand. That Sorcerer shortened his stride at the right moment was entirely due to his own judgment; standing well away from the jump, he rose like a stag out of the tussocky ground, and as he swung my twelve stone six into the air the obstacle revealed itself to him and me as consisting not of one bank but of two, and between the two lay a deep grassy lane, half choked with furze. I have often been asked to state the width of the bohereen, and can only reply that in my opinion it was at least eighteen feet; Flurry Knox and Dr Hickey, who did not jump it, say that it is not more than five. What Sorcerer did with it I cannot say; the sensation was of a towering flight with a kick back in it, a biggish drop, and a landing on cee-springs, still on the downhill grade. That was how one of the best horses in Ireland took one of Ireland's most ignorant riders over a very nasty place.

A sombre line of fir-wood lay ahead, rimmed with a grey wall, and in another couple of minutes we had pulled up on the Aussolas road, and were watching the hounds struggling over the wall into Aussolas demesne.

'No hurry now,' said Flurry, turning in his saddle to watch the Cockatoo jump into the road, 'he's to ground in the big earth inside. Well, Major, it's well for you that's a big-jumped horse. I thought you were a dead man a while ago when you faced him at the bohereen!'

I was disclaiming intention in the matter when Lady Knox and the others joined us.

'I thought you told me your wife was no sportswoman,' she said to me, critically scanning Sorcerer's legs for cuts the while, 'but when I saw her a minute ago she had abandoned her bicycle and was running across country like—'

'Look at her now!' interrupted Miss Sally. 'Oh!—oh!' In the interval between these exclamations my incredulous eyes beheld my wife in mid-air, hand in hand with a couple of stalwart country boys, with whom she was leaping in unison from the top of a bank on to the road.

Every one, even the saturnine Dr Hickey, began to laugh; I rode back to Philippa, who was exchanging compliments and congratulations with her escort.

'Oh, Sinclair!' she cried, 'wasn't it splendid? I saw you jumping, and everything! Where are they going now?'

'My dear girl,' I said, with marital disapproval, 'you're killing yourself. Where's your bicycle?'

'Oh, it's punctured in a sort of lane, back there. It's all right; and then they'—she breathlessly waved her hand at her attendants—'they showed me the way.'

'Begor! you proved very good, Miss!' said a grinning cavalier.

'Faith she did!' said another, polishing his shining brow with his white flannel coat-sleeve, 'she lepped like a haarse!'

'And may I ask how you propose to go home?' said I.

'I don't know and I don't care! I'm not going home!' She cast an entirely disobedient eye at me. 'And your eye-glass is hanging down your back and your tie is bulging out over your waist-coat!'

The little group of riders had begun to move away.

'We're going on into Aussolas,' called out Flurry; 'come on, and make my grandmother give you some breakfast, Mrs Yeates; she always has it at eight o'clock.'

The front gates were close at hand, and we turned in under the tall beech-trees, with the unswept leaves rustling round the horses' feet, and the lovely blue of the October morning sky filling the spaces between smooth grey branches and golden leaves. The woods rang with the voices of the hounds, enjoying an untrammelled rabbit hunt, while the Master and the Whip, both on foot, strolled along unconcernedly with their bridles over their arms, making themselves agreeable to my wife, an occasional touch of Flurry's horn, or a crack of Dr Hickey's whip, just indicating to the pack that the authorities still took a friendly interest in their doings.

Down a grassy glade in the wood a party of old Mrs Knox's young horses suddenly swept into view, headed by an old mare, who, with her tail over her back, stampeded ponderously past our cavalcade, shaking and swinging her handsome old head, while her youthful friends bucked and kicked and snapped at each other round her with the ferocious humour of their kind.

'Here, Jerome, take the horn,' said Flurry to Dr Hickey; 'I'm going to see Mrs Yeates up to the house, the way these tomfools won't gallop on top of her.'

From this point it seems to me that Philippa's adventures are more worthy of record than mine, and as she has favoured me with a full account of them, I venture to think my version may be relied on.

Mrs Knox was already at breakfast when Philippa was led, quaking, into her formidable presence. My wife's acquaintance with Mrs Knox was, so far, limited to a state visit on either side, and she found but little comfort in Flurry's assurances that his grandmother wouldn't mind if he brought all the hounds in to breakfast, coupled with the statement that she would put her eyes on sticks for the Major.

Whatever the truth of this may have been, Mrs Knox received her guest with an equanimity quite unshaken by the fact that her boots were in the fender instead of on her feet, and that a couple of shawls of varying dimensions and degrees of age did not conceal the inner presence of a magenta flannel dressing-jacket. She installed Philippa at the table and plied her with food, oblivious as to whether the needful implements with which to eat it were forthcoming or not. She told Flurry where a vixen had reared her family, and she watched him ride away, with some biting comments on his mare's hocks screamed after him from the window.

The dining-room at Aussolas Castle is one of the many rooms in Ireland in which Cromwell is said to have stabled his horse (and probably no one would have objected less than Mrs Knox had she been consulted in the matter). Philippa questions if the room had ever been tidied up since, and she endorses Flurry's observation that 'there wasn't a day in the year you wouldn't get feeding for a hen and chickens on the floor.' Opposite to Philippa, on a Louis Quinze chair, sat Mrs Knox's woolly dog, its suspicious little eyes peering at her out of their setting of pink lids and dirty white wool. A couple of young horses outside the windows tore at the mattered creepers on the walls, or thrust faces that were half-shy, half-impudent, into the room. Portly pigeons waddled to and fro on the broad window-sill, sometimes flying in to a perch on the picture-frames, while they kept up incessantly a hoarse and pompous cooing.

Animals and children are, as a rule, alike destructive to conversation; but Mrs Knox, when she chose, *bien entendu*, could have made herself agreeable in a Noah's ark, and Philippa has a gift of sympathetic attention that personal experience has taught me to regard with distrust as well as respect, while it has often made me realise the worldly wisdom of Kingsley's injunction:

'Be good, sweet maid, and let who will be clever.'

Family prayers, declaimed by Mrs Knox with alarming austerity, following close on breakfast, Philippa and a vinegar-faced henchwoman forming the family. The prayers were long, and through the open window as they progressed came distantly a whoop or two; the declamatory tones staggered a little, and then continued at a distinctly higher rate of speed.

'Ma'am! Ma'am!' whispered a small voice at the window.

Mrs Knox made a repressive gesture and held on her way. A sudden outcry of hounds followed, and the owner of the whisper, a small boy with a face freckled like a turkey's egg, darted from the window and dragged a donkey and bath-chair into view. Philippa admits to having lost the thread of the discourse, but she thinks that the 'Amen' that immediately ensued can hardly have come in its usual place. Mrs Knox shut the book abruptly, scrambled up from her knees, and said, 'They've found!'

In a surprisingly short space of time she had added to her attire her boots, a fur cape, and a garden hat, and was in the bath-chair, the small boy stimulating the donkey with the success peculiar to his class, while Philippa hung on behind.

The woods of Aussolas are hilly and extensive, and on that particular morning it seemed that they held as many foxes as hounds. In vain was the horn blown and the whips cracked, small rejoicing parties of hounds, each with a fox of its own, scoured to and fro: every labourer in the vicinity had left his work, and was sedulously heading every fox with yells that would have befitted a tiger hunt, and sticks and stones when occasion served.

'Will I pull out as far as the big rosydandhrum, ma'am?' inquired the small boy; 'I seen three of the dogs go in it, and they yowling.'

'You will,' said Mrs Knox, thumping the donkey on the back with her umbrella; 'here! Jeremiah Regan! Come down out of that with that pitchfork! Do you want to kill the fox, you fool?'

'I do not, your honour, ma'am,' responded Jeremiah Regan, a tall young countryman, emerging from a bramble brake.

'Did you see him?' said Mrs Knox eagerly.

'I seem himself and his ten pups drinking below at the lake ere yesterday, your honour, ma'am, and he as big as a chestnut horse!' said Jeremiah.

'Faugh! Yesterday!' snorted Mrs Knox; 'go on to the rhododendrons, Johnny!'

The party, reinforced by Jeremiah and the pitchfork, progressed at a high rate of speed along the shrubbery path, encountering *en route* Lady Knox, stooping on to her horse's neck under the sweeping branches of the laurels.

'Your horse is too high for my coverts, Lady Knox,' said the Lady of the Manor, with a malicious eye at Lady Knox's flushed face and dinged hat; 'I'm afraid you will be left behind like Absalom when the hounds go away!'

'As they never do anything here but hunt rabbits,' retorted her ladyship, 'I don't think that's likely.'

'Rabbits, my dear!' she said scornfully to Philippa. 'That's all she knows about it. I declare it disgusts me to see a woman of that age making such a Judy of herself! Rabbits indeed!'

Down in the thicket of rhododendron everything was very quiet for a time. Philippa strained her eyes in vain to see any of the riders; the horn blowing and the whip cracking passed on almost out of hearing. Once or twice a hound worked through the rhododendrons, glanced at the party, and hurried on, immersed in business. All at once Johnny, the donkey-boy, whispered excitedly:

'Look at he! Look at he!' and pointed to a boulder of grey rock that stood out among the dark evergreens. A big yellow cub was crouching on it; he instantly slid into the shelter of the bushes, and the irrepressible Jeremiah, uttering a rending shriek, plunged into the thicket after him. Two or three hounds came rushing at the sound, and after this Philippa says she finds some difficulty in recalling the proper order of events; chiefly, she confesses, because of the wholly ridiculous tears of excitement that blurred her eyes.

'We ran,' she said, 'we simply tore, and the donkey galloped, and as for that old Mrs Knox, she was giving cracked screams to the hounds all the time, and they were screaming too; and then somehow we were all out on the road!'

What seems to have occurred was that three couple of hounds, Jeremiah Regan, and Mrs Knox's equippage, amongst them somehow hustled the cub out of Aussolas demesne and up on to a hill on the farther side of the road. Jeremiah was sent back by his mistress to fetch Flurry, and the rest of the party pursued a thrilling course along the road, parallel with that of the hounds, who were hunting slowly through the gorse on the hillside.

'Upon my honour and word, Mrs Yeates, my dear, we have the hunt to ourselves!' said Mrs Knox to the panting Philippa, as they pounded along the road. 'Johnny, d'ye see the fox?'

'I do, ma'am!' shrieked Johnny, who possessed the usual field-glass vision bestowed upon his kind. 'Look at him over-right us on the hill above! Hi! The spotty dog have him! No, he's gone from him! *Gwan out o' that!*' This to the donkey, with blows that sounded like the beating of carpets, and produced rather more dust.

They had left Aussolas some half a mile behind, when, from a strip of wood on their right, the fox suddenly slipped over the bank on to the road just ahead of them, ran up it for a few yards and whisked in at a small entrance gate, with the three couple of hounds yelling on a red-hot scent, not thirty yards behind. The bath-chair party whirled in at their heels, Philippa and the donkey considerably blown, Johnny scarlet through his freckles, but as fresh as paint, the old lady blind and deaf to all things save the chase. The hounds went raging through the shrubs beside the drive, and away down a grassy slope towards a shallow glen, in the bottom of which ran a little stream, and after them over the grass bumped the bath-chair. At the stream they turned sharply and ran up the glen towards the avenue, which crossed it by means of a rough stone viaduct.

''Pon me conscience, he's into the old culvert!' exclaimed Mrs Knox; 'there was one of my hounds choked there once, long ago! Beat on the donkey, Johnny!'

At this juncture Philippa's narrative again becomes incoherent, not to say breathless. She is, however, positive that it was somewhere about here that the upset of the bath-chair occurred, but she cannot be clear as to whether she picked up the donkey or Mrs Knox, or whether she herself was picked up by Johnny while Mrs Knox picked up the donkey. From my knowledge of Mrs Knox I should say she picked up herself and no one else. At all events, the next salient point is the palpitating moment when Mrs Knox, Johnny, and Philippa successively applying an eye to the opening of the culvert by which the stream trickled under the viaduct, while five dripping hounds bayed and leaped around them, discovered by more sense than that of sight that the fox was in it, and furthermore that one of the hounds was in it too.

'There's a sthrong grating before him at the far end,' said Johnny, his head in at the mouth of the hole, his voice sounding as if he were talking into a jug, 'the two of them's fighting in it; they'll be choked surely!'

'Then don't stand gabbling there, you little fool, but get in and pull the hound out!' exclaimed Mrs Knox, who was balancing herself on a stone in the stream.

'I'd be in dread, ma'am,' whined Johnny.

'Balderdash!' said the implacable Mrs Knox. 'In with you!'

I understand that Philippa assisted Johnny into the culvert, and presume that it was in so doing that she acquired the two Robinson Crusoe bare footprints which decorated her jacket when I next met her.

'Have you got hold of him, yet, Johnny?' cried Mrs Knox up the culvert.

'I have, ma'am, by the tail,' responded Johnny's voice, sepulchral in the depths.

'Can you stir him, Johnny?'

'I cannot, ma'am, and the wather is rising in it.'

'Well, please God, they'll not open the mill dam!' remarked Mrs Knox philosophically to Philippa, as she caught hold of Johnny's dirty ankles. 'Hold on to the tail, Johnny!'

She hauled, with, as might be expected, no appreciable result. 'Run, my dear, and look for somebody, and we'll have that fox yet!'

Philippa ran, whither she knew not, pursued by fearful visions of bursting mill-dams, and maddened foxes at bay. As she sped up the avenue she heard voices, robust male voices, in a shrubbery, and made for them. Advancing along an embowered walk towards her was what she took for one wild instant to be a funeral; a second glance showed her that it was a party of clergymen of all ages, walking by twos and threes in the dappled shade of the over-arching trees. Obviously she had intruded her sacrilegious presence into a Clerical Meeting. She acknowledges that at this awe-inspiring spectacle she faltered, but the thought of Johnny, the hound, and the fox, suffocating, possibly drowning together in the culvert, nerved her. She does not remember what she said or how she said it, but I fancy she must have conveyed to them the impression that old Mrs Knox was being drowned, as she immediately found herself heading a charge of the Irish Church towards the scene of disaster.

Fate has not always used me well, but on this occasion it was mercifully decreed that I and the other members of the hunt should be privileged to arrive in time to see my wife and her rescue party precipitating themselves down the glen.

'Holy Biddy!' ejaculated Flurry, is she running a paper-chase with all the parsons? But look! For pity's sake will you look at my grandmother and my Uncle Eustace?'

Mrs Knox and her sworn enemy the old clergyman, whom I had met at dinner the night before, were standing, apparently in the stream, tugging at two bare legs that projected from a hole in the viaduct, and arguing at the top of their voices. The bath-chair lay on its side with the donkey grazing beside it, on the bank a stout Archdeacon was tendering advice, and the hounds danced and howled round the entire group.

'I tell you, Eliza, you had better let the Archdeacon try,' thundered Mr Hamilton.

'Then I tell you I will not!' vociferated Mrs Knox, with a tug at the end of the sentence that elicited a subterranean lament from Johnny. 'Now who was right about the second grating? I told you so twenty years ago!'

Exactly as Philippa and her rescue party arrived, the efforts of Mrs Knox and her brother-in-law triumphed. The struggling, sopping form of Johnny was slowly drawn from the hole, drenched, speechless, but clinging to the stern of a hound, who, in its turn, had its jaws fast in the hind-quarters of a limp, yellow cub.

'Oh, it's dead!' wailed Philippa, 'I *did* think I should have been in time to save it!'

'Well, if that doesn't beat all!' said Dr Hickey.

THE POLICY OF THE CLOSED DOOR

Some Experiences of an Irish RM
E. Œ. Somerville and Martin Ross
1890

The disasters and humiliations that befell me at Drumcurran Fair may yet be remembered. They certainly have not been forgotten in the regions about Skebawn, where the tale of how Bernard Shute and I stole each other's horses has passed into history. The grand-daughter of the Mountain Hare, bought by Mr Shute with such light-hearted enthusiasm, was restored to that position between the shafts of a cart that she was so well fitted to grace; Moonlighter, his other purchase, spent the two months following on the fair in 'favouring' a leg with a strained sinew, and in receiving visits from the local vet, who, however uncertain in his diagnosis of Moonlighter's leg, had accurately estimated the length of Bernard's foot.

Miss Bennett's mare Cruiskeen, alone of the trio, was immediately and thoroughly successful. She went in harness like a hero, she carried Philippa like an elder sister, she was never sick or sorry; as Peter Cadogan summed her up, 'That one'd live where another 'd die.' In her safe keeping Philippa made her *début* with hounds at an uneventful morning's cubbing, with no particular result, except that Philippa returned home so stiff that she had to go to bed for a day, and arose more determined than ever to be a fox-hunter.

The opening meet of Mr Knox's foxhounds was on November 1, and on that morning Philippa on Cruiskeen, accompanied by me on the Quaker, set out for Ardmeen Cross, the time-honoured fixture for All Saints' Day. The weather was grey and quiet, and full of all the moist sweetness of an Irish autumn. There had been a great deal of rain during the past month; it had turned the bracken to a purple brown, and had filled the hollows with shining splashes of water. The dead leaves were slippery under foot, and the branches above were thinly decked with yellow, where the pallid survivors of summer still clung to their posts. As Philippa and I sedately approached the meet the red coats of Flurry Knox and his whip, Dr Jerome Hickey, were to be seen on the road at the top of the hill; Cruiskeen put her head in the air, and stared at them with eyes that understood all they portended.

'Sinclair,' said my wife hurriedly, as a straggling hound, flogged in by Dr Hickey, uttered a grievous and melodious howl, 'remember, if they find, it's no use to talk to me, for I shan't be able to speak.'

I was sufficiently acquainted with Philippa in moments of enthusiasm to exhibit silently the corner of a clean pocket-handkerchief; I have seen her cry when a police constable won a bicycle race in Skebawn; she has wept at hearing Sir Valentine Knox's health drunk with musical honours at a tenants' dinner. It is an amiable custom, but, as she herself admits, it is unbecoming.

An imposing throng, in point of numbers, was gathered at the crossroads, the riders being almost swamped in the crowd of traps, outside cars, bicyclists, and people on foot. The field was an eminently representative one. The Clan Knox was, as usual, there in force, its more aristocratic members dingily respectable in black coats and tall hats that went impartially to weddings, funerals, and hunts, and, like a horse that is past mark of mouth, were no longer to be identified with any special epoch; there was a humbler squireen element in tweeds and flat-brimmed pot-hats, and a good muster of farmers, men of the spare, black-muzzled, West of Ireland type, on horses that ranged from the cart mare, clipped trace high, to shaggy and leggy three-year-olds, none of them hunters, but all of them able to hunt. Philippa and I worked our way to the heart of things, where was Flurry, seated on his brown mare, in what appeared to be a somewhat moody silence. As we exchanged greetings I was aware that his eye was resting with extreme disfavour upon two approaching figures. I put up my eye-glass, and perceived that one of them was Miss Sally Knox, on a tall grey horse; the other was Mr Bernard Shute, in all the flawless beauty of his first pink coat, mounted on Stockbroker, a well-known, hard-mouthed, big-jumping bay, recently purchased from Dr Hickey.

During the languors of a damp autumn the neighbourhood had been much nourished and sustained by the privilege of observing and diagnosing the progress of Mr Shute's flirtation with Miss Sally Knox. What made it all the more enjoyable for the lookers-on—or most of them—was, that although Bernard's courtship was of the nature of a proclamation from the housetops, Miss Knox's attitude left everything to the imagination. To Flurry Knox the romantic but despicable position of slighted rival was comfortably allotted; his sole sympathisers were Philippa and old Mrs Knox of Aussolas, but no one knew if he needed sympathisers. Flurry was a man of mystery.

Mr Shute and Miss Knox approached us rapidly, the latter's mount pulling hard.

'Flurry,' I said, 'isn't that grey the horse Shute bought from you last July at the fair?'

Flurry did not answer me. His face was as black as thunder. He turned his horse round, cursing two country boys who got in his way, with low and concentrated venom, and began to move forward, followed by the hounds. If his wish was to avoid speaking to Miss Sally it was not to be gratified.

'Good-morning, Flurry,' she began, sitting close down to Moonlighter's ramping jog as she rode up beside her cousin. 'What a hurry you're in! We passed no end of people on the road who won't be here for another ten minutes.'

'No more will I,' was Mr Knox's cryptic reply, as he spurred the brown mare into a trot.

Moonlighter made a vigorous but frustrated effort to buck, and indemnified himself by a successful kick at a hound.

'Bother you, Flurry! Can't you walk for a minute?' exclaimed Miss Sally, who looked about as large, in relation to her horse, as the conventional tomtit on a round of beef. 'You might have more sense than to crack your whip under this horse's nose! I don't believe you know what horse it is even!'

I was not near enough to catch Flurry's reply.

'Well, if you didn't want him to be lent to me you shouldn't have sold him to Mr Shute!' retorted Miss Knox, in her clear, provoking little voice.

'I suppose he's afraid to ride him himself,' said Flurry, turning his horse in at a gate. 'Get ahead there, Jerome, can't you? It's better to put them in at this end than to have every one riding on top of them!'

Miss Sally's cheeks were still very pink when I came up and began to talk to her, and her grey-green eyes had a look in them like those of an angry kitten.

The riders moved slowly down a rough pasture-field, and took up their position along the brow of Ardmeen covert, into which the hounds had already hurled themselves with their customary contempt for the convenances. Flurry's hounds, true to their nationality, were in the habit of doing the right thing in the wrong way.

Untouched by autumn, the furze bushes of Ardmeen covert were darkly green, save for a golden fleck of blossom here and there, and the glistening grey cobwebs that stretched from spike to spike. The look of the ordinary gorse covert is familiar to most people as a tidy enclosure of an acre or so, filled with low plants of well-educated gorse; not so many will be found who have experience of it as a rocky, sedgy wilderness, half a mile, square, garrisoned with brigades of furze bushes, some of them higher than a horse's head, lean, strong, and cunning, like the foxes that breed in them, impenetrable, with their bristling spikes, as a hedge of bayonets. By dint of infinite leisure and obstinate greed, the cattle had made paths for themselves through the bushes to the patches of grass that they hemmed in; their hoofprints were guides to the explorer, down muddy staircases of rock, and across black intervals of umplumbed bog. The whole covert slanted gradually down to a small river that raced round three sides of it, and beyond the stream, in agreeable contrast, lay a clean and wholesome country of grass fields and banks.

The hounds drew slowly along and down the hill towards the river, and the riders hung about outside the covert, and tried—I can answer for at least one of them—to decide which was the least odious of the ways through it, in the event of the fox breaking at the far side. Miss Sally took up a position not very far from me, and it was easy to see that she had her hands full with her borrowed mount, on whose temper the delay and suspense were visibly telling. His ironic-grey neck was white from the chafing of the reins; had the ground under his feet been red-hot he could hardly have sidled and hopped more uncontrollably; nothing but the most impassioned conjugation of the verb to condemn could have supplied any human equivalent for the manner in which he tore holes in the sedgy grass with a furious forefoot. Those who were even superficial judges of character gave his heels a liberal allowance of sea-room, and Mr Shute, who could not be numbered among such, and had, as usual, taken up a position as near Miss Sally as possible, was rewarded by a double knock on his horse's ribs that was a cause of heartless mirth to the lady of his affections.

Not a hound had as yet spoken, but they were forcing their way through the gorse forest and shoving each other jealously aside with growing excitement, and Flurry could be seen at intervals, moving forward in the direction they were indicating. It was at this juncture that the ubiquitous Slipper presented himself at my horse's shoulder.

''Tis for the river he's making, Major,' he said, with an upward roll of his squinting eyes, that nearly made me sea-sick. 'He's a Castle Knox fox that came in this morning, and ye should get ahead down to the ford!'

A tip from Slipper was not to be neglected, and Philippa and I began a cautious progress through the gorse, followed by Miss Knox as quietly as Moonlighter's nerves would permit.

'Wishful has it!' she exclaimed, as a hound came out into view, uttered a sharp yelp, and drove forward.

'Hark! hark!' roared Flurry with at least three *r*'s reverberating in each 'hark;' at the same instant came a holloa from the farther side of the river, and Dr Hickey's renowned and blood-curdling screech was uplifted at the bottom of the covert. Then babel broke forth, as the hounds, converging from every quarter, flung themselves shrieking on the line. Moonlighter went straight up on his hind-legs, and dropped again with a bound that sent him crushing past Philippa and Cruiskeen; he did it a second time, and was almost on to the tail of the Quaker, whose bulky person was not to be hurried in any emergency.

'Get on if you can, Major Yeates!' called out Sally, steadying the grey as well as she could in the narrow pathway between the great gorse bushes.

Other horses were thundering behind us, men were shouting to each other in similar passages right and left of us, the cry of the hounds filled the air with a kind of delirium. A low wall with a stick laid along it barred the passage in front of me, and the Quaker firmly and immediately decided not to have it until some one else had dislodged the pole.

'Go ahead!' I shouted, squeezing to one side with heroic disregard of the furze bushes and my new tops.

The words were hardly out of my mouth when Moonlighter, mad with thwarted excitement, shot by me, hurtled over the obstacle with extravagant fury, landed twelve feet beyond it on clattering slippery rock, saved himself form falling with an eel-like forward buck on to sedgy ground, and bolted at full speed down the muddy cattle track. There are corners—rocky, most of them—in that cattle track, that Sally has told me she will remember to her dying day; boggy holes of any depth, ranging between two feet and half-way to Australia, that she says she does not fail to mention in the General Thanksgiving; but at the time they occupied mere fractions of the strenuous seconds in which it was hopeless for her to do anything but try to steer, trust to luck, sit hard down into the saddle and try to stay there. (For my part, I would as soon try to adhere to the horns of a charging bull as to the crutches of a side-saddle, but happily the necessity is not likely to arise.) I saw Flurry Knox a little ahead of her on the same track, jamming his mare into the furze bushes to get out of her way; he shouted something after her about the ford, and started to gallop for it himself by a breakneck short cut.

The hounds were already across the river, and it was obvious that, ford or no ford, Moonlighter's intentions might be simply expressed in the formula 'Be with them I will.' It was all down-hill to the river, and among the furze bushes and rocks there was neither time nor place to turn him. He rushed at it with a shattering slip upon a streak of rock, with a heavy plunge in the deep ground by the brink; it was as bad a take-off for twenty feet of water as could well be found. The grey horse rose out of the boggy stuff with all the impetus that pace and temper could give, but it was not enough. For one instant the twisting, sliding current was under Sally, the next a veil of water sprang up all round her, and Moonlighter was rolling and lurching in the desperate effort to find foothold in the rocky bed of the stream.

I was following at the best pace I could kick out of the Quaker, and saw the water swirl into her lap as her horse rolled to the near-side. She caught the mane to save herself, but he struggled on to his legs again, and came floundering broad-side on to the further bank. In three seconds she had got out of the saddle and flung herself at the bank, grasping the rushes, and trying, in spite of the sodden weight of her habit, to drag herself out of the water.

At the same instant I saw Flurry and the brown mare dashing through the ford, twenty yards higher up. He was off his horse and beside her with that uncanny quickness that Flurry reserved for moments of emergency, and, catching her by the arms, swung her on to the bank as easily as if she had been the kennel terrier.

'Catch the horse!' she called out, scrambling to her feet.

'Damn the horse!' returned Flurry, in the rage that is so often the reaction from a bad scare.

I turned along the bank and made for the ford; by this time it was full of hustling, splashing riders, through whom Bernard Shute, furiously picking up a bad start, drove a devastating way. He tried to turn his horse down the bank towards Miss Knox, but the hounds were running hard, and, to my intense amusement, Stockbroker refused to abandon the chase, and swept his rider away in the wake of his stable companion, Dr Hickey's young chestnut. By this time two country boys had, as is usual in such cases, risen from the earth, and fished Moonlighter out of the stream. Miss Sally wound up an acrimonious argument with her cousin by observing that she didn't care what he said, and placing her water-logged boot in his obviously unwilling hand, in a second was again in the saddle, gathering up the wet reins with the trembling, clumsy fingers of a person who is thoroughly chilled and in a violent hurry. She set Moonlighter going, and was away in a moment, galloping him at the first fence at a pace that suited his steeplechasing ideas.

'Mr Knox!' panted Philippa, who had by this time joined us, 'making her go home!'

'She can go where she likes as far as I'm concerned,' responded Mr Knox, pitching himself on his mare's back and digging in the spurs.

Moonlighter had already glided over the bank in front of us, with a perfunctory flick at it with his heels; Flurry's mare and Cruiskeen jumped it side by side with equal precision. It was a bank of some five feet high; the Quaker charged it enthusiastically, refused it abruptly, and, according to his infuriating custom at such moments, proceeded to tear hurried mouthfuls of grass.

'Will I give him a couple o' belts, your Honour?' shouted one of the running accompaniment of country boys.

'You will!' said I, with some further remarks to the Quaker that I need not commit to paper.

Swish! Whack! The sound was music in my ears, as the good, remorseless ash sapling bent round the Quaker's dappled hind-quarters. At the third stripe he launched both his heels in the operator's face; at the fourth he reared undecidedly; at the fifth he bundled over the bank in a manner purged of hesitation.

'Ha!' yelled my assistants, 'that'll put the fear o' God in him!' as the Quaker fled headlong after the hunt. 'He'll be the betther o' that while he lives!'

Without going quite as far as this, I must admit that for the next half-hour he was astonishingly the better of it.

The Castle Knox fox was making a very pretty line of it over the seven miles that separated him from his home. He headed through a grassy country of Ireland's mild and brilliant green, fenced with sound and buxom banks, enlivened by stone walls, uncompromised by the presence of gates, and yet comfortably laced with lanes for the furtherance of those who had laid to heart Wolsey's valuable advice: 'Fling away ambition: by that sin fell the angels.' The flotsam and jetsam of the hunt pervaded the landscape: standing on one long bank, three dismounted farmers flogged away at the refusing steeds below them, like anglers trying to rise a sulky fish; half-a-dozen hats, bobbing in a string, showed where the road riders followed the delusive windings of a bohireen. It was obvious that in the matter of ambition they would not have caused Cardinal Wolsey a moment's uneasiness; whether angels or otherwise, they were not going to run any risk of falling.

Flurry's red coat was like a beacon two fields ahead of me, with Philippa following in his tracks; it was the first run worthy of the name that Philippa had ridden, and I blessed Miss Bobby Bennett as I saw Cruiskeen's undefeated fencing. An encouraging twang of the Doctor's horn notified that the hounds were giving us a chance; even the Quaker pricked his blunt ears and swerved in his stride to the sound. A stone wall, a rough patch of heather, a boggy field, dinted deep and black with hoof marks, and the stern chase was at an end. The hounds had checked on the outskirts of a small wood, and the field, thinned down to a panting dozen or so, viewed us with the disfavour shown by the first flight towards those unexpectedly add to their select number. In the depths of the wood Dr Hickey might be heard uttering those singular little yelps of encouragement that to the irreverent suggest a milkman in his dotage. Bernard Shute, who neither knew nor cared what the hounds were doing, was expatiating at great length to an uninterested squireen upon the virtues and perfections of his new mount.

'I did all I knew to come and help you at the river,' he said, riding up to the splashed and still dripping Sally, 'but Stockbroker wouldn't hear of it. I pulled his ugly head round till his nose was on my boot, but he galloped away just the same!'

'He was quite right,' said Miss Sally! 'I didn't want you in the least.'

As Miss Sally's red gold coil of hair was turned towards me during this speech, I could only infer the glance with which it was delivered, from the fact that Mr Shute responded to it with one of those firm gazes of adoration in which the neighbourhood took such an interest, and crumbled away into incoherency.

A shout from the top of a hill interrupted the amenities of the check; Flurry was out of the wood in half-a-dozen seconds, blowing shattering blasts upon his horn, and the hounds rushed to him, knowing the 'gone away' note that was never blown in vain. The brown mare came out through the trees and the undergrowth like a woodcock down the wind, and jumped across a stream on to a more than questionable bank; the hounds splashed and struggled after him, and, as they landed, the first ecstatic whimpers broke forth. In a moment it was full cry, discordant, beautiful, and soul-stirring, as the pack spread and sped, and settled to the line. I saw the absurd dazzle of tears in Philippa's eyes, and found time for the insulting proffer of the clean pocket-handkerchief, as we all galloped hard to get away on good terms with the hounds.

It was one of those elect moments in fox-hunting when the fittest alone have survived; even the Quaker's sluggish blood was stirred by good company, and possibly by the remembrance of the singing ash-plant, and he lumbered up tall stone-faced banks and down heavy drops, and cross wide ditches, in astounding adherence to the line cut out by Flurry. Cruiskeen went like a book—a story for girls, very pleasant and safe, but rather slow. Moonlighter was pulling Miss Sally on to the sterns of the hounds, flying his banks, rocketing like a pheasant over three-foot walls—committing, in fact, all the crimes induced by youth and overfeeding; he would have done very comfortably with another six or seven stone on his back.

Why Bernard Shute did not come off at every fence and generally die a thousand deaths I cannot explain. Occasionally I rather wished he would, as, from my secure position in the rear, I saw him charging his fences at whatever pace and place seemed good to the thoroughly demoralised Stockbroker, and in so doing cannon heavily against Dr Hickey on landing over a rotten ditch, jump a wall with his spur rowelling Charlie Knox's boot, and cut in at top speed in front of Flurry, who was scientifically cramming his mare up a very awkward scramble. In so far as I could think of anything beyond Philippa and myself and the next fence, I thought there would be trouble for Mr Shute in consequnce of this last feat. It was a half-hour long to be remembered, in spite of the Quaker's ponderous and unalterable gallop, in spite of the thump with which he came down off his banks, in spite of the confiding manner in which he hung upon my hand.

We were nearing Castle Knox, and the riders began to edge away from the hounds towards a gate that broke the long barrier of the demesne wall. Steaming horses and purple-faced riders clattered and crushed in at the gate; there was a moment of pulling up and listening, in which quivering tails and pumping sides told their own story. Cruiskeen's breathing suggested a cross between a grampus and a gramaphone; Philippa's hair had come down, and she had a stitch in her side. Moonlighter, fresher than ever, stamped and dragged at his bit; I thought little Miss Sally looked very white. The bewildering clamour of the hounds was all through the wide laurel plantations. At a word from Flurry, Dr Hickey shoved his horse ahead and turned down a ride, followed by most of the field.

'Philippa', I said severely, 'you've had enough, and you know it.'

'Do go up to the house and make them give you something to eat,' struck in Miss Sally, twisting Moonlighter round to keep his mind occupied.

'And as for you, Miss Sally,' I went on, in the manner of Mr Fairchild, 'the sooner you get off that horse and out of those wet things the better.'

Flurry, who was just in front of us, said nothing, but gave a short and most disagreeable laugh. Philippa accepted my suggestion with the meekness of exhaustion, but under the circumstances it did not surprise me that Miss Sally did not follow her example.

Then ensued an hour of woodland hunting at its worst and most bewildering. I galloped after Flurry and Miss Sally up and down long glittering lanes of laurel, at every other moment burying my face in the

Quaker's coarse white mane to avoid the slash of the branches, and receiving down the back of my neck showers of drops stored up from the rain of the day before; playing an endless game of hide-and-seek with the hounds, and never getting any near to them, as they turned and doubled through the thickets of evergreens. Even to my limited understanding of the situation it became clear at length that two foxes were on foot; most of the hounds were hard at work a quarter of a mile away, but Flurry, with a grim face and a faithful three couple, stuck to the failing line of the hunted fox.

There came a moment when Miss Sally and I—who through many vicissitudes had clung to each other—found ourselves at a spot where two rides crossed. Flurry was waiting there, and a little way up one of the rides a couple of hounds were hustling to and fro, with the thwarted whimpers half breaking from them; he held up his hand to stop us, and at that identical moment Bernard Shute, like a bolt from the blue, burst upon our vision. It need scarcely be mentioned that he was going at full gallop—I have rarely seen him ride at any other pace—and as he bore down upon Flurry and the hounds, ducking and dodging to avoid the branches, he shouted something about a fox having gone away at the other side of the covert.

'Hold hard!' roared Flurry; 'don't you see the hounds, you fool?'

Mr Shute, to do him justice, held hard with all the strength in his body, but it was of no avail. The bay horse had got his head down and his tail up, there was a piercing yell from a hound as it was ridden over, and Flurry's brown mare will not soon forget the moment when Stockbroker's shoulder took her on the point of the hip and sent her staggering into the laurel branches. As she swung round, Flurry's whip went up, and with a swift backhander the cane and the looped thong caught Bernard across his broad shoulders.

'O Mr Shute!' shrieked Miss Sally, as I stared dumbfoundered; 'did that branch hurt you?'

'All right! Nothing to signify!' he called out as he bucketed past, tugging at his horse's head. 'Thought some one had hit me at first! Come on, we'll catch 'em up this way!'

He swung perilously into the main ride and was gone, totally unaware of the position that Miss Sally's quickness had saved.

Flurry rode straight up to his cousin, with a pale, dangerous face.

'I suppose you think I'm to stand being ridden over and having my hounds killed to please you,' he said; 'but you're mistaken. You were very smart, and you may think you've saved him his licking, but you needn't think he won't get it. He'll have it in spite of you, before he goes to his bed this night!'

A man who loses his temper badly because he is badly in love is inevitably ridiculous, far though he may be from thinking himself so. He is also a highly unpleasant person to argue with, and Miss Sally and I held our peace respectfully. He turned his horse and rode away.

Almost instantly the three couple of hounds opened in the underwood near us with a deafening crash, and not twenty yards ahead the hunted fox, dark with wet and mud, slunk across the ride. The hounds were almost on his brush; Moonlighter reared and chafed; the din was redoubled, passed away to a little distance, and suddenly seemed stationary in the middle of the laurels.

'Could he have got into the old ice-house?' exclaimed Miss Sally, with reviving excitement. She pushed ahead, and turned down the narrowest of all the rides that had that day been my portion. At the end of the green tunnel there was a comparatively open space; Flurry's mare was standing in it, riderless, and Flurry himself was hammering with a stone at the padlock of a door that seemed to lead into the heart of a laurel clump. The hounds were baying furiously somewhere back of the entrance, among the laurel stems.

'He's got in by the old ice drain,' said Flurry, addressing himself sulkily to me, and ignoring Miss Sally. He had not the least idea of how absurd was his scowling face, draped by the luxuriant hart's-tongues that overhung the doorway.

The padlock yielded, and the opening door revealed a low, dark passage, into which Flurry disappeared, lugging a couple of hounds with him by the scruff of the neck; the remaining two couple bayed implacably at the mouth of the drain. The croak of a rusty bolt told of a second door at the inner end of the passage.

'Look out for the steps, Flurry, they're all broken,' called out Miss Sally in tones of honey.

There was no answer. Miss Sally looked at me; her face was serious, but her mischievous eyes made a confederate of me.

'He's in an *awful* rage!' she said. 'I'm afraid there will certainly be a row.'

A row there certainly was, but it was in the cavern of the ice-house, where the fox had evidently been discovered. Miss Sally suddenly flung Moonlighter's reins to me and slipped off his back.

'Hold him!' she said, and dived into the doorway under the overhanging branches.

Things happened after that with astonishing simultaneousness. There was a shrill exclamation from Miss Sally, the inner door was slammed and bolted, and at one and the same moment the fox darted from the entry, and was away into the wood before one could wink.

'What's happened?' I called out, playing the refractory Moonlighter like a salmon.

Miss Sally appeared at the doorway, looking half scared and half delighted.

'I've bolted him in, and I won't let him out till he promises to be good! I was only just in time to slam the door after the fox bolted out!'

'Great Scott!' I said helplessly.

Miss Sally vanished again into the passage, and the imprisoned hounds continued to express their emotions in the echoing vault of the ice-house. Their master remained mute as the dead, and I trembled.

'Flurry!' I heard Miss Sally say. 'Flurry, I—I've locked you in!'

This self-evident piece of information met with no response.

'Shall I tell you why?'

A keener note seemed to indicate that a hound had been kicked.

'I don't care whether you answer me or not, I'm going to tell you!'

There was a pause; apparently telling him was not as simple as had been expected.

'I won't let you out till you promise me something. Ah, Flurry, don't be so cross! What do you say?—Oh, that's a ridiculous thing to say. You know quite well it's not on his account!'

There was another considerable pause.

'Flurry!' said Miss Sally again, in tones that would have wiled a badger from his earth. 'Dear Flurry—'

At this point I hurriedly flung Moonlighter's bridle over a branch and withdrew.

My own subsequent adventures are quite immaterial, until the moment when I encountered Miss Sally on the steps of the hall door at Castle Knox.

'I'm just going in to take off these wet things,' she said airily.

This was no way to treat a confederate.

'Well?' I said, barring her progress.

'Oh—he—he promised. It's all right,' she replied, rather breathlessly.

There was no one about; I waited resolutely for further information. It did not come.

'Did he try to make his own terms?' said I, looking hard at her.

'Yes, he did.' She tried to pass me.

'And what did you do?'

'I refused them!' she said, with the sudden stagger of a sob in her voice, as she escaped into the house.

Now what on earth was Sally Knox crying about?

'WARE HOLES
Sir Arthur Conan Doyle
1898

A SPORTIN death! My word it was!
An' taken in a sportin' way.
Mind you, I wasn't there to see;
I only tell you what they say.

They found that day at Shillinglee
An' ran 'im down to Chilinghurst;
The fox was goin' straight and free
For ninety minutes at the burst.

They 'ad a check at Ebernoe
An' made a cast across the Down,
Until they got a view 'ullo
An' chased 'im up to Kindford town.

From Kindford 'e run Brander way,
An' took 'em over 'alf the weald.
If you 'ave tried the Sussex clay,
You'll guess it weeded out the field,

Until at last I don't suppose
As 'alf a dozen at the most,
Came safe to where the grassland goes
Switchbackin' southwards to the coast.

Young Captain 'Eadley 'e was there,
An' Jim the whip an 'Percy Day;
The Purcells an' Sir Charles Adair,
An' this 'ere gent from London way.

For 'e 'ad gone amazing fine,
Two 'undred pounds between 'is knees;
Eight stone 'e was, an' rode at nine,
As light an' limber as you please.

'E was a stranger to the 'unt,
There weren't a person as 'e knew there;
But 'e could ride, that London gent—
'E sat 'is mare as if 'e grew there.

They seed the 'ounds upon the scent,
But found a fence across their track,
An' 'ad to fly it, else it meant
A turnin' an' a 'arking back.

'E was the foremost at the fence,
And as 'is mare just cleared the rail
'E turned to them that rode be'ind,
For three was at 'is very tail.

"Ware 'oles!" says 'e, an' with the word,
Still sittin' easy on 'is mare,
Down, down 'e went, an' down an' down,
Into the quarry yawnin' there.

Some say it was two' undred foot,
The bottom lay as black as ink.
I guess they 'ad some ugly dreams
Who reined their 'orses on the brink.

'E'd only time for that one cry;
"Ware 'oles!" says 'e, an' saves all three.
There may be better deaths to die,
But that one's good enough for me.

For, mind you, 'twas a sportin' end,
Upon a right good sportin' day;
They think a deal of 'im down 'ere,
That gent that came from London way.

HOW THE BRIGADIER SLEW THE FOX

Adventures of Gerard
Sir Arthur Conan Doyle
1903

In all the great hosts of France there was only one officer towards whom the English of Wellington's army retained a deep, steady, and unchangeable hatred. There were plunderers among the French, and men of violence, gamblers, duellists, and *roués*. All these could be forgiven, for others of their kidney were to be found among the ranks of the English. But one officer of Massena's force had committed a crime which was unspeakable, unheard of, abominable; only to be alluded to with curses late in the evening, when a second bottle had loosened the tongues of men. The news of it was carried back to England, and country gentlemen who knew little of the details of the war grew crimson with passion when they heard of it, and yeomen of the shires raised freckled fists to Heaven and swore. And yet who should be the doer of this dreadful deed but our friend the brigadier, Etienne Gerard, of the Hussars of Conflans, gay-riding, plume-tossing, debonair, the darling of the ladies and of the six brigades of light cavalry.

But the strange part of it is that this gallant gentleman did this hateful thing, and made himself the most unpopular man in the Peninsula, without ever knowing that he had done a crime for which there is hardly a name amid all the resources of our language. He died of old age, and never once in that imperturbable self-confidence which adorned or disfigured his character knew that so many thousand Englishmen would gladly have hanged him with their own hands. On the contrary, he numbered this adventure among those other exploits which he has given to the world, and many a time he chuckled and hugged himself as he narrated it to the eager circle who gathered round him in that humble *café* where, between his dinner and his dominoes, he would tell, amid tears and laughter, of that inconceivable Napoleonic past when France, like an angel of wrath, rose up, splendid and terrible, before a cowering continent. Let us listen to him as he tells the story in his own way and from his own point of view.

You must know, my friends (said he), that it was toward the end of the year eighteen hundred and ten that I and Massena and the others pushed Wellington backwards until we had hoped to drive him and his army into the Tagus. But when we were still twenty-five miles from Lisbon we found that we were betrayed, for what had this Englishman done but build an enormous line of works and forts at a place called Torres Vedras, so that even we were unable to get through them! They lay across the whole peninsula, and our army was so far from home that we did not dare to risk a reverse, and we had already learned at Busaco that it was no child's play to fight against these people. What could we do, then, but sit down in front of these lines and blockade them to the best of our power? There we remained for six months, amid such anxieties Massena said afterwards that he had not one hair which was not white upon his body. For my own part, I did not worry much about our situation, but I looked after our horses, who were in great need of rest and green fodder. For the rest, we drank the wine of the country and passed the time as best we might. There was a lady at Santarem—but my lips are sealed. It is the part of a gallant man to say nothing, though he may indicate that he could say a great deal.

One day Massena sent for me, and I found him in his tent with a great plan pinned upon the table. He looked at me in silence with that single piercing eye of his, and I felt by his expression that the matter was serious. He was nervous and ill at ease, but my bearing seemed to reassure him. It is good to be in contact with brave men.

'Colonel Etienne Gerard,' said he, 'I have always heard that you are a very gallant and enterprising officer.'

It was not for me to confirm such a report, and yet it would be folly to deny it, so I clinked my spurs together and saluted.

'You are also an excellent rider.'

I admitted it.

'And the best swordsman in the six brigades of light cavalry.'

Massena was famous for the accuracy of his information.

'Now,' said he, 'if you will look at this plan you will have no difficulty in understanding what it is that I wish you to do. These are the lines of Torres Vedras. You will perceive that they cover a vast space, and you will realise that the English can only hold a position here and there. Once through the lines, you have twenty-five miles of open country which lie between them and Lisbon. It is very important to me to learn how Wellington's troops are distributed throughout that space, and it is my wish that you should go and ascertain.'

His words turned me cold.

'Sir,' said I, 'it is impossible that a colonel of light cavalry should condescend to act as a spy.'

He laughed and clapped me on the shoulder 'You would not be a Hussar if you were not a hot-head,' said he. 'If you will listen you will understand that I have not asked you to act as a spy. What do you think of that horse?'

He had conducted me to the opening of his tent, and there was a Chasseur who led up and down a most admirable creature. He was a dapple grey, not very tall—a little over fifteen hands perhaps—but with the short head and splendid arch of the neck which comes with the Arab blood. His shoulders and haunches were so muscular, and yet his legs so fine, that it thrilled me with joy just to gaze upon him. A fine horse or a beautiful woman, I cannot look at them unmoved, even now when seventy winters have chilled my blood. You can think how it was in the year '10.

'This,' said Massena, 'is Voltigeur, the swiftest horse in our army. What I desire is that you should start to-night, ride round the lines upon the flank, make your way across the enemy's rear, and return upon the other flank, bringing me news of his dispositions. You will wear a uniform, and will, therefore, if captured, be safe from the death of a spy. It is probable that you will get through the lines unchallenged, for the posts are very scattered. Once through, in daylight you can outride anything which you meet, and if you keep off the roads you may escape entirely unnoticed. If you have not reported yourself by to-morrow night I will understand that you are taken, and I will offer them Colonel Petrie in exchange.'

Ah, how my heart swelled with pride and joy as I sprang into the saddle and galloped this grand horse up and down to show the marshal the mastery which I had of him! He was magnificent—we were both magnificent, for Massena clapped his hands and cried out in his delight. It was not I, but he, who said that a gallant beast deserves a gallant rider. Then, when for the third time, with my panache flying and my dolman streaming behind me, I thundered past him, I saw upon his hard old face that he had no longer any doubt that he had chosen the man for his purpose. I drew my sabre, raised the hilt to my lips in salute, and galloped on to my own quarters. Already the news had spread that I had been chosen for a mission, and my little rascals came swarming out of their tents to cheer me. Ah! it brings the tears to my old eyes when I think how proud they were of their colonel. And I was proud of them also. They deserved a dashing leader.

The night promised to be a stormy one, which was very much to my liking. It was my desire to keep my departure most secret, for it was evident that if the English heard that I had been detached from the army they would naturally conclude that something important was about to happen. My horse was taken, therefore, beyond the picket line, as if for watering, and I followed and mounted him there. I had a map, a compass, and a paper of instructions from the marshal, and with these in the bosom of my tunic, and a sabre at my side, I set out upon my adventure. A thin rain was falling, and there was no moon, so you may imagine that it was not very cheerful. But my heart was light at the thought of the honour which had been done me, and the glory which awaited me. This exploit should be one more in that brilliant series which was to change my sabre into a baton. Ah, how we dreamed, we foolish fellows, young, and drunk with success! Could I have foreseen that night as I rode, the chosen man of 60,000 that I should spend my life planting cabbages on a hundred francs a month! Oh, my youth, my hopes, my comrades! But the wheel turns and never stops. Forgive me, my friends, for an old man has his weakness.

My route, then, lay across the face of the high ground of Torres Vedras, then over a streamlet, past a farmhouse which had been burned down and was now only a landmark, then through a forest of young cork oaks, and so to the monastery of San Antonio, which marked the left of the English position. Here I turned south and rode quietly over the downs, for it was at this point that Massena thought that it would be most easy for me to find my way unobserved through the position. I went very slowly, for it was so dark that I could not see my hand in front of me. In such cases I leave my bridle loose, and let my horse pick its own way. Voltigeur went confidently forward, and I was very content to sit upon his back, and to peer about me, avoiding every light. For three hours we advanced in this cautious way, until it seemed to me that I must have left all danger behind me. I then pushed on more briskly, for I wished to be in the rear of the whole army by daybreak. There are many vineyards in these parts which in winter became open plains, and a horseman finds few difficulties in his way.

But Massena had underrated the cunning of these English, for it appears that there was not one line of defence, but three, and it was the third which was the most formidable, through which I was at that instant passing. As I rode, elated at my own success, a lantern flashed suddenly before me, and I saw the glint of polished gunbarrels and the gleam of a red coat.

'Who goes there?' cried a voice—such a voice! I swerved to the right and rode like a madman, but a dozen squirts of fire came out of the darkness, and the bullets whizzed all round my ears. That was no new sound to me, my friends, though I will not talk like a foolish conscript and say that I have ever liked it. But at least it had never kept me from thinking clearly, and so I knew that there was nothing for it but to gallop hard and try my luck elsewhere. I rode around the English picket, and then, as I heard nothing more of them, I concluded rightly that I had at last come through their defences. For five miles I rode south, striking a tinder from time to time to look at my pocket compass. And then in an instant—I feel the pang once more as my memory brings back the moment—my horse, without a sob or stagger, fell stone dead beneath me!

I had not known it, but one of the bullets from that infernal picket had passed through his body. The gallant creature had never winced nor weakened, but had gone while life was in him. One instant I was secure on the swiftest, most graceful horse in Massena's army. The next he lay upon his side, worth only the price of his hide, and I stood there that most helpless, most ungainly of creatures, a dismounted Hussar. What could I do with my boots, my spurs, my trailing sabre? I was far inside the enemy's lines. How could I hope to get back again? I am not ashamed to say that I, Etienne Gerard, sat upon my dead horse and sank my face in my hands in my despair. Already the first streaks were whitening in the east. In half an hour it would be light. That I should have won my way past every obstacle, and then at this last instant be left at the mercy of my enemies, my mission ruined, and myself a prisoner—was it not enough to break a soldier's heart?

But courage, my friends! We have these moments of weakness, the bravest of us; but I have a spirit like a slip of steel, for the more you bend it the higher it springs. One spasm of despair, and then a brain of ice and a heart of fire. All was not yet lost. I, who had come through so many hazards, would come through this one also. I rose from my horse and considered what had best be done.

And first of all it was certain that I could not get back. Long before I could pass the lines it would be broad daylight. I must hide myself for the day, and devote the next night to my escape. I took the saddle, holsters, and bridle from my poor Voltigeur, and I concealed them among some bushes, so that no one finding him could know that he was a French horse. Then, leaving him lying there, I wandered on in search of some place where I might be safe for the day. In every direction I could see camp fires upon the sides of the hills, and already figures had begun to move around them. I must hide quickly or I was lost. But where was I to hide? It was a vineyard in which I found myself, the poles of the vines still standing, but the plants gone. There was no cover there. Beside, I should want some food and water before another night had come. I hurried wildly onwards through the waning darkness, trusting that chance would be my friend. And I was not disappointed. Chance is a woman, my friends, and she has her eye always upon a gallant Hussar.

Well, then, I stumbled through the vineyard, something loomed in front of me, and I came upon a great square house with another long, low building upon one side of it. Three roads met there, and it was easy to see that this was the *posada*, or wine-shop. There was no light in the windows, and everything was dark and silent, but, of course, I knew that such comfortable quarters were certainly occupied, and probably by someone of importance. I have learned, however, that the nearer the danger may really be the safer the place, and so I was by no means inclined to trust myself away from this shelter. The low building was evidently the stable, and into this I crept, for the door was unlatched. The place was full of bullocks and sheep, gathered there, no doubt, to be out of the clutches of marauders. A ladder led to a loft, and up this I climbed, and concealed myself very snugly among some bales of hay upon the top. This loft had a small open window, and I was able to look down upon the front of the inn and also upon the road. Then I crouched and waited to see what would happen.

It was soon evident that I had not been mistaken when I had thought that this might be the quarters of some person of importance. Shortly after daybreak an English light dragoon arrived with a despatch, and from then onwards the place was in a turmoil, officers continually riding up and away. Always the same name was upon their lips: 'Sir Stapleton—Sir Stapleton.' It was hard for me to lie there with a dry moustache and watch the great flagons which were brought out by the landlord to these English officers. But it amused me to look at their fresh-coloured, clean-shaven, careless faces, and to wonder what they would think if they knew that so celebrated a person was lying so near to them. And then, as I lay and watched, I saw a sight which filled me with surprised.

It is incredible the insolence of these English! What do you suppose Milord Wellington had done when he found that Massena had blockaded him and that he could not move his army? I might give you many guesses. You might say that he had raged, that he had despaired, that he had brought his troops together and spoken to them about glory and the fatherland before leading them to one last battle. No, Milord did none of these things. But he sent a fleet ship to England to bring him a number of fox-dogs, and he with his officers settled himself down to chase the fox. It is true what I tell you. Behind the lines of Torres Vedras these mad Englishmen made the fox-chase three days in the week. We had heard of it in the camp, and now I myself was to see that it was true.

For, along the road which I have described, there came these very dogs, thirty or forty of them, white and brown, each with its tail at the same angle, like the bayonets of the Old Guard. My faith, but it was a pretty sight! And behind and amidst them there rode three men with peaked caps and red coats, whom I understood to be the hunters. After them came many horsemen with uniforms in twos and threes, talking together and laughing. They did not seem to be going above a trot, and it appeared to me that it must indeed be a slow fox which they hoped to catch. However, it was their affair, not mine, and soon they had all passed my window and were out of sight. I waited and I watched, ready for any chance which might offer.

Presently an officer, in a blue uniform not unlike that of our flying artillery, came cantering down the road—an elderly, stout man he was, with grey side-whiskers. He stopped and began to talk with an orderly officer of dragoons, who waited outside the inn, and it was then that I learned the advantage of the English which had been taught me. I could hear and understand all that was said.

'Where is the meet?' said the officer, and I thought that he was hungering for his bifstek. But the other answered him that it was near Altara, so I saw that it was a place of which he spoke.

'You are late, Sir George,' said the orderly.

'Yes, I had a court-martial. Has Sir Stapleton Cotton gone?'

At this moment a window opened, and a handsome young man in a very splendid uniform looked out of it.

'Halloa, Murray!' said he. 'These cursed papers keep me, but I will be at your heels.'

'Very good, Cotton. I am late already, so I will ride on.'

'You might order my groom to bring round my horse,' said the young general at the window to the orderly below, while the other went on down the road.

The orderly rode away to some outlying stable, and then in a few minutes there came a smart English groom with a cockade in his hat, leading by the bridle a horse—and, oh, my friends, you have never known the perfection to which a horse can attain until you have seen a first-class English hunter. He was superb: tall, broad, strong, and yet as graceful and agile as a deer. Coal black he was in colour, and his neck, and his shoulder, and his quarters, and his fetlocks—how can I describe him all to you? The sun shone upon him as on polished ebony, and he raised his hoofs in a little playful dance so lightly and prettily, while he tossed his mane and whinnied with impatience. Never have I seen such a mixture of strength and beauty and grace. I had often wondered how the English Hussars had managed to ride over the Chasseurs of the Guards in the affair at Astorga, but I wondered no longer when I saw the English horses.

There was a ring for fastening bridles at the door of the inn, and the groom tied the horse there while he entered the house. In an instant I had seen the chance which Fate had brought to me. Were I in that saddle I should be better off than when I started. Even Voltigeur could not compare with this magnificent creature. To think is to act with me. In one instant I was down the ladder and at the door of the stable. The next I was out and the bridle was in my hand. I bounced into the saddle. Somebody, the master or the man, shouted wildly behind me. What cared I for his shouts! I touched the horse with my spurs, and he bounded forward with such a spring that only a rider like myself could have sat him. I gave him his head and let him go—it did not matter to me where, so long as we left this inn far behind us. He thundered away across the vineyards, and in a very few minutes I had placed miles between myself and my pursuers. They could no longer tell, in that wild country, in which direction I had gone. I knew that I was safe, and so, riding to the top of a small hill, I drew my pencil and note-book from my pocket, and proceeded to make plans of those camps which I could see, and to draw the outline of the country.

He was a dear creature upon whom I sat, but it was not easy to draw upon his back, for every now and then his two ears would cock, and he would start and quiver with impatience. At first I could not understand this trick of his, but soon I observed that he only did it when a peculiar noise—'Yoy, yoy, yoy'—came from somewhere among the oak woods beneath us. And then suddenly this strange cry changed into a most terrible screaming, with the frantic blowing of a horn. Instantly he went mad—this horse. His eyes blazed. His mane bristled. He bounded from the earth and bounded again, twisting and turning in a frenzy. My pencil flew one way and my note-book another. And then, as I looked down into the valley, an extraordinary sight met my eyes. The hunt was streaming down it. The fox I could not see, but the dogs were in full cry, their noses down, their tails up, so close together that they might have been one great yellow and white moving carpet. And behind them rode the horsemen—my faith, what a sight! Consider every type which a great army could show: some in hunting dress, but the most in uniforms; blue dragoons, red dragoons, red-trousered hussars, green riflemen, artillerymen, gold-slashed lancers, and most of all red, red, red, for the infantry officers ride as hard as the cavalry. Such a crowd, some well mounted, some ill, but all flying along as best they might, the subaltern as good as the general, jostling and pushing, spurring and driving, with every thought thrown to the winds save that they should have the blood of this absurd fox! Truly, they are an extraordinary people, the English! But I had little time to watch the hunt or to marvel at these islanders, for of all these mad creatures the very horse upon which I sat was the maddest. You understand that he was himself a hunter and that the crying of these dogs was to him what the call of a cavalry trumpet in the street yonder would be to me. It thrilled him. It drove him wild. Again and again he bounded into the air, and then, seizing the bit between his teeth, he plunged down the slope, and galloped after the dogs. I swore, and tugged, and pulled, but I was powerless. This English general rode his horse was a snaffle only, and the beast had a mouth of iron. It was useless to pull him back. One might as well try to keep a Grenadier from a wine bottle. I gave it up in despair, and, settling down in the saddle, I prepared for the worst which could befall.

What a creature he was! Never have I felt such a horse between my knees. His great haunches gathered under him with every stride, and he shot forward every faster and faster, stretched like a greyhound, while the wind beat in my face and whistled past my ears. I was wearing our undress jacket, a uniform simple and dark in itself—though some figures give distinction to any uniform—and I had taken the precaution to remove the long panache from my busby. The result was that, amidst the mixture of costumes in the hunt, there was no reason why mine should attract attention, or why these men, whose thoughts were all with the chase, should give any heed to me. The idea that a French officer might be riding with them was too absurd to enter their minds. I laughed as I rode, for, indeed, amid all the danger, there was something of comic in the situation.

I have said that the hunters were very unequally mounted, and so, at the end of a few miles, instead of being one body of men, like a charging regiment, they were scattered over a considerable space, the better riders well up to the dogs, and the others trailing away behind. Now, I was as good a rider as any, and my horse was the best of them all, and so you can imagine that it was not long before he carried me to the front. And when I saw the dogs streaming over the open, and the red-coated huntsman behind them, and only seven or eight horsemen between us, then it was that the strangest thing of all happened, for I, too, went mad—I, Etienne Gerard! In a moment it came upon me, this spirit of sport, this desire to excel, this hatred of the fox. Accursed animal, should he then defy us? Vile robber, his hour was come! Ah, it is a great feeling, this feeling of sport, my friends, this desire to trample the fox under the hoofs of your horse. I have made the fox-chase with the English. I have also, as I may tell you some day, fought the box-fight with the Bustler, of Bristol. And I say to you that this sport is a wonderful thing—full of interest as well as madness.

The farther we went the faster galloped my horse, and soon there were but three men as near the dogs as I was. All thought of fear of discovery had vanished. My brain throbbed, my blood ran hot—only one thing upon earth seemed worth living for, and that was to overtake this infernal fox. I passed one of the horsemen—a Hussar like myself. There were only two in front of me now—the one in a black coat, the other the blue artilleryman whom I had seen at the inn. His grey whiskers streamed in the wind, but he rode magnificently. For a mile or more we kept in this order, and then, as we galloped up a steep slope, my lighter weight brought me to the front. I passed them both, and when I reached the crown I was riding level with the little, hard-faced English huntsman. In front of us were the dogs, and then, a hundred paces beyond them, was a brown wisp of a thing, the fox itself, stretched to the uttermost. The sight of him fired my blood. 'Aha, we have you then, assassin!' I cried, and shouted my encouragement to the huntsman. I waved my hand to show him that there was one upon whom he could rely.

And now there were only the dogs between me and my prey. These dogs, whose duty it is to point out the game, were now rather a hindrance than a help to us, for it was hard to know how to pass them. The huntsman felt the difficulty as much as I, for he rode behind them and could make no progress towards the fox. He was a swift rider, but wanting in enterprise. For my part, I felt that it would be unworthy of the Hussars of Conflans if I could not overcome such a difficulty as this. Was Etienne Gerard to be stopped by a herd of fox-dogs? It was absurd. I gave a shout and spurred my horse.

'Hold hard, sir! Hold hard!' cried the huntsman.

He was uneasy for me, this good old man, but I reassured him by a wave and smile. The dogs opened in front of me. One or two may have been hurt, but what would you have? The egg must be broken for the omelette. I could hear the huntsman shouting his congratulations behind me. One more effort, and the dogs were all behind me. Only the fox was in front.

Ah, the joy and pride of that moment! To know that I had beaten the English at their own sport. Here were three hundred all thirsting for the life of this animal, and yet it was I who was about to take it. I thought of my comrades of the light cavalry brigade, of my mother, of the Emperor, of France. I had brought honour to each and all. Every instant brought me nearer to the fox. The moment for action had arrived, so I unsheathed my sabre. I waved it in the air, and the brave English all shouted behind me.

Only then did I understand how difficult is this fox-chase, for one may cut again and again at the creature and never strike him once. He is small, and turns quickly from a blow. At every cut I heard those shouts of encouragement behind me, and they spurred me to yet another effort. And then at last the supreme moment of my triumph arrived. In the very act of turning I caught him fair with such another back-handed cut as that with which I killed the aide-de-camp of the Emperor of Russia. He flew into two pieces, his head one way and his tail another. I looked back and waved the blood-stained sabre in the air. For the moment I was exalted—superb!

Ah! how I should have loved to have waited to have received the congratulations of these generous enemies. There were fifty of them in sight, and not one of them who was not waving his hand and shouting. They are not really such a phlegmatic race, the English. A gallant deed in war or in sport will always warm their hearts. As to the old huntsman, he was the nearest to me, and I could see with my own eyes how overcome he was by what he had seen. He was like a man paralysed—his mouth open, his hand, with outspread fingers, raised in the air. For a moment my inclination was to return and embrace him. But already the call of duty was sounding in my ears, and these English, in spite of all the fraternity which exists among sportsmen, would certainly have made me prisoner. There was no hope for my mission now, and I had done all that I could do. I could see the lines of Massena's camp no very great distance off, for, by a lucky chance, the chase had taken us in that direction. I turned from the dead fox, saluted with my sabre, and galloped away.

But they would not leave me so easily, these gallant huntsmen. I was the fox now, and the chase swept bravely over the plain. It was only at the moment when I started for the camp that they could have known that I was a Frenchman, and now the whole swarm of them were at my heels. We were within gunshot of our pickets before they would halt, and then they stood in knots and would not go away, but shouted and waved their hands at me. No, I will not think that it was in enmity. Rather would I fancy that a glow of admiration filled their breasts, and that their one desire was to embrace the stranger who had carried himself so gallantly and well.

When I galloped back into the French lines with the blood of the creature still moist upon my blade, the outposts who had seen what I had done raised a frenzied cry in my honour, whilst these English hunters still yelled behind me, so that I had the applause of both armies. It made the tears rise to my eyes to feel that I had won the admiration of so many brave men. These English are generous foes. That very evening there came a packet under a white flag addressed 'To the Hussar officer who cut down the fox.' Within I found the fox itself in two pieces, as I had left it. There was a note also, short but hearty as the English fashion is, to say that as I had slaughtered the fox it only remained for me to eat it. They could not know that it was not our French custom to eat foxes, and it showed their desire that he who had won the honours of the chase should also partake of the game. It is not for a Frenchman to be outdone in politeness, and so I returned it to these brave hunters, and begged them to accept it as a side-dish for the next *dejeuner de la chasse*. It is thus that chivalrous opponents make war.

THE FOX MEDITATES
Rudyard Kipling

When Samson set my brush a' fire,
   To spoil the Timnites' barley,
I made my point for Leicestershire,
   And left Philistia early.
Through Gath and Rankesborough Gorse, I fled,
   And took the Coplow Road, sir!
And was a Gentleman in Red
   When all the Quorn wore woad, sir!

When Rome lay massed on Hadrian's Wall,
   And nothing much was doing,
Her bored Centurions heard my call
   O' nights when I went wooing.
They raised a pack—they ran it well
   (For I was there to run 'em)
From Aesica to Carter Fell,
   And down North Tyne to Hunnum.

When William landed, hot for blood,
   And Harold's hosts were smitten,
I lay at earth in Battle Wood
   While Domesday Book was written.
Whatever harm he did to man,
   I owe him pure affection,
For in his righteous reign began
   The first of Game protection.

When Charles, my namesake, lost his mask,
   And Oliver dropped his'n,
I set those Northern Squires a task,
   To keep 'em out of prison.
In boots as big as milking-pails,
   With holsters on the pommel,
They chevied me across the Dales
   Instead of fighting Cromwell.

When thrifty Walpole took the helm,
   And hedging came in fashion,
The March of Progress gave my realm
   Enclosure and Plantation.
'Twas then, to soothe their discontent,
   I showed each pounded Master,
However fast the Commons went,
   I went a little faster!

When Pigg and Jorrocks held the stage,
   And Steam had linked the Shires,
I broke the staid Victorian age
   To posts, and rails and wires.
Then fifty mile was none too far
   To go by train to cover,
Till some dam' sutler pupped a Car,
   And decent sport was over!

When men grew shy of hunting stag
   For fear the Law might try 'em,
The car put up an average bag
   Of twenty dead per diem.
Then every road was made a rink
   For Coroners to sit on;
And so began, in skid and stink,
   The real blood-sports of Britain!

THE BAG

Reginald in Russia
'Saki' (H. H. Munro)
1910

'The Major is coming in to tea,' said Mrs Hoopington to her niece. 'He's just gone round to the stables with his horse. Be as bright and lively as you can; the poor man's got a fit of the glooms.'

Major Pallaby was a victim of circumstances, over which he had no control, and of his temper, over which he had very little. He had taken on the Mastership of the Pexdale Hounds in succession to a highly popular man who had fallen foul of his committee, and the Major found himself confronted with the overt hostility of at least half the hunt, while his lack of tact and amiability had done much to alienate the remainder. Hence subscriptions were beginning to fall off, foxes grew provokingly scarcer, and wire obtruded itself with increasing frequency. The Major could plead reasonable excuse for his fit of the glooms.

In ranging herself as a partisan on the side of Major Pallaby Mrs Hoopington had been largely influenced by the fact that she had made up her mind to marry him at an early date. Against his notorious bad temper she set his three thousand a year, and his prospective succession to a baronetcy gave a casting vote in his favour. The Major's plans on the subject of matrimony were not at present in such an advanced stage as Mrs Hoopington's, but he was beginning to find his way over to Hoopington Hall with a frequency that was already being commented on.

'He had a wretchedly thin field out again yesterday,' said Mrs Hoopington. 'Why you didn't bring one or two hunting men down with you, instead of that stupid Russian boy, I can't think.'

'Vladimir isn't stupid,' protested her niece; 'he's one of the most amusing boys I ever met. Just compare him for a moment with some of your heavy hunting men—'

'Anyhow, my dear Norah, he can't ride.'

'Russians never can; but he shoots.'

'Yes; and what does he shoot? Yesterday he brought home a woodpecker in his game-bag.'

'But he'd shot three pheasants and some rabbits as well.'

'That's no excuse for including a wood-pecker in his game-bag.'

'Foreigners go in for mixed bags more than we do. A Grand Duke pots a vulture just as seriously as we should stalk a bustard. Anyhow, I've explained to Vladimir that certain birds are beneath his dignity as a sportsman. And as he's only nineteen, of course, his dignity is a sure thing to appeal to.'

Mrs Hoopington sniffed. Most people with whom Vladimir came in contact found his high spirits infectious, but his present hostess was guaranteed immune against infection of that sort.

'I hear him coming in now,' she observed. 'I shall go and get ready for tea. We're going to have it here in the hall. Entertain the Major if he comes in before I'm down, and, above all, be bright.'

Norah was dependent on her aunt's good graces for many little things that made life worth living, and she was conscious of a feeling of discomfiture because the Russian youth whom she had brought down as a welcome element of change in the country-house routine was not making a good impression. That young gentleman, however, was supremely unconscious of any shortcomings, and burst into the hall, tired, and less sprucely groomed than usual, but distinctly radiant. His game-bag looked comfortably full.

'Guess what I have shot,' he demanded.

'Pheasants, wood-pigeons, rabbits,' hazarded Norah.

'No; a large beast; I don't know what you call it in English. Brown, with a darkish tail.' Norah changed colour.

'Does it live in a tree and eat nuts?' she asked, hoping that the use of the adjective 'large' might be an exaggeration.

Vladimir laughed.

'Oh no; not a *biyelka*.'

'Does it swim and eat fish?' asked Norah, with a fervent prayer in her heart that it might turn out to be an otter.

'No,' said Vladimir, busy with the straps of his game-bag; 'it lives in the woods, and eats rabbits and chickens.'

Norah sat down suddenly, and hid her face in her hands.

'Merciful Heaven!' she wailed; 'he's shot a fox!'

Vladimir looked up at her in consternation. In a torrent of agitated words she tried to explain the horror of the situation. The boy understood nothing, but was thoroughly alarmed.

'Hide it, hide it!' said Norah frantically, pointing to the still unopened bag. 'My aunt and the Major will be here in a moment. Throw it on the top of that chest; they won't see it there.'

Vladimir swung the bag with fair aim; but the strap caught in its flight on the outstanding point of an antler fixed in the wall, and the bag, with its terrible burden, remained suspended just above the alcove where tea would presently be laid. At that moment Mrs Hoopington and the Major entered the hall.

'The Major is going to draw our covers to-morrow,' announced the lady, with a certain heavy satisfaction. 'Smithers is confident that we'll be able to show him some sport; he swears he's seen a fox in the nut copse three times this week.'

'I'm sure I hope so; I hope so,' said the Major moodily. 'I must break this sequence of blank days. One hears so often that a fox has settled down as a tenant for life in certain covers, and then when you go to turn him out there isn't a trace of him. I'm certain a fox was shot or trapped in Lady Widden's woods the very day before we drew them.'

'Major, if anyone tried that game on in my woods they'd get short shrift,' said Mrs Hoopington.

Norah found her way mechanically to the tea-table and made her fingers frantically busy in rearranging the parsley round the sandwich dish. On one side of her loomed the morose countenance of the Major, on the other she was conscious of the scared, miserable eyes of Vladimir. And above it all hung *that*. She dared not raise her eyes above the level of the tea-table, and she almost expected to see a spot of accusing vulpine blood drip down and stain the whiteness of the cloth. Her aunt's manner signalled to her the repeated message to 'be bright'; for the present she was fully occupied in keeping her teeth from chattering.

'What did you shoot to-day?' asked Mrs Hoopington suddenly of the unusually silent Vladimir.

'Nothing—nothing worth speaking of,' said the boy.

Norah's heart, which had stood still for a space, made up for lost time with a most distubring bound.

'I wish you'd find something that was worth speaking about,' said the hostess; 'every one seems to have lost their tongues.

'When did Smithers last see that fox?' said the Major.

'Yesterday morning; a fine dog-fox, with a dark brush,' confided Mrs Hoopington.

'Aha, we'll have a good gallop after that brush to-morrow,' said the Major, with a transient gleam of good humour. And then gloomy silence settled again round the tea-table, a silence broken only by despondent munchings and the occasional feverish rattle of a teaspoon in its saucer. A diversion was at last afforded by Mrs Hoopington's fox-terrier, which had jumped on to a vacant chair, the better to survey the delicacies of the table, and was now sniffing in an upward direction at something apparently more interesting than cold tea-cake.

'What is exciting him?' asked his mistress, as the dog suddenly broke into short, angry barks, with a running accompaniment of tremulous whines.

'Why,' she continued, 'it's your game-bag, Vladimir! What *have* you got in it?'

'By Gad,' said the Major, who was now standing up; 'there's a pretty warm scent!'

And then a simultaneous idea flashed on himself and Mrs Hoopington. Their faces flushed to distinct but harmonious tones of purple, and with one accusing voice they screamed, 'You've shot the fox!'

Norah tried hastily to palliate Vladimir's misdeed in their eyes, but it is doubtful whether they heard her. The Major's fury clothed and reclothed itself in words as frantically as a woman up in town for one day's shopping tries on a succession of garments. He reviled and railed at fate and the general scheme of things, he pitied himself with a strong, deep pity too poignant for tears, he condemned every one with whom he had ever come in contact to endless and abnormal punishments. In fact, he conveyed the impression that if a destroying angel had been lent to him for a week it would have had very little time for private study. In the lulls of his outcry could be heard the querulous monotone of Mrs Hoopington and the sharp staccato barking of the fox-terrier. Vladimir, who did not understand a tithe of what was being said, sat fondling a cigarette and repeating under his breath from time to time a vigorous English adjective which he had long ago taken affectionately into his vocabulary. His mind strayed back to the youth in the old Russian folk-tale who shot an enchanted bird with dramatic results. Meanwhile, the Major, roaming round the hall like an imprisoned cyclone, had caught sight of and joyfully pounced on the telephone apparatus, and lost no time in ringing up the hunt secretary and announcing his resignation of the Mastership. A servant had by this time brought his horse round to the door, and in a few seconds Mrs Hoopington's shrill monotone had the field to itself. But after the Major's display her best efforts at vocal violence missed their full effect; it was as though one had come straight out from a Wagner opera into a rather tame thunderstorm. Realizing, perhaps, that her tirades were something of an anticlimax, Mrs Hoopington broke suddenly into some rather necessary tears and marched out of the room, leaving behind her a silence almost as terrible as the turmoil which had preceded it.

'What shall I do with—*that?*' asked Vladimir at last.

'Bury it,' said Norah.

'Just plain burial?' said Vladimir, rather relieved. He had almost expected that some of the local clergy would have insisted on being present, or that a salute might have to be fired over the grave.

And thus it came to pass that in the dusk of a November evening the Russian boy, murmuring a few of the prayers of his Church for luck, gave hasty but decent burial to a large polecat under the lilac trees at Hoopington.

MY FIRST DAY'S FOX-HUNTING

Memoirs of a Fox-hunting Man
Siegfried Sassoon
1928

It was a grey and chilly world that I went out into when I started for my first day's fox-hunting. The winter-smelling air met me as though with a hint that serious events were afoot. Silently I stood in the stable-yard while Dixon led Sheila out of her stall. His demeanour was business-like and reticent. The horses and their accoutrements were polished up to perfection, and he himself, in his dark-grey clothes and hard black hat, looked a model of discretion and neatness. The only one who lacked confidence was myself.

Stuffing a packet of sandwiches into my pocket and pulling on my uncomfortably new gloves, I felt half aware of certain shortcomings in my outward appearance. Ought one really to go out hunting in a brown corduroy suit with a corduroy jockey-cap made to match the suit? Did other boys wear that sort of thing? . . . I was conscious, too, that Dixon was regarding me with an unusually critical eye. Mute and flustered, I mounted. Sheila seemed very fresh, and the saddle felt cold and slippery. As we trotted briskly through the village everything had an austerely unfamiliar look about it, and my replies to Dixon were clumsy and constrained.

Yet the village was its ordinary village self. The geese were going single file across the green, and Sibson, the lame shoeing-smith, was clinking his hammer on the forge as usual. He peered out at us as we passed, and I saluted him with a slightly forlorn wave of the hand. He grinned and ducked his head. Sheila had had her shoes looked to the day before, so he knew all about where we were going.

As we jogged out of the village, Dixon gazed sagaciously at the sky and said with a grim smile, 'I'll bet they run like blazes to-day; there's just the right nip in the air,' and he made the horses cock their ears by imitating the sound of a hunting-horn—a favourite little trick of his. Secretly I wondered what I should do if they 'ran like blazes'. It was all very well for *him*—he'd been out hunting dozens of times!

As we neared the meet I became more and more nervous. Not many of the hunting people came from our side of the country, and we saw no other horsemen to distract my attention until we rounded a bend of the road, and there at last was Finchurst Green, with the hounds clustering in a corner and men in red coats and black coats moving to and fro to keep their horses from getting chilled. But this is not the last meet that I shall describe, so I will not invent details which I cannot remember, since I was too awed and excited and self-conscious to be capable of observing anything clearly.

Once we had arrived, Dixon seemed to become a different Dixon, so dignified and aloof that I scarcely dared to speak to him. Of course I knew what it meant: I was now his 'young gentleman' and he was only the groom who had brought me to 'have a look at the hounds'. But there was no one at the meet who knew me, so I sat there, shy and silent—aware of being a newcomer in a strange world which I did not understand. Also I was quite sure that I should make a fool of myself. Other people have felt the same, but this fact would have been no consolation to me at the time, even if I could have realized it.

My first period of suspense ended when with much bobbing up and down of hats the cavalcade moved off along the road. I looked round for Dixon, but he allowed me to be carried on with the procession; he kept close behind me, however. He had been sensible enough to refrain from confusing me with advice before we started, and I can see now that his demeanour continued to be full of intuitive tactfulness. But he was talking to another groom, and I felt that I was being scrutinized and discussed. I was riding alongside of a large, lolloping lady in a blue habit; she did not speak to me; she confined herself to a series of expostulatory remarks to her horse which seemed too lively and went bouncing along sideways with its ears back, several times bumping into Sheila, whose behaviour was sedately alert.

Soon we turned in at some lodge gates, crossed the corner of an undulating park, and then everyone pulled up outside a belt of brown woodland. The hounds had disappeared, but I could hear the huntsman's voice a little way off. He was making noises which I identified as not altogether unlike those I had read about in Surtees. After a time the chattering crowd of riders moved slowly into the wood which appeared to be a large one.

My first reaction to the 'field' was one of mute astonishment. I had taken it for granted that there would be people 'in pink', but these enormous confident strangers overwhelmed my mind with the visible authenticity of their brick-red coats. It all felt quite different to reading Surtees by the schoolroom fire.

But I was too shy to stare about me, and every moment I was expecting an outburst of mad excitement in which I should find myself galloping wildly out of the wood. When the outbreak of activity came I had no time to think about it. For no apparent reason the people around me (we were moving slowly along a narrow path in the wood) suddenly set off at a gallop and for several minutes I was aware of nothing but the breathless flurry of being carried along, plentifully spattered with mud by the sportsman in front of me. Suddenly, without any warning, he pulled up. Sheila automatically followed suit, shooting me well up her neck. The next moment everyone turned round and we all went tearing back by the way we had come. I found Dixon in front of me now, and he turned his head with a grin of encouragement.

Soon afterwards the hunt came to a standstill in an open space in the middle of the wood: the excitement seemed to be abating, and I felt that fox-hunting wasn't so difficult as I'd expected it to be. A little way below I could hear a confused baying of the hounds among the trees. Then, quite close to where I had halted, a tall man in a blue velvet cap and vermilion coat came riding out from among the undergrowth with one arm up to shield his face from the branches. His face was very red and he seemed upset about something. Turning in my direction he bawled out in an angry voice, 'What the bloody hell do you think you're here for?'

For a moment I sat petrified with terror and amazement. He was riding straight at me, and I had no time to wonder what I done to incur his displeasure. So I stared helplessly until I was aware that he had passed me and was addressing someone immediately behind my horse's heels. . . . Looking round I saw a surly-featured elderly man with side-whiskers: he was on foot and wore the weathered garments of a gamekeeper.

'What the hell do you mean by leaving the main-earth unstopped?' the infuriated voice continued.

'Very sorry, m'lord', the man mumbled, 'but I never heard you was coming till this morning, and——'

'Don't answer me back. I'll get you sacked for this when Major Gamble comes down from Scotland. I tell you I'm sick of you and your god-damned pheasants,' and before the man could say any more the outraged nobleman was pushing his way into the undergrowth again and was bawling 'Go on to Hoath Wood, Jack,' to the invisible huntsman.

I looked at Dixon, whose horse was nibbling Sheila's neck. 'That's the Master', he said in a low voice, adding, 'his lordship's a rough one with his tongue when anyone gets the wrong side of him.' Silently I decided that Lord Dumborough was the most terrifying man I had ever encountered. . . .

Dixon was explaining that our fox had gone to ground and I heard another man near me saying: 'That blighter Gamble thinks of nothing but shooting. The place is crawling with birds, and the wonder is that we ever found a fox. Last time we were here we drew the whole place blank, and old D. cursed the keeper's head off and accused him of poisoning the foxes, so I suppose he did it to get a bit of his own back!' Such was my introduction to the mysteries of 'earth-stopping'. . . .

The comparatively mild activities of the morning had occupied a couple of hours. We now trotted away from Major Gamble's preserves. It was about three miles to Hoath Wood; on the way several small spinneys were drawn blank, but Hoath Wood was a sure find, so Dixon said, and a rare place to get a gallop from. This caused a perceptible evaporation of the courage which I had been accumulating, and when there was a halt for the hunt-servants to change on to their second horses I made an attempt to dispel my qualms by pulling out my packet of sandwiches.

While I was munching away at these I noticed for the first time another boy of about my own age. Dixon was watching him approvingly. Evidently this was a boy to be imitated, and my own unsophisticated eyes already told me that. He was near enough to us for me to be able to observe him minutely. A little aloof from the large riders round him, he sat easily, but very upright, on a corky chestnut pony with a trimmed stump of a tail and a neatly 'hogged' neck.

Reconstructing that far-off moment, my memory fixes him in a characteristic attitude. Leaning slightly forward from the waist, he straightens his left leg and scrutinizes it with an air of critical abstraction. He seems to be satisfied with his smart buff breeches and natty brown gaiters. Everything he has on is neat and compact. He carries a small crop with a dark leather thong, which he flicks at a tuft of dead grass in a masterly manner. An air of self-possessed efficiency begins with his black bowler hat, continues in his neatly-tied white stock, and gets its finishing touch in the short, blunt, shining spurs on his black walking boots. (I was greatly impressed by the fact that he wore spurs.) All his movements were controlled and modest, but there was a suggestion of arrogance in the steady, unrecognizing stare which he gave me when he became conscious that I was looking at him so intently. Our eyes met, and his calm strutiny reminded me of my own deficiencies in dress. I shifted uneasily in my saddle, and the clumsy unpresentable old hunting-crop fell out of my hand. Dismounting awkwardly to pick it up, I wished that it, also, had a thong, (though this would make the double reins more difficult to manage) and I hated my silly jockey-cap and the badly-fitting gaiters which pinched my legs and always refused to remain in the correct position (indicated by Dixon). When I had scrambled up on to Sheila again—a feat which I could only just accomplish without assistance—I felt what a poor figure I must be cutting in Dixon's eyes while he compared me with that other boy, who had himself turned away with a slight smile and was now soberly following the dappled clustering pack and its attendant red-coats as they disappeared over the green, rising ground on their way to Hoath Wood.

By all the laws of aunthood we should by now have been well on our way home. But Dixon was making a real day of it. The afternoon hunt was going to be a serious affair. There never appeared to be any doubt about that. The field was reduced to about forty riders, and the chattersome contingent seemed to have gone home. We all went into the covert and remained close together at one end. Dixon got off and tightened my girths, which had got very loose (as I ought to have noticed). A resolute-looking lady in a tall hat drew her veil down after taking a good pull at the flask which she handed back to her groom. Hard-faced men rammed their hats on to their heads and sat silently in the saddle as though, for the first time in the day, they really meant business. My heart was in my mouth and it had good reason to be there. Lord Dumborough was keeping an intent eye on the ride which ran through the middle of the covert.

'Cut along up to the top end, Charlie,' he remarked without turning his head; and a gaunt, ginger-haired man in a weather-stained scarlet coat went off up the covert in a squelchy canter.

'That's Mr. Macdoggart,' said Dixon in a low voice, and my solemnity increased as the legendary figure vanished on its mysterious errand.

Meanwhile the huntsman was continuing his intermitent yaups as he moved along the other side of the wood. Suddenly his cheers of encouragement changed to a series of excited shoutings. 'Hoick-holler, hoick-holler, hoick-holler!' he yelled, and then blew his horn loudly; this was followed by an outbreak of vociferation from the hounds, and soon they were in full cry across the covert. I sat there petrified by my private feelings; Sheila showed no symptoms of agitation; she merely cocked her ears well forward and listened.

And then, for the first time, I heard a sound which has thrilled generations of fox-hunters to their marrow. From the far side of the wood came the long shrill screech (for which it is impossible to find an adequate word) which signifies that one of the whips has viewed the fox quitting the covert. 'Gone Away' it meant. But before I had formulated the haziest notion about it. Lord Dumborough was galloping up the ride and the rest of them were pelting after him as though nothing could stop them. As I happened to be standing well inside the wood and Sheila took the affair into her own control, I was swept along with them, and we emerged on the other side among the leaders.

I cannot claim that I felt either excitement or resolution as we bundled down a long slope of meadowland and dashed helter-shelter through an open gate at the bottom. I knew nothing at all except that I was out of breath and that the air was rushing to meet me, but as I hung on to the reins I was aware that Mr. Macdoggart was immediately in front of me. My attitude was an acquiescent one. I have always been inclined to accept life in the form in which it has imposed itself upon me, and on that particular occasion, no doubt, I just felt that I was 'in for it'. It did not so much as occur to me that in following Mr. Macdoggart I was setting myself rather a high standard, and when he disappeared over a hedge I took it for granted that I must do the same. For a moment Sheila hesitated in her stride. (Dixon told me afterwards that I actually hit her as we approached the fence, but I couldn't remember having done so.) Then she collected herself and jumped the fence with a peculiar arching of her back. There was a considerable drop on the other side. Sheila had made no mistake, but as she landed I left the saddle and flew over her head. I had let go of the reins, but she stood stock-still while I sat on the wet ground. A few moments later Dixon popped over a gap lower down the fence and came to my assistance, and I saw the boy on the chestnut pony come after him and gallop on in a resolute but unhurrying way. I scrambled to my feet, feeling utterly ashamed.

'What ever made you go for it like that?' asked Dixon, who was quite disconcerted.

'I saw Mr. Macdoggart going over it, and I didn't like to stop,' I stammered. By now the whole hunt had disappeared and there wasn't a sound to be heard.

'Well, I suppose we may as well go on.' He laughed as he game me a leg up. 'Fancy you following Mr Macdoggart over the biggest place in the fence. Good thing Miss Sherston couldn't see you.'

The idea of my aunt seemed to amuse him, and he slapped his knee and chuckled as he led me onward at a deliberate pace. Secretly mortified by my failure I did my best to simulate cheerfulness. But I couldn't forget the other boy and how ridiculous he must have thought me when he saw me rolling about on the ground. I felt as if I must be covered with mud. About half an hour later we found the hunt again, but I can remember nothing more except that it was beginning to get dark and the huntsman, a middle-aged, mulberry-faced man named Jack Pitt, was blowing his horn as he sat in the middle of his hounds. The other boy was actually talking to him—a privilege I couldn't imagine myself promoted to. At that moment I almost hated him for his cocksuredness.

Then, to my surprise, the Master himself actually came up and asked me how far I was from home. In my embarrassment I could only mutter that I didn't know, and Dixon interposed with 'About twelve miles, m'lord,' in his best manner.

'I hear he's quite a young thruster.' . . . The great man glanced at me for a moment with curiosity before he turned away. Not knowing what he meant I went red in the face and thought he was making fun of me.

Now that I have come to the end of my first day's hunting I am tempted to moralize about it. But I have already described it at greater length than I had intended, so I will only remind myself of the tea I had an an inn on the way home. The inn was kept by a friend of Dixon's—an ex-butler who 'had been with Lord Dumborough for years'. I well remember the snug fire-lit parlour where I ate my two boiled eggs, and how the innkeeper and his wife made a fuss over me. Dixon, of course, transferred me to them in my full status of 'one of the quality', and then disappeared to give the horses their gruel and get his own tea in the kitchen. I set off on the ten dark miles home in a glow of satisfied achievement, and we discussed every detail of the day except my disaster. Dixon had made enquiries about 'the other young gentleman', and had learnt that his name was Milden and that he was staying at Dumborough Park for Christmas. He described him as a proper little sportsman; but I was reticent on the subject. Nor did I refer to the question of our going out with the hounds again. By the time we were home I was too tired to care what anybody in the world thought about me.

CUBBING

Memoirs of a Fox-hunting Man
Siegfried Sassoon
1928

Ringwell cubbing days are among my happiest memories. Those mornings now reappear in my mind, lively and freshly painted by the sunshine of an autumn which made amends for the rainy weeks which had washed away the summer. Four days a week we were up before daylight. I had heard the snoring stable-hands roll out of bed with yawns and grumblings, and they were out and about before the reticent Henry came into my room with a candle and a jug of warm water. (How Henry managed to get up was a mystery.) Any old clothes were good enough for cubbing, and I was very soon downstairs in the stuffy little living-room, where Denis had an apparatus for boiling eggs. While they were bubbling he put the cocoa-powder in the cups, two careful spoonfuls each, and not a grain more. A third spoonful was unthinkable.

Not many minutes afterwards we were out by the range of loose-boxes under the rustling trees, with quiet stars overhead and scarcely a hint of morning. In the kennels the two packs were baying at one another from their separate yards, and as soon as Denis had got his horse from the gruff white-coated head-groom, a gate released the hounds—twenty-five or thirty couple of them, and all very much on their toes. Out they streamed like a flood of water, throwing their tongues and spreading away in all directions with waving sterns, as though they had never been out in the world before. Even then I used to feel the strangeness of the scene with its sharp exuberance of unkennelled energy. Will's hearty voice and the crack of his whip stood out above the clamour and commotion which surged around Denis and his horse. Then, without any apparent lull or interruption, the whirlpool became a well-regulated torrent flowing through the gateway into the road, along which the sound of hoofs receded with a purposeful clip-clopping. Whereupon I hoisted myself on to an unknown horse—usually an excited one—and set off higgledy-piggledy along the road to catch them up. Sometimes we had as many as twelve miles to go, but more often we were at the meet in less than an hour.

The mornings I remember most zestfully were those which took us up on to the chalk downs. To watch the day breaking from purple to dazzling gold while we trotted up a deep-rutted lane; to inhale the early freshness when we were on the sheep-cropped uplands; to stare back at the low country with its cock-crowing farms and mist-coiled waterways; thus to be riding out with a sense of spacious discovery—was it not something stolen from a lie-a-bed world and the luckless city workers—even though it ended in nothing more than the killing of a leash of fox-cubs? (for whom, to tell the truth, I felt an unconfessed sympathy). Up on the downs in fine September weather sixteen years ago....

It is possible that even then, if I was on a well-behaved horse I could half forget why we were there, so pleasant was to to be alive and gazing around me. But I would be dragged out of my day-dream by Denis when he shouted to me to wake up and get round to the far side of the covert; for on such hill days we often went straight to one of the big gorses without any formality of a meet. There were beech woods, too, in the mellow sunshine, with summer's foliage falling in ever-deepening drift among their gnarled and mossy roots.

A HUNTING DAY

Foxiana
Isaac Bell, MFH
1929

Looks a rare sort of day. But there's a scent. Coming along hounds were raking on, determined looking, and their mouths shut tight. Never saw the thorn look blacker. Everything smelling so strong. See how the smoke hangs. I can smell the Colonel's cigar from across the road.

Let's move hounds away from the exhausts of these motors. It makes them sneeze—gets into their coats and all helps to foil scent. I can smell that idoform. That's where I dressed Caroline's cut foot. Forgot to wash it off this morning. We want no other scent with us than 'Fox.' I do hate the smell of bath salts and hair wash. Delicate organ a hound's nose, can't be too careful.

Blackthorne Gorse the first draw. What a good day it is to 'hear.' Listen to the clatter of the horses on the stony lane! The slamming of that gate. The barking of that collie. *And* that man driving cattle. Pity our first covert's down-wind of it all!

* * *

Nip on, Jack, and sharp too! The old customer may hear us and steal away. I've a jolly good mind to hold them round the covert before putting in, in case he's hooked it . . . No, I shan't. . . . There are several foxes in the thorns, and if the old customer has slipped away he is not the sort that will let us work up to him and fresh find him in some other covert. No, he's perpetual motion. Like the tide, 'waits for no man.' It would be a stern chase all day.

Nothing like getting away on his brush, and hustle him from the start. That's the first thing towards killing him. Next comes hitting him off quick at the first check. Never let 'em get their second wind. The nearer you stay to your fox the better the scent, and if he is blowing you get a 'breath scent' as well as the body and pad scent. So it's hustle him along. The final act is brought about by the sagacity of your older hounds running harder when they recognise the weakening scent of a sinking fox and by the help the horsemen give you, if they keep well off hounds; and by allowing no noise or row in the establishment. Those are my ideas on the matter. Sounds easy. But here we are outside the covert.

* * *

No, my lasses! Keen as you are, not one of you must be off into covert before I tip you the wink. *Lew-in!* How the covert fence crackles as they jump on and off! I suppose a pack weighs nearly a ton. Anyhow, last week when I was half up that hole trying to get hold of the fox the hounds got suddenly excited and jumped down on the top of me. Like a cart-load of bricks. My back, I can feel it still.

What's that speaking? Only young Lightning. Rabbit, probably. *Ware riot, Lightning!* Have a care! She's a high mettled young bitch. Shan't say too much to her. Besides, she'll very likely help to put the fox up by her row. *It's done it, too.* Just as I said. But he jumped up just where Lightning was speaking, so she was right. I am sorry I chided her. However she'll forgive me—and I've learnt that she's got an uncommon good nose in brambles. *Huic, huic, huic at him!* They're all round him. What a chorus! By Jove they're out of covert.

But Jack is there and he would have viewed him away? No, that's it. He's turned up inside the covert fence and they have flashed out downwind on his scent, which has blown out. Steadee, Jack! Don't rate 'em back, let 'em make their swing by themselves; the fox is inside and they'll be back on to him like a knife if you leave 'em alone. Much better let 'em do it for themselves—and get the experience. *Garneawuuay!!*—At the far end. Well it's a flying start this time, for I've got hold of them before they got back into the gorse.

Must be careful now. No 'bad hurry,' but nip down with them well before me a little to one side, and my horse up-wind of them on the covert side—and then come down onto the line almost parallel with it. Nothing looks more ridiculous than striking it 'heel.' It's often done by the hounds behind your horse—specially if there's a heavy tongued one among 'em.

Where's my second whipper-in? Now, Bill, they're 'all on!' But don't get forrard. This fox looks like a cub—and a ringer probably. So stay about here for a while, and if he doubles back later through the horse foil and if I'm not on his line—just give *one* halloa. See him to the covert and then nip on in case you see him through. Don't put me on another, however. You've had a good look at him and should recognise him a year hence even in the Zoo. *Forrard, forrard!*

Blow these cattle! It's checked them. However, I prefer cattle to sheep foil. Hounds can drive through cattle further *and* give one a better 'direction' where to get out on the clean ground and hit it quick—especially if there's a bit of a breeze. *Yooi bitches forrard!* Not a head up all through this check. Trying all the time. They think they did it all themselves, too—bless 'em. Never noticed me just inclining them out of the field.

What a head they are carrying. Watch Gossamer. Hope she is not getting a bit stingy with her tongue. No, she's all right, thank goodness. She was just a bit wide of the line and driving back into the wind. She's got it now. *Hark forrard to Gossamer.* What a lovely tongue! By Jove, it's a cracker. Glad I'm on a good horse. Pancake is dropping back. It's those two days 'in' with a cut foot has done that. She's always been our top bitch. Just shows what 'condition' means. Jezebel has dropped back. Never thought she *would* do it when the 'tap was turned full on.' It's those shoulders—and those over-knuckling knees. It's a pity, for her heart is as brave as a lion's. She was first prize bitch—and the Captain says to me, 'Walter,' he says, 'when you can draw twenty couples like this you'll be a proud man.' 'Not so sure about *that*,' I says. 'I'll tell you how she goes on after Christmas. There's some items in her conformation I don't quite like. I won't say what they are, because I fancy it's those items made you give her first prize, Captain—and you might be annoyed with me.' A good job for me and a bad job for the foxes we ain't got a pack of all of the sort the Captain likes! They're all right eight days out of ten, but it's when you meet the real scent, breast high, that these young nippy ladies of ours run the other sort clean off their legs. Sort of flummox 'em—outclass them. It's like running a hunter at Ascot, to put Gossamer with that lot. In her own class she'd be a star turn.

Spinster's at head now. Did you notice the sprint she put in to get there? How they chaffed me for keeping her from going in the draft! She was light and plain at the knees. But I kept her, for she was out of Susan, who was out of Sunfish, out of Sunday, out of Susie, who was by our Sultan, who was by Brocklesby Wrangler out of old Sinuous, who went slap back to Squire Chaplin's Blankney lot—and of course back to Lord Henry's. Somehow they never seem to throw 'em with much bone, and several visitors last year said to me, 'Walter, if you want to get a nice pack get out of that sort.' But, bless you, they never seem to wear out. No trouble in kennel or in the field; all you want is a jolly good horse to see 'em dust their fox along.

Here's the turnpike. It's checked 'em right enough, but they are trying hard. We came at it on a right-hand slant—so it's ten-to-one that where he has crossed out is to the right of where he got in. It's usually a cert, I find. Not much chance of a good hit on a road these days—what with motor car foil and tarmac—so while the leaders are driving down the road I'll just slip these five couple or so out under these rails, and they can be trying on the grass while the others are driving down the road. They've got it! *Forrard, forrard.* Not much time wasted so far! We've been dusting him along exactly 38 minutes by the watch—watch they gave me when I left the Bleakshire for here, by the way.

* * *

Must have been nearly ten minutes in these roots. Yes, sir. Thank you, sir, I saw that fox go away, all right. But it's been so dry that I shouldn't be surprised if there are all several foxes here; and I don't want to change if I can help. *Whooohoopwhoop!* A good job I let 'em hunt the line and didn't lift 'em. Tragic nailed him in the roots. Fairly bust up with the pace, he must have been. It was a fresh one went away.

MEDITATIONS OF MR BLOWHARD
Foxiana
Isaac Bell, MFH
1929

I'm mounted the best, and everything liberal, with a Master who's all for sport. He understands hunting and he understands hounds, and I don't want a better to breed our pack; but if he wants me to show the followers sport, he's got to leave a lot to me.

Yes, he knows all about hunting—as far as a gen'leman can; but of course he's not been through the mill as I have. I was second whipper-in to old Croaks for six seasons, when Jack Sprite was first. You understand what *that* meant. 'Sharp' was the word and no mistake. All 'fair hunting' you know, no 'patchouli' or 'rosewater,' *but sharp*, as I say. Good hunting, but as 'near the wind' as didn't hurt hounds, or disgrace our good name.

Croaks would grumble all the way home if we hadn't caught our fox. Whenever we found, if he passed either of us whippers-in it was, 'D— you, look alive! Work your soul out till we catch 'im.' Ah! And that's the sprit, too.

Croaks had a great command over his hounds. In some coverts he would let 'em spread out and draw as wide as you ever saw a pack draw; in others he would almost 'tuft'—keeping about thirteen couples or so at his heels all the while. It was a knack he had, and it wasn't very long before hounds learnt it from him, tufting or spreading out to draw, according to the sort of covert it was or its condition at the time of year. I saw 'em do it straight off for Jack Sprite the first day ever he hunted them, one time when Croaks got hurt. Shows how hounds learn things.

Croaks was the quickest to get away on his fox I ever saw. Odd times he would take 'em out of covert and swing them round to the holloa, cutting off p'raps half-a-mile—according to the wind. And I will say, I never once saw him strike heel way. Other days he would hunt the line right out, cheering them away. I asked him, one night riding home, when he happened to be particular pleased with me for helping him to kill his fox, 'why did you hunt the line out—instead of getting them out, like the time before, and getting a nick on your fox?'

'It was a different type of scent, lad,' he answered. It was a *holding* scent. And it would have upset them to no purpose if I'd interfered. The other time, though they did run harder in the open, scent was really of a more volatile sort. On a holding scent, d'you see, the length of a field or a minute lost (though I grudge both) is not so important as getting hounds well settled down to hunting their fox. But what we call a *volatile* scent is a quickly vanishing one. A holding scents gets only *gradually* weaker, like the taper on a good ash stick; but the volatile scent has a knack of going 'snap'—like an elastic band.

'If the scent is of the quick-vanishing sort, how long to leave hounds alone is what you've got to decide. One minute behind your fox you can race him, but three minutes later hounds won't so much as be able to tell you he has ever been that way. The time when I let 'em hunt it out we were in the thin end of the covert; but the time I took 'em out the opposite end from the holloa there was all that thick stuff before us. Nice guy I'd have looked if they'd got on to another fox in covert and you holloaing the old customer away.

'Some folks,' he warned me, 'will tell you Croaks can get hounds to come to him even when they're in *full cry* on another fox. Don't you believe it, lad (and I wouldn't like my hounds to do it, either). But say nowt. What I *can* do is to time the right moment for getting their heads up. That moment may only last for a couple of seconds, but if the moment comes—I recognise it. I expect,' he went on, 'you'll be a huntsman yourself some day. Remember this: NEVER TRY TO DO WITH YOUR HOUNDS WHAT YOU ARE NOT CERTAIN YOU *CAN* DO. And with that,' he ended, 'I've told you the whole secret.'

With Croaks our orders were never to holloa if hounds were running hard in covert when another fox went away. We were to keep our eye on him as far as we could, and then to nip in and tell Croaks. He rarely made any answer. 'Does he look a good 'un?' was the most he ever said. As to what he would do—that, as I came to see, all depended on the scent. I remember when, on a rare scenting day, we viewed a famous old fox away—an old fox with two white pads. Hounds were tied to another in covert, so I came up and told him about it. 'Stay with me, lad,' he said, 'and if they get out on a ride—or if the fox makes a turn and they check for a second—we'll have 'em out on the white-legged 'un.'

It was a full twelve minutes before the fox crossed the big ride, hounds in full cry. Quick as thought Croaks gallops straight on his line, foiling it towards the pack. One holloa, and he has the pack away, laying them on to our white-padded friend. As I say, there was a *holding scent*. Hounds struck it; but they knew it for a weaker one and a different one from that which they'd left. *Romulus, Remus* and *Clinker* all tried to drive back into covert, and I can well remember how old Croaks praised me for putting them on to the body at once. For with such a heavy tongue as that $1\frac{1}{2}$ couple had, they would have swung the whole pack to them.

Croak's methods were always varying. During cub-hunting he was, in general, very steady and quiet, and made hounds work every inch themselves. 'Learning them the game,' he called it, or sometimes, 'developing nose and brains.' But he would sometimes, suddenly, do something one didn't expect of him. 'Just to sharpen 'em up,' he would explain to us whippers-in—after (as usually happened) he had killed his cub by that piece of unexpected interference.

Yes, I learnt a lot from Croaks. Later on I was 'first' to George Ketch, and I picked up a lot from him, too. He had all Croaks's methods. He had whipped in to him for four seasons, and Croaks always said he never had to say a word to George in the field. He worked him, as he always declared, 'with his eyes.'

Ketch was gipsy bred. Such a voice, such a note on his horn! He could make hounds' hackles rise, of if they rioted or did wrong he could make 'em almost weep. They'd do anything for him. He didn't seem to pay much attention to them when out with them—always let 'em rake along in front. Never spoke to hounds unless it was to make them *do something*. Never gossiped to 'em like some fellows do. But when he did speak—they did what he wanted them to do.

Ketch worked his way up. He would often talk to me about it. 'I'm not in Croaks's position,' he'd remind me—'huntsman to a nobleman's private pack. I'm huntsman to a big subscription pack; and if I don't keep 'em moving and show sport I'll get the sack. I am a favourite as long as I give them fun. If I strike a bad season—an *unlucky* season of bad foxes, bad stopping, or bad scent—it'll just be 'No, Ketch, I'm sorry, but we must make a change. We're engaging young so-and-so from the Brokeshire, who is showing such sport!'

'Before all, it's sport I must show; and, much as I should like to, I can't afford to hunt hounds in the style of amateur gentlemen with lots of money in the provinces. I love my hounds,' he would say, 'and if I had my way I'd never deceive them. And because, for bread-and-butter's sake, I *do* have to deceive 'em at times, I must make it up to them so doubly well that they either look on me as inspired, or else are so happy with themselves that they forgive me.'

Ketch was a man who thought a lot, and he'd a wide understanding of what his job required of him. 'Besides hunting hounds,' he would tell me, 'you must almost compare me to a man staging a great day's amusement, and I can only do that if a lot of the 'staging' part is left to me. I mustn't be bound strictly to the order of drawing coverts, or to the cub-hunting of them. I mustn't be strictly bound at all. I'll serve my Master loyally, but he must understand that I can't work to hard and fast rules.'

As for Stickpoodle Wood, until Ketch came no one had a good word for that covert. In fact, when Patsy Slow was huntsman, if hounds were to draw Stickpoodle Wood the field went home. But there was nothing the matter with the covert—the foxes were the trouble and a rotten bad breed they were.

Ketch went to Stickpoodle, early, cub-hunting—and by dint of hard mornings, holding up, mobbing and digging, I think we pretty well exterminated almost every fox in the place. The Master was away in Scotland, and when he came back he said we'd killed too many. Ketch said he thought there were plenty more left. But *how* he thought that I *don't* know. For, besides killing every cub in the covert he had dug and killed four vixens. Bad vixens make bad sport. The country was well foxed and all that season, whenever we ran into Stickpoodle, we drove our fox clean through it—he being a stranger. And later on, when we began to find there again, the foxes would go straight away and give runs. 'Bad vixens, bad sport'—there's no truer word than that.

Ketch always had in mind the stage-managing side of his job. It was because of those reasons that he determined that one of our coverts he wouldn't cub-hunt at all, if he could work it. This covert had a strong litter, and in it we had turned down a number of cubs which the Master had sent from Scotland.

This covert helped us out several times, and enabled Ketch to reward his hounds by laying hold of a soft fox after days of much lifting, wide casting, and 'changing.' Days which otherwise would have got hounds disappointed and made them not come so well on with him in those long casts. I remember one day, especially, when one of those coverts stood Ketch in good stead. We had a large crowd out, and the Master said we must show them a rare good day. We drew Blankthornes, but previously in the season we had caught the two good foxes it had held, after hunts; and now there was only a ringing vixen there for us. We made a few rings outside and back to the covert. Ketch soon spotted that she would keep up these dodging tactics till dark, so the next time, when we checked in cattle a few fields away from the covert, Ketch decided not to let hounds try back.

He told us whippers-in to work forward and wide, and to keep a lookout for a fox on the move or for any holloas. On he raked for a mile-and-a-half over a good country, hounds coming along keenly. Getting below Ryehill (a favourite line for foxes to cross), he touched a line. It was too stale to bring off anything, but Ketch was letting hounds work it, when I came back to tell him that a labourer had seen a fox close by Ringpool, some ten minutes ago another mile on. Ketch had the map of the country always well in his eye, and he took hounds over the places easiest for them at a good canter, never waisting a moment. We hit this line—it was a bit fresher than the one we had left—and we ran on well over a stiff line for a while, but then scent began fizzling out. The fences had thinned the field, and there were a number of loose horses, and Ketch was still two miles from the covert which held those Scotch cubs. Casting right-handed he got on to the road that led to the covert, and, pegging along at a good seven-mile-an-hour trot, he sent us whippers-in 'on' with orders,—'*We've got to get hold of one of them.*' Then he slipped hounds into the covert. We held them up, and hounds laying hold of one, Ketch took him out of the covert and broke him up—just as the straggling field came along. It was voted a good hunt of one-and-a-half hours, a six-mile point, and a kill.

'It didn't amuse me,' said Ketch, 'but it gave sport to a big field; it sent them all home happy: and my hounds were rewarded by blood for coming on with me so well. But those are not everday tactics,' he added. 'And I take a good look at the field, to see who is out, before I try them on. *For it don't go down with some!*'

THE COCK-AND-PYE DAY

The Hawbucks
John Masefield
1929

They agreed as they drove to the Cock-and-Pye, that it was a perfect morning for hunting: there was dry going, scent, coolness and an almost windless air; and enough signs of spring beginning to give zest to the winter beauty. Nick dropped George at the Cock-and-Pye, and then drove on alone to a neighbouring farm where Sir Edward's horse was waiting for him. George got Kilkenny from the inn stables. As he rode out into the wide space in front of the inn he saw Steer reined in out of the way, moodily snicking at grass blades with his thong. He rode up to greet Steer, but found him in the pangs of despair.

It's no good, George,' he said, "'Thou can'st not minister to a mind diseased.' I don't really care two pence even about hunting on a day like this.'

At this instant George caught sight of the Harridew party, and rode off to greet them: Steer seeing to whom he was going turned his horse's head, so that he might see no more.

All the Harridews were there; Carrie on the Night-Jar looking more divinely lovely than ever; old Harridew, looking for Vaughan; and Jane on her cob, with a bundle of charities for some outlying sufferer to whom she meant to ride as hounds drew.

'Where are they drawing, George?' Jane asked.

'Ghost Heath, I think,' he said: 'either that or the East Hope.'

'You'll look after Carrie, George, won't you?' she said.

'I'll look after her: never fear.'

'I'm afraid the man Vaughan is rather annoying her.'

'I'll see that he doesn't, while I'm with her,' he promised. After this he greeted Carrie. He did not see Vaughan, but heard his cheery voice from somewhere in the inn yard. He did not see Nick, who was probably with Sir Edward, down the road.

'It ought to be a lovely hunt,' he said. 'How's the Night-Jar?'

'Almost too beautiful. Here's Charles Cothill.'

Charles were lunging and plunging past upon his chestnut, among cries of 'Why ride a circus horse?' or 'Cheer up, Charles: we see the cobbler's wax. A little further down the road he nearly got among the hounds: ribaldry followed him.

'I hope that's not the chestnut he's riding in the Point-to-Point,' George said.

'It is,' Carrie said. 'He's a beauty, isn't he?'

'He looks as though he'd extend Kilkenny,' George said.

Almost at that moment there was a sudden leaping into life among the pack. Robin crossed the road past them with the pack at his heels, and little dry sideways yaps of 'Hounds, please, gemmen, hounds, please.' Sir Peter went past, and all followed through out of the road into the pasture, where worn-out old pear trees rotted, with great shrubs of mistletoe on their boughs.

They had gone about a quarter of a mile when Vaughan suddenly cut in on Carrie's right. 'Good morning, Carrie,' he said. 'They're drawing Ghost Heath. You come along with me by the short cut here.'

'You cut along by the short cut, Vaughan,' George said: 'and leave Miss Harridew alone.'

'I'm not speaking to you, Childrey,' Vaughan said, 'Carrie and I quite understand each other. Besides, she promised to ride with me to-day, and I've come to claim her promise.'

At this moment the old bear, old Harridew, rode up. He thrust in between Carrier and Vaughan. 'Excuse me, Mr Childrey,' he said to George. 'I have a word to say here.'

He was a fine big figure of a man who looked his very best in scarlet on horseback. 'He would have made a good figurehead for a ship,' Steer Harpit had said. His pride, intolerance and unintelligence would have been less noticed in wood than in flesh. Now that he was fulfilling one of the main functions of his life, which was that of the protective angry bull, he looked almost beautiful. He was not a man to mince matters. 'Mr Vaughan,' he said, 'your attentions to my daughter are offensive to her. They are to stop. If they don't, I'll horse-whip you with these hands.'

'Mr Harridew,' Vaughan said; 'there's no need to advertise my suit for your daughter's hand in quite so public a fashion. And your threats are unworthy of you. I don't think of your threats, because in such a cause I'll risk them, or a hundred such.'

'I'm not going to argue the point,' Harridew said. 'I'm a man of my word, and so you'll find me.'

'Right, sir,' Vaughan said. 'I'm a man of my word, too, and my word is pledged to Carrie, and so you'll find that.'

There was no answer to this, for they had reached a gully in the covert, where Vaughan was forced to drop behind. In the next field he found himself alongside Len Stokes, a grazier. Carrie was riding ahead, between her father and George. Two or three other men were just behind her, hoping for a word, and thankful for the sight of her. Mike was one of them, young Cothill another.

'Who's the third chap on the black?' Vaughan asked.

'Young Crowmarsh,' Stokes muttered.

'Gad,' Vaughan said, 'Our young virgin's guarded like a prize she-cat; but this resolute Tom will get past, they'll find.'

'You'll get the family battle-axe, if you're not careful,' Stokes said. 'And I won't blame the man who gives it to you. You might be useful as a cross, Vaughan, but as permanent mating-stock, I'd rather use a sheep dog.'

'I'll bet you an even pony,' Vaughan said, 'that the old man will be blessing me at the altar before the year's out.'

'I won't rob you,' Stokes said. 'But one of you will have the other in the dock before that: I'll bet on that.'

'In the dock? What for?'

'You, for I won't say what,' Stokes said. 'But the Squire for attempted murder.'

They turned up the windy hill pasture among the old, weathered thorn trees, now stripped of their berries. Little streamers of wool clung to some of the thorn-stems were sheep had rubbed: there were sheep snuggles here and there, where for centuries sheep had snuggled down out of the wind. Further on was the oval building of small unmortared stones. Lobs Pound the place was called: a pre-historic work, so thickly grown with sloes that there was no getting into it; the stones of it seemed to have decayed into the earth, so that it looked like a natural mound.

'Lobs Pound,' Carrie said, as they drew near. 'We always come here in the autumn for sloes, for the annual store of gin.'

'Look, a weasel,' George said. He promptly sucked his wrist so as to make a squeaking noise, like enough to the cry of a rabbit to hold the weasel on the wall till Carrie could see it.

'He's out early,' George said. 'And now here we come to the point of the wood.'

The wood thrust a sort of snout towards them on the hill-top, and spread away on each side. The nearer parts had been stubbed down a year or two before, leaving only small stuff: beyond were big trees and many yews. An old gate, hanging on its lower hinge, was open. Its effect, against the yews, was sinister. Robin riding forward through it into covert seemed to be entering something evil.

Three poachers, Brassy, Pimply, and the Tiddler, who meant to do business in the wood after the hunt had gone, slipped round the east side of the covert after the second whip: a good many of the field followed them: among them Nick and Sir Edward, to George's joy.

'What is the fox going to do, George?' Carrie asked.

'Run, like fun,' he said.

'Yes; but where?'

'Round the wood. No fox will break at once from a covert as big as this.'

'Yes, but where will he break?'

'They're on to a fox,' George answered, as a hound whimpered, and Robin harked them to it. 'Yes, there are three more: the fun's beginning.'

The horn blew to encourage hounds and the clear voice cheered them to it: hounds were plainly on a fox in covert, and moving away. Half-a-dozen excited riders pushed past George and Carrie, over the crest of the hill, and away down the further slope. One of them called out, 'That sounds like business: I'll get to them.' Two or three others, caught by the infection of action, followed.

'Hadn't we better go?' Carrie asked. 'They're going.'

'Don't you,' George said. 'He won't break from that side. Come on down the hill with these.'

'There'll be no fox in this confounded place,' the Squire said. 'They're running a polecat or a badger.'

'Badger your maiden aunt,' a man said, pushing past.

Most of the rest of the field had begun to file down a woodcutter's cart-track which led through a spinney of hazel and spindle to the pastures below. 'We'll follow on with these,' George said, turning Kilkenny.

'Hadn't we better hurry?' Carrie said. 'Look, they're away down below.'

'Not they,' George said. 'They're still running him in covert. They'll rouse up a leash more foxes here.'

'But look, George: they're riding.'

Looking down hill through the tall shoots of the hazels, on which already a few catkins hung, they had a glimpse of two men in scarlet cantering fast on the pasture below. The horsemen in the cart-track quickened into a trot at the sight of the canterers. 'Don't you trot, Carrie,' George said, 'you won't be left behind. He won't break yet.' The hounds were still in covert, but among much riot and the scents of half-a-dozen foxes who had been there during the night. As George and Carrie passed out of the cart-track into the pasture, they came upon Steer, reined in to one side, staring at Carrie with haggard eyes. It smote upon George's heart that Steer was taking his loss very bitterly to heart. 'I must ride over to see him,' he thought. After he had passed he looked back at his old friend, and saw that he had turned from the hunt, and was riding slowly away.

'He must be feeling pretty sore,' George thought, 'not to be able to hunt.' He would have liked to ride after him, to comfort him; but he was with Carrie, the most envied man there, hounds were on to the fox, and there was the field bunched together and attentive behind the figure of Tom the whip.

Tom moved slowly forwards: the field now began to shog off towards the right, to avoid a neck of the wood. They came into a wooded hollow, said to have been one of Sir Christopher Wren's quarries, for some (not remembered) building. A lane led out of this; a hundred yards further on it forked into two tracks. The riders pressed down the track to the left. 'Don't follow them down there, Carrie,' George said. 'Keep out, up here.'

'But they're all going, George. And I don't want to be left behind.'

'Come here,' George said. 'There's no way out of that lane except at thick thorn fence, fifteen feet high. Besides, it leads into the covert. They'll all have to come back. Now watch that strip of grass for the fox.'

They watched, while the hounds cried in covert and the welter of horses in the lane having joggled a while began to joggle back.

'There he goes, Carrie,' George said suddenly, leaning forward, following an intent trembling eagerness in Kilkenny. 'Look. There: there, by the fence. A travelling dog. Do you see him?'

There went the fox, indeed, a little red flashing thing, looking much smaller than he was, because he was already fully extended. He gave no sense of enjoying it (as people said he did) but a vivid image of the terror of death. On the instant the cry in the covert swelled up into the ecstasy, and on the top of it came the ringing halloa of 'Gone awa-wa-woy' from Tom. A horn blew, and a wave of motion surged out. A great bitch-hound, which George knew to be Daffodil (having marked her and heard her called) came over the fence where the fox had crossed it, in the very place, giving a terrible impression of infallibility. She was throwing her tongue in little excited cries. With her, just behind her, crying like her, and at one with her in their certainty, came Tarry-breeks, and Arrogant, and Queenie, with their sterns down straight and their heads up. Then instantly, from all over the place, came romping joyous helter-skelter hounds, who had done none of the work and didn't know where the fox was, but knew that their leaders knew, and knew where their leaders were.

'There you are, Carrie,' George said. 'He's off for Larks Leybourne, and we're in the very front row. There comes Bob.'

There came Bob, over the fence below them; he blew a blast as he landed, jamming his horn into his boot, cast an eye ahead, and gave a cheer to his beauties. Halloas came from all over the covert.

'No need to wait, Carrie,' George said. 'Come on. Now for glory.'

They were off, as it were on the right bank of a stream of racing hounds, out of sight of the rest of the field and leading it. He saw Carrie's face all lit up with excitement and delight. They rode through a gate and across a field. They saw hounds going over a fence in front of them, and came over after them on to wet pale pasture, with Bob on their left forty yards away, and a young magpie hound tearing between them to get up. 'Along to the right: follow me, Carrie,' George cried. He knew that bit of the world rather better than most. They thundered muckily out of the field into a cart-track.

The whine and the drone of a threshing machine came on their ears as they splashed through the muck into a farmyard. A thresher stood by a staddled rick, hard at it. A man on a wagon paused with his fork in air as they came in sight. Three or four men stopped work on the instant, but the two were past, the ducks waddling and the poultry scuttering in front of them. They splashed into a cow track which looked like a bog. George led through this, and in another fifty yards was out on the pasture again, in a big field, in which the cows were ranged in line in the far corner, lowering and tossing heads, from the passing of the pack an instant before. 'Lucky, those gates,' George cried; 'we stole a march on Bob there.' Indeed, Bob had only just entered the field far away to the left and behind them. 'Are these bulls? Carrie asked. 'We won't stay to see,' George said. 'I'll give you a lead. It's nothing of a fence.'

It was nothing of a fence, there was no need of any lead, they went across it into a big field sloping down before them. The sun came out suddenly, so that it seemed to both, as they landed, that they had leaped into a world of light, or into a world lit by their own enjoyment. The field was all lit: the pools of the little stream beside them gleamed blue: in front there was a steelier gleam from the Yell Brook overlapping its banks. Away to the left was Sir Peter: far in front was a glimpse of hounds. A big brown horse with his stirrups flying high came over the fence beside White Rabbit. As yet no one was in it with George and Carrie: they were leaders of what was surely the quickest burst ever made into the very cream of the country. To George there came an image which he never forgot of the lovely Carrie at her loveliest, at one with her lovely black horse, against a slope of a hill, in which a field of pale plough lay above a field of red plough, with elm-trees black-twigged against the sky, rooks building in them, and intense green under the hedge.

He had a glimpse of hounds swerving to the right. No one else in the hunt could have seen it: the lie of the ground must have hidden it from Sir Peter and Bob. He called to Carrie, 'Keep on after me.' He charged across into the red plough, took it slantingly, came out on to pasture, with the tail of the pack ahead, and came down to a double-gated cattle bridge over the Yell. 'Saves you jumping the Yell,' he called, as he opened the gates for her, one after the other. 'By George! we're in luck to-day.'

They rode across a narrow field, scrambled up a bank, broke through a young thorn fence, and found how well in luck they were. They were in sight of hounds; the only people who were, though behind them, to their left, were twenty doing their best at the jumping of the Yell. 'What became of father?' Carrie called. 'Scuppered, probably,' George called. The two horses went side by side, stride for stride, as full of joy as their riders. The red-brick Nonesuch Farm hove up on the left. Two women and three little children came running to the little rose garden to see. A cowman pointed with his hat, but there was no need for him to point: they were in the same field with hounds (three hounds), the sun was shining, Carrie was there, and the horses going like angels. A covey of partridges whirred away to the right.

As they went over a fence an owl in an apple-stump hooted above them with a cry that was like the laughter of the morning.

They came up to the disused mill of Nonesuch, where old, knobby cob-nut trees grew over the stank. They crossed the dark pool and saw hounds ahead going up the grass of Gallows Hill, swerving away from them. They strode out from the mill to the stretch of the grass: larks were aloft and others went as they galloped. 'If there be a heaven upon earth,'

George sang, 'it is this, it is this, it is this.' 'It is,' Carrie cried. But the heaven to him was the ecstacy in Carrie's face.

They went over the crest of Gallows Hill into red clay plough, where four plough-teams were halted, with men at the horses' heads, all staring in the same direction. Rooks were rising over the fields on ahead: they splashed along the drain in that direction. They came up to a fence beyond which the hounds were at fault. Bob was with them now, so was Tom. Sir Peter was up a moment later, with Charles Cothill and a man in a rat-catcher. There was no stay: Bob held them on over a raddled deep stream on to what was called the battlefield, where men had been killed in the Wars of the Roses. Nob Manor, Bunny's brother, rode up alongside George. 'Have you seen Nick?' George asked. 'Your damned writ-serving brother, you mean?' Nob said. 'Yes, he got left the other side the covert.' Here the hounds got the scent full again and were off past the Norman church and away on to Tineton Waste, a grazing worth half a crown an acre, from which they saw their fox's point, the Wan Dyke, in the downland above Larks Leybourne.

They went through a dozen fields and across a spinney, skirted some orchards, and came out on to Long Hinton Green, both blowsy and hot, with wisps of Carrie's hair loose and the horses dark with sweat. In front was a swell of downland with three black trees upon it, so spaced and sized that they looked like a ship's masts under sail.

They went lollopping up the downs past the fir-trees, and then away over the expanse, where nothing grew but the grass, a few thorns, a few junipers, and gorse too sparse to hide a fox. Larks went up and rabbits scuttered away from them till they came to Blowbury, where the vast down suddenly became immense and all covert seemed to cease. For two miles there seemed nothing but grass, with the wind running over it in ripples swifter than water ripples. The horses felt the glory of it. To George, beside the glory, was the ecstasy of being with Carrie, sailing from wonder to wonder on this adventure of speed. Whatever the fox may have felt, those four spirits at speed were knitted into the one joy, and George's eyes were as like as stars to Carrie's.

Up at Maesbury an archæologist, grubbing for flints in the plough, and finding only bits of Samian ware (which he despised), saw the fox go past in a furrow, which perhaps left colder scent than the grass. A moment later he saw the hounds (he was the only man who did, at this point) coming unfailingly ten yards to leeward of the fox's track. He blessed his stars that those eyes and hackled necks were not after him. Later he realised that he had never seen anything like it, for will bent upon destruction. A minute later he saw the hunt go by in a scattered chivalry much the worse for wear, and wondered who the golden girl was who rode the black horse so well.

They galloped past Maesbury into Thirty Acre for the last half mile to Wan Dyke Hill. They saw the fox's point ahead, with the Seven Standing Stones on the far side of the bourne, and a big barrow half ploughed out. George and Carrie were well up still, but others were ahead of them. That did not matter much now, for they had held their own in such a run as they had never had. George was thinking that he would share this in Carrie's memory for ever, and that life had touched its peak, or almost its peak. If Carrie would have him it would be the peak.

They rode at a little dark fence, which had a lot of privet among its thorn. What happened, George never quite knew, and Carrie, who had jumped in front of him, could not tell him; but Kilkenny put in his toes and shot George into the privet, where he kicked for an instant, still holding the reins, in a scratched, wrenched, and startled state, wondering what on earth was the matter. As he groped himself up, feeling that no bone was broken and no vital button gone, Carrie came circling back, crying, 'Oh, George, are you hurt?'

'No thanks,' he said. 'All right. Go on, go on. Don't spoil your run. You were a brick to turn.'

'Whatever happened?' she said. 'I had a sort of sideways glimpse of you falling. You seemed to go a fearful purler. Are you sure you're all right?'

'Right as rain, thanks. But go on to see the end. They'll kill him on his earth here.' He came up to Kilkenny, who was inclined to swerve away: he mounted and put him over the fence.

'Too bad, my stopping your run,' he said. 'Now I've put you out of it all. However, he's dead by this time.'

'We'll take it quietly, George,' Carrie said, 'till I see whether you really are all right.'

Hounds had disappeared upon the Wan Dyke; five riders showed ahead of them, splashing through the flood where the bourne had overflowed. The hill behind them seemed sprinkled with riders converging upon them. 'Pull round to the right of the hill, Carrie,' George said. 'It's less steep that side.'

'Now tell me truly, George, how you feel,' Carrie asked.

'Honestly, all right, thanks: nothing wrong, not even scratched. I didn't quite know where I was for a second: now I'm myself again. I'm only vexed that I've spoiled your run.'

'Spoiled my run,' she said. 'You've given me the run of my life. I've never, never had such a day.'

They heard the note of a horn from somewhere in the Wan Dyke. In a minute or two they came upon the hunt drawn out of the way of hounds in a boggy green patch near a pool. Hounds were checked on the hillside: Bob was with them, speaking to one or two by name, and watching their work intently. Some men were dismounted and had turned their reeking horses to the wind. Some second horsemen came up and made their exchanges. Mrs Ridden rode up in her masterful, manly way. 'That was a pretty good skurry, Sir Peter,' she cried. 'Not much wrong with that. But make a long lift, Sir Peter, or he'll be on to Cheddesdon Warren.'

'He's probably lying down in a rut within a hundred yards of us,' someone answered. A man came up on a heaving horse: he mopped his brow and took a sup of cherry brandy. 'Pretty little nip, that,' he said 'Gad, did anybody time it? Up to the Quorn, by Gad!'

There came a movement from the pack as Bob lifted them: all followed after him along the side of the wood, which grew battered, starved oak trees shining with lichens. Charles Copse, the gentle and beautiful, rode up to Carrie. 'If you and Mr Childrey go anywhere near my place,' he said, 'my wife will be so glad if you'll go in for lunch or coffee or something. Do go in. Was it you who took a toss there, Mr Childrey? I hope you're none the worse.'

'No, rather not, thanks.'

'What happened?'

'Can't think,' George said. 'I suddenly went wallop.'

Hounds spoke to a scent a few minutes later: off they went at head over the rolling grass of Godsdown. Someone said, 'A fresh fox'; but George, whose eyes were very quick, saw the fox ahead, and answered: 'No, the old one. See him there. That's a hunted fox.' Not many saw him there, but the gallop began again. Men said, 'No fox on earth will stand up another two miles.' Others said: 'A good game fox, but hounds have earned him. They'll kill this side the brook.'

But now the salt was gone out of the gallop for George and Carrie, they kept on, but could not keep up. Hounds made a swerve, which threw them out. They found themselves alone, out of sight of even a rider. 'He's running short,' George said; 'he can't be far from us. And I must get one of his pads for you.' A man in a red coat hove in sight: they followed him till some boys gave them a direction. In following the direction they passed out of any trace of the hunt: they saw no rooks rising, no cattle bunching, no sheep running into line: they heard no whimper nor blast of horn.

'We're out of it,' George said.

'Where are we?'

'That's Mourne End Wood up above us. If we get up the hill we may see what's going on. Yes: look there some of them go; yes, and there are hounds. We'll see the end of it. The Night-Jar looks as if he'd had about enough.'

'So does yours,' Carrie said.

'We'll stop while there's something in them,' George said. 'We're a long way from home.'

They rode up a sunken trackway, listening for the burst of the pack running into their fox. They heard no hounds, but a coarse voice cheering hounds some considerable distance to windward of them. They came into Mourne Camp, with a yew wood on their left and a sighing fir plantation on the right. There was now no noise of the hunt whatsoever. A blue jay flashed his wings and swore at them.

'They haven't killed,' George said, 'so they must be running. It's odd that we don't hear them.'

They rode on into the darkness of the wood, hearing no sound of the hunt. Suddenly, with a crashing in the dead leaves of a beech-clump, a hare went across their track and fled away from them.

'Did you catch that reek of fox?' George asked at one point. 'It was almost as strong as a touch.'

'No, I missed it,' Carrie said.

Presently they came out of the wood into a grass valley, with a deep sunk brook in the bottom: away to the left a ditcher stood watching something: soon he left his watching and came down to clear a choked drain. 'Which way did hounds go?' George called.

'Thiccy,' the man said, pointing.

'Were they on to a fresh fox?'

'Ah.'

'Did you see the fox?'

'How?'

'Did you see the fox?'

'No. No, I didn't see the fox.' He paused to consider this, then added: 'No, I couldn't have seen the fox, for he was gone; gone afore I could have seen him.'

'Were hounds running fast?'

The man mopped his brow, spat, and straightened himself wearily, as he put down his ditching spade. 'I'll show 'ee,' he said, leading the way up the slope for a few yards. 'I wasn't paying much attention, if you'll understand me, being a man as has had troubles: but I heard hounds back a piece. They went across the far field, where that red coat is riding.

'How long have they been gone?' George asked. 'Five minutes?'

'Ah, it might a bin.'

'Were hounds going fast?'

'How?'

'Were hounds running fast?'

'Ah. Like a vlight a twites.'

'What I expected,' George said to Carrie. 'They've changed foxes in covert. He turned to the ditcher. 'I suppose you didn't see a beaten fox, a fox that had been hunted, come through the fence here?'

'No,' the man said. 'And if I had done, I wouldn't tell 'ee. If you want to kill the poor thing, kill him; not run him down same as you would do a man.'

'I shouldn't do the same to a man,' George said.

'Why do it to a poor beast, then? God Almighty gave him feelings, I hope.' He turned wearily to the muck and thrust the ditching spade into it. 'I've got my work to attend to,' he added.

The man had a coloured cutty pipe stuck in his hatbrim. 'I see you smoke,' George said. 'Will you have a cigar?

'Yes, and two if you've got the same; and I'll cut 'em up and pipe 'em.'
George gave him the cigars.

'What's your name?' he asked.

'Jackment. Will Jackment, of what they call Jackment's Piece.

> "Jackment's Piece my dwelling-place is
> And muck's my occupation."'

'Would you like to change your occupation?' George asked.

'No. I would not,' the man said. 'Time was when I would have; but now I say. 'Give me muck,' I say, 'acos it'll always be there; long after all these new-fangled things are gone down into the bonfire.' And so I tell 'ee plain.'

At this he turned to the muck in a way that stopped the talk.

'I liked that chap,' George said, as they rode away.

'I thought him very rude,' Carrie said. 'Why did you give him your cigars?'

'Because I've had a topping day and want to share it.'

'I expect you'll find that he drinks,' Carrie said.

'He's a jolly good ditcher,' George said. 'And of an old family, too; one of the Jaquemains who got a grant of this county from the Conqueror; he's related to you, probably: he must be a Norman.'

'I'm sure he's not related to me,' Carrie said, somewhat stiffly.

About thirty yards ahead of them a blue jay was swearing in a tree in covert; some small birds were chattering excitedly in the fence of the wood.

'What are the birds mobbing?' Carrie asked.

'An owl or a squirrel,' George said. As they rode past the excited birds, George peered at the fence, which of black thorn, with the stalks of bracken in it. George had good country eyes, quick to catch subtle changes. He saw nothing as he passed, but just after he had passed he saw something move, ever so slightly, as though with relief at a danger gone. He said nothing for half a minute; then he said: 'That was our fox in the hedge, lying down to die. He'll never get up after such a gruelling. They changed in the wood, as I said.'

Father always says that Sir Peter ought to breed more for speed,' Carrie said. 'They ought to have pulled him down at Lark's Leybourne.'

'What would you like to do now, Carrie? We might see something more of them at Nun's Wood, or would you care to shog along to Copse Hold, which can't be more than a couple of miles?'

'I'm game to go along, George,' she said. 'But we'd never get back from Nun's Wood. Let's go to see Mrs Copse.'

'Right,' he said; 'we will.'

They were alone together in that lonely valley between the woods: the cup of George's happiness was almost full.

THE RECTOR OF ST TIMOTHY'S

The Silver Horn
Gordon Grand
1934

The Rector of St Timothy's, known throughout the parish as St Timothy's in the Fields, had been awake since dawn. In truth he had seen each new day creep across Helmscote Heath towards the rectory for a full score of years, for it is a custom of old age to bear witness to the dawn.

On this particular Saturday morning he was loath to arise and face the day's events. On the other hand the thoughts and reflections which assailed him in bed seemed to make getting up the lesser evil. For the third time that morning he fumbled under his pillow for his watch, reached for his glasses, and consulted the time. There yet remained fifteen minutes before Mary Madden would come up with his hot water.

Fifty-two years ago he had received the living of St Timothy's from the present Squire's father and moved into the rectory with his young wife, and Mary Madden had come to them as a maid of then eighteen years. During all these years Mary had brought up his hot water in the same tall pewter jug wrapped about with a piece of grey flannel. What continuity of service, he thought, and again his mind reverted to the unhappy recollections of the previous evening, and the equally trying drama to be enacted during the present day.

Tasker Oaks, the ever improvident village saddler, had died leaving a wife and three small children in perilous circumstances,—with no apparent means of support. The Rector had been to the 'Hall' the evening before pleading with the Squire to permit the widow to occupy Willow Cottage rent-free for the balance of the year. Their talk had been extremely unpleasant for both of them. The Squire had been petulant and shown little sympathy or interest in the situation and had advanced his own increasing financial distress—tenants in arrears of rent, unemployment, mounting taxes, prohibitive costs of repairs, and the many demands of a newly acquired and fastidious wife. At eighty-one it is not easy to be combative and argumentative and the Rector came away with a feeling of having failed through his own impotency; yet he knew how much had been at stake for Nancy Oaks.

As he lay abed he concluded for the thousandth time that it was due to the effects of the late War. To him his span of life divided itself into but two periods—the well-regulated, dependable, comprehensible years preceding the War—the years patterned by his ancestors, a time when one knew exactly what to expect from one's self, one's neighbours, and one's government—a pleasant era in which literature, art, music, sport and all social contacts changed and evolved with so slow a trend that one's susceptibilities were hardly aware of change. And then these post-war days—an uncongenial, incomprehensible period for old age to keep step with. An age in which he seemed to have little to offer which men and women wanted or appeared to need.

The Squire himself had caused him untold concern. He had neglected the age-old precept that country should marry country, and as a result his lady had no insight into the problems of the estate. The 'Hall' was but a place to visit periodically and to entertain in during the hunting season. Many of his parishioners lived in houses and cottages on the estate and the sympathy of the landlord for the needs and problems of the tenants was as necessary as the revolving of the seasons. Without this understanding help the ever-recurring misfortunes of life were often turned into tragedies.

Tasker Oaks was to be buried that morning, and in an effort to spare Nancy some expense the Rector had offered to drive her in his chaise to Abbots Appleby, nine miles away, where Tasker Oak's kith and kind lay buried these three hundred years; Will Holcombe was to follow on with the coffin.

It was a long drive for his aged white horse and he knew well that before they would have cleared the village Nancy would ask him what the Squire had said, and he would have to tell her that she and the children would have to move, and there would be a long silence, and then she would ask what she and the bairns would do and where they would go, and he would have no answer for her and so would say that he would think it over. He would set himself to think it over but no thoughts would come to him, and to his humiliation and in spite of all his resolve, his old mind would get diverted by some inconsequential thing such as a bird flying overhead, yearling colts heckling each other in a pasture, or even a clump of brown winter weeds growing along the roadside, and so he would finally say to Nancy that he would think things over for a few days and then come to see her.

To one in the late evening of life it is essential that civilization and its manifestations should not become too complex and incomprehensible, because one has not over-long in which to readjust one's views and faith; and yet this matter of Nancy Oaks was perplexing in the extreme. He could not reconcile his mind to a civilization which could neglect so splendid an institution as Nancy and her children, for to him she typified the very best of rural England.

He heard Mary Madden coming upstairs with the hot water and wondered whether it was only the reflection of his own thoughts which made her steps sound slow and dull that morning. He heard her enter the bathroom, pull back the curtains, do the same in his dressing room, and start the fire; then come to his door, rap and say, 'It's a quarter past eight, Sir, and a pleasant day, only a mite overcast.'

As he started to shave he noticed that the new Hunt fixture card had been propped up against the mirror, held in place by a diminutive bronze figure of the great sire, Stockwell, which had served this purpose for half a century. This kindly act of arranging the fixture cards, which Mary persisted in, always amused and pleased him. It was an effort on Mary's part to suggest that he had not actually given up hunting, but, rather, was not going out that season.

From habit he invariably consulted the card each morning to see where hounds were meeting, and to call to mind the scene as it would be enacted, and would ever and anon say to himself in good part, 'Well if I *were* hunting I could not go out today. There is too much to be done.' On mornings when the weather precluded any possibility of hounds going out, Mary would say at breakfast, 'There will be no hunting today, Sir,' just as though he might have planned to hunt, and he would say, 'No, Mary, no hunting today. Perhaps it will be better by the next hunting day.'

Five years ago on his seventy-sixth birthday he had formally abandoned the sport. That day had marked his sixty-fifth year in the field, for he had had his first day to hounds on his eleventh birthday. How well he remembered that first day. His grandfather had been Master of Hounds and had given him a new shilling for jumping his pony over a goodly brook. Then his memory reverted to the day five years ago, his last day to hounds, and how people of all degrees had expressed regret that he was giving up the sport, and young and old had said kindly things of good cheer to him. Before starting downstairs he glanced at the card and saw that the fixture for the day was Thornhill Upper Bridge at 11 am.

After attending to his mail and one or two matters pertaining to the morrow's service he called for Nancy Oaks and together they started their sombre drive to Abbots Appleby. Their conversation had been much as he had feared it would be, and he had been of little present help. He had known Nancy since she was a wee tot playing up and down the village street, and her burdens and perplexities weighed heavily upon him.

After passing through Wedmere Cross they mounted the long hill which leads over the Peak of Medford. On the summit the Rector rested his white cob and waited for Will Holcombe's slower horse to come up with them.

Looking to the west he could follow the valley of the river Tro until it narrowed into a gorge five miles away and disappeared north around Holderness Head. 'Thornhill Upper Bridge at 11 am,' flashed through his mind. If Tim Templer had found in West End Spinney, hounds might now be running some place in the valley between Holderness Head and Medford Bottom. He stood up in the chaise and peered long and intently. He was a tall, slightly stooped, frail man with white hair, and there was a shade of longing in his fine face.

As he stood thus scanning the valley, the pale, wintry sun disentangled itself from masses of grey clouds and filled the valley with light, and there, some two miles up the vale, was the glint of scarlet and presently he distinguished hounds racing on towards him. He started the cob on its tortuous course down the hill, and as the banks were high no further view was had of hounds, but as the chaise approached Medford Bottom, which is a mile wide at that point, he heard hounds on the right and coming towards them. He focused his eyes on the long straight road in front of him for the fox was bound to cross somewhere in the bottom.

Of a sudden he was startled by the horn of a great motor bus, hastily pulled to the side of the road and the bus sped past, leaving the air rancid with fumes. He again fixed his eyes on the road and saw a small red object slip from the hedge row into the road and run in the air-fouled wake of the fast disappearing bus. Smart—very smart—mused the Rector. That will worry them.

He brought the cob to a standstill to wait for the field to cross the road and gallop on wishing to spare Nancy any contact with the Hunt, but as he waited he watched the fox. On and on it ran. Never, thought the Rector, will hounds unsnarl that line and, in such mild manner as is permissible to a rector of advanced age, he asked for divine condemnation upon cement roads, internal combustion engines, all standard and other brands of petrol, and in particular the fumes left by each—then he saw the fox turn left-handed and disappear through a break in the hedge.

The Rector heard hounds carry the line with fine cry to the edge of the road—then there was silence. First one hound and then another entered the road, and threw their heads right and left, but without a whimper. Some of the more impetuous hounds given to wider casts, carried their search across the road. He knew that Tim Templer would let them try it alone before he helped them, and so hounds sought for the thin thread of scent growing every thinner with each passing moment.

The humble funeral cortège was concealed from the field by a growth of alder bushes. The Rector of St Timothy's was too heavy of heart at that moment to feel in tune with the hunt. What sympathy he felt was all for the hounds. They were baffled, through the innovations of the times. He rebelled at the thought of exposing Nancy in her grief to the countryside at play, but twice Nancy had asked him in her gentle, faltering voice if they might not be late. He knew that Tim Templer would make every conceivable cast before he would abandon the fox, and so he finally decided to drive on and be through with it.

He put the grey cob in action, beckoned Will Holcombe to follow on, and so came into view of the field. They were standing a hundred yards or more from the road watching Tim cast his hounds. A hundred scarlet coats and shimmering silk hats. As the chaise came into view Tim stopped his horse and ceased talking to his hounds. The Squire said to him, 'Tim, I have no doubt the Rector knows what became of that fox, but who would dare ask him now?' But Tim was not listening to the

MFH. The narrow, lively slits in his weather-beaten face that served him as eyes were staring at the chaise. They grey cob was creeping his deliberate way across the long straight cement road while Will Holcombe's aged sorrel mare followed with her doleful burden.

Attracted by his huntsman's gazing, the Squire looked over at the Rector and saw that his round black hat was being held far aloft. The Squire removed his velvet cap and stood thus until the Rector might again replace his hat. On and on the chaise proceeded until it was far beyond the field and still the hunt went back to their chattering, but Tim Templer's narrow eyes were twinkling and the Master continued to hold his cap in his hand. He too was staring. Then of a sudden Tim heard him say, 'I have it. By God, what a prince the old man is!' The chaise at last reached a place where a break or gap appeared in the hedge at the left of the road, and they saw the round black hat tilt far out to the left, and then return to its owner's head. Master and huntsman smiled at each other, and Tim called his hounds to him.

When the chaise disappeared from view an impatient huntsman took his hounds at a gallop to a break in the hedge, and as the Rector turned a bend in the road he heard hounds open and knew they were flying on; in spite of himself a gentle smile broke over his deep-lined face.

It was dusk when Tim Templer and his two whippers-in passed through the village to the kennels. The Rector was returning from dropping a letter in the post. At sight of him Tim stopped his horse and removing his cap, said, 'Please, Sir, if you're to be at home and could find it convenient, Sir, I would like to speak with you a piece as soon as I see to the hounds.'

Within the hour the huntsman was in the rectory library and telling of the greatest run in the history of the hunt, and how the fox had run eight and twenty miles, and how the Squire had said on the way home that there was little to choose in distance between their run and the great Waterloo Run of the Pychley in '62 when they found in Waterloo Gorse and had to stop hounds after three hours and forty-five minutes close to Blaiston, except that he and the Squire had killed their fox. In his enthusiasm Tim unfolded the course hounds ran and opened a great panorama of country which his listener followed mile upon mile.

Of a sudden Tim stopped, 'Excuse me, Sir. I didn't come to tell you all this. I clean forgot myself. I came for something else.'

'Timothy Templer, never interrupt a story like that. Particularly that kind of story. Where did you kill?'

'On the edge of a bit of gorse just afore the river turns to slip away in Fernsworth Fenns. We were well into Mr Stackpole's country. The furthest from home ever I've been on a horse. There was only the Squire and that American gentlemen, Mr Weatherford, what has the Grange at Dunmorrow, with me when we killed and we waited there a spell and the gentlemen kept coming up for as long as ever we waited for they were strung back all the ways to the ford at Weston, and never a second horse to be found when they were needed. If there was a half-bred horse within five miles of the kill I never saw him.

'What I came to say, Sir, was as how the gentlemen were uncommonly generous with me on account of how it was such a grand run and gave me six pounds, and, Sir, I was thinking some of poor Tasker and his widow and them children. He was never much of a one to save a shilling was Tasker, but we was friends a goodish long time. He did the fixing up of the tack up at the kennels. I was thinking as how I'd like to give you three pounds if you could find a way to get it to Nancy, for she would never take it from me, Sir, and Slem Whimple and the Connors boy who are whipping to me this season say as how they would like to add ten shillings apiece, so that's four pounds, and here it is, Sir, if you'd be pleased to take it, and I must be getting along. Old Crusader that I rode today wouldn't as much as take a sniff at his oats and I'll be having a look at him. I don't know as how you'd like to have me mention it, Sir. Maybe you wouldn't, but you were a powerful help to me today, Sir. The smell of that motor bus and the way the wind was blowing on the cement road made it pretty hard for the hounds. Good night, Sir, and thank you.'

The morning of the Third Sunday in Lent commenced as all Sunday mornings had commenced in the rectory of St Timothy's in the Fields time out of mind, except that the Rector himself was not quite in the 'pink'. The long cold drive of the day before had been somewhat of a strain on him and he felt stiff and draggy as he walked across the lawn to the church. Then he forgot the memorandum of announcements he was to make and had to retrace his steps. When he reached the vestry room the choir was assembled and ready to commence the processional and he could hear the organ playing the last bars of Bach's Chorale, *What Tongue Can Tell Thy Greatness, Lord*.

The verger helped him on with his cassock and surplice as he had done for so many years, and he heard the organ commence the grand old marching hymn, *Ride on, Ride on to Victory*. The verger in his black robe stepped forward and opened the heavy oak door leading to the church and the Morning Service of St Timothy's in the Fields had commenced.

How well he knew the sight that would meet his eyes. A scant half of the pews would be occupied and these principally by old people from up and down the village street with here and there an elderly spinster from the country houses.

He followed the words of the hymn and did not look up until he had reached his place in the choir stalls, and then let his eye wander off over his congregation. To his amazement there was not an empty pew and scarce an unoccupied seat.

A great alarm spread over him. He had been conscious lately of many evidences of a fast failing memory. Could he by any chance have miscalculated the period since Ash Wednesday? Could this be Easter Sunday? Within his remembrance the church had never been so filled except at Easter. It was with infinite relief that he finally fixed it in his mind that it was but the Third Sunday in Lent.

By the time he had finished reading the First Lesson appointed for that Sunday he had regained his composure, but to his further amazement he kept discovering one fox-hunting person after another in the congregation. For the first time in many months the Squire and his lady were in the family pew. By the conclusion of the service he had discovered practically all of the first-flight, hard-riding members of the Hunt.

When the choir again reached the vestry room and were singing the last verse of the Recessional the verger closed the batten door, which caused the singing to sound as though it came from afar off and the Morning Service was over. The verger handed him the green cloth bag containing the offering and he took his perplexed way home, but even as he did so he could not free his mind from the thought that the day must have been set apart in people's minds as a memorial the very nature of which had slipped his memory and that surely there was something he should have made reference to in the service.

Upon reaching his study he proceeded to arrange the contents of the green bag upon his desk preparatory to counting it. In the bag he discovered a large envelope addressed to him in handwriting which he recognized as that of Mr Merrill Meredith, a substantial landowner, a keen sportsman and an old friend. He opened the envelope which he found to contain a letter from Meredith and another from the Squire.

The Meredith letter ran:

A group of your old friends dining together at John Weatherford's last evening following the longest and most spectacular run of this or any other season for our hounds talked long and affectionately of you, and wishing to give more tangible proof of their regard subscribed the sum of sixty-five pounds to a fund to be used as you may think best in the relief of any case or cases of distress in our village. My cheque for this amount is enclosed.

With expressions of warm personal regard, I remain,
    Very sincerely yours,
      MERRILL MEREDITH.

The Squire wrote:

My dear Dominie:

I tender my apologies and regrets for the affair of Friday evening. Please accept them. How many times I wonder have you forgiven and overlooked since I was a wee shaver. I know I am a continual disappointment to you. Please say to Nancy Oaks that she may occupy the cottage rent free for as long as you feel she should have it. If anything untowards happens to her or the children and I not be available I have instructed Smithers to honour any demands you may make on him for this purpose.

Please don't take it amiss but you were magnificent, really magnificent, yesterday on the Medford road.

The Rector had long since finished his dinner yet sat quietly alone in his armchair at the head of the table and peace and contentment were in his face. When Mary entered he asked her to hand him a cigar. 'There it is in your very hand, Sir, and you aturning it around and around.' 'Oh yes, so it is Mary. I was thinking of something else. And Mary, would you send the cook's little boy over to Nancy Oaks to say I would like to see her just before the Vesper Service, and Mary please bring me a scrap of paper. My memory is not very good—any little piece—an old envelope will do.'

When on Monday morning the verger was tidying up and putting the books away in the chancel he picked up an envelope addressed to the rector from Hemple & Mellick, Coal, Wood, Feed and Building Supplies, and was about to dispose of it when he saw a note on the back.

'I want them to sing *Faith, Perfect Faith* at this evening's service.'

THE MISTER

Sherston's Progress
Siegfried Sassoon
1936

By the time I had been at Limerick a week I knew that I had found something closely resembling peace of mind. My body stood about for hours on parade, watching young soldiers drill and do physical training, and this made it easy for me to spend my spare time refusing to think. I felt extraordinarily healthy, and I was seldom alone. There had been no difficulty in reverting to what the people who thought they knew me would have called my 'natural self'. I merely allowed myself to become what they expected me to be. As someone good-naturedly remarked, I had 'given up lecturing on the prevention of war-weariness'—(which meant, I suppose, that the only way to prevent it was to stop the War). The 'New Barracks', which had been new for a good many years, were much more cheerful than the huts at Clitherland, and somehow made me feel less like a temporary soldier. Looking at the lit windows of the barrack square on my first evening in Ireland, I felt profoundly thankful that I wasn't at Slateford. And the curfew-tolling bells of Limerick Cathedral sounded much better than the factory hooters around Clitherland Camp. I had been talking to four officers who had been with me in the First Battalion in 1916, and we had been reviving memories of what had become the more or less good old days at Mametz. Two of them had been wounded in the Ypres battle three months before, and their experiences had apparently made Mametz Wood seem comparatively pleasant, and the 'unimaginable touch of time' had completed the mellowing process.

Toward the end of my second week the frost and snow changed to soft and rainy weather. One afternoon I walked out to Adare and saw for the first time the Ireland which I had imagined before I went there. Quite unexpectedly I came in sight of a wide shallow river, washing and hastening past the ivied stones of a ruined castle among some ancient trees. The evening light touched it all into romance, and I indulged in ruminations appropriate to the scene. But this was not enough, and I soon began to make enquiries about the meets of the Limerick Hounds.

No distance, I felt, would be too great to go if only I could get hold of a decent hireling. Nobody in the barracks could tell me where to look for one. The genial majors permanent at the Depot were fond of a bit of shooting and fishing, but they had no ambition to be surmounting stone walls and big green banks with double ditches. Before long however, I had discovered a talkative dealer out at Croome, and I returned from my first day's hunting feeling that I'd had more than my money's worth.

The whole thing had been most exhilarating. Everyone rode as if there wasn't a worry in the world except hounds worrying foxes. Never had I galloped over such richly verdant fields or seen such depth of blue in distant hills. It was difficult to believe that such a thing as 'trouble' existed in Ireland, or that our majors were talking in apprehensive undertones about being sent out with mobile columns—the mere idea of our mellow majors going out with mobile columns seemed slightly ludicrous.

But there it was. The Irish were being troublesome—extremely troublesome—and no one knew much more than that, except that our mobile columns would probably make them worse.

Meanwhile there was abundance of real dairy butter, and I sent some across to Aunt Evelyn every week.

At the end of the third week in January my future as an Irish hunting man was conclusively foreshortened. My name came through on a list of officers ordered to Egypt. After thinking it over, I decided, with characteristic imbecility, that I would much rather go to France. I had got it fixed in my mind that I was going to France, and to be informed that I was going to Egypt instead seemed an anti-climax. I talked big to myself about Palestine being only a side-show; but I also felt that I should put up a better performance with a battalion where I was already known. So I wired to the CO of our second battalion asking him to try and get me posted to them; but my telegram had no result, and I heard afterwards that the CO had broken his leg the day after it arrived, riding along a frost-slippery street in Ypres. I don't suppose that the War Office would have posted me to him in any case; and I only record it as one of life's little contrasts—that while I was enjoying myself with the Limerick Hounds, one of our most gallant and popular senior officers—himself a fine horseman—was being put out of action while riding quietly along a road in the town which held the record for being knocked to ruins by crumps.

A day or two later, greatly to my disgust, I was despatched to Cork to attend an anti-gas course. I didn't take my studies very seriously, as I'd heard it all before and there was nothing new to learn. So on the fourth and last day I cut the exam and had a hunt with the Muskerry Hounds. I had introduced myself to a well-known horse-dealer in Cork who hunted the hounds, and the result was that I had a nice little scramble over a rough country about eighteen miles away from the army hut where I ought to have been putting on paper such great thoughts as 'gas projectors consist of drums full of liquid gas fired by trench-mortars set at an angle of forty-five degrees'.

In the afternoon the hounds were drawing slowly along some woods above the river which flowed wide and rain-swollen down long glens and reaches in a landscape that was all grey-green and sad and lonely. I thought what a haunted ancient sort of land it was. It seemed to go deep into my heart while I looked at it, just as it had done when I gazed at the castle ruins at Adare.

In the county club that evening I got into conversation with a patrician-faced old parson. We were alone by the smoking-room fire, and after he'd been reminiscing delightfully about hunting it transpired that he had a son in the Cameronians. And I discovered that this son of his had been one of the officers in the headquarters dug-out in the Hindenburg trench while I was waiting to go up to the bombing attack in which I was wounded.

We agreed that this was a remarkable coincidence. It certainly felt like a queer little footnote to my last year's experience, and the old gentleman laughed heartily when I said to him 'If life was like *Alice in Wonderland*, I suppose I should have said to your son—not "I think I once met your father in Ireland" but "I think in nine months' time I shall be talking your father in the county club at Cork".' We then decided that on the whole it was just as well that the Almighty had arranged that *homo sapiens* should be denied the power of foreseeing the future.

Next day I was back at Limerick by the middle of the afternoon. Going into the ante-room I found no one there except Kegworthy. It was Sunday, and the others were all out or having a bit of extra sleep.

'There's been an old boy up here asking for you. He said he'd come back again later,' said Kegworthy, adding as an afterthought, 'Have a drink.'

I mention the afterthought because it was a too-frequent utterance of his. Kegworthy was one of the most likeable men at the Depot; there were only two formidable things about him: his physique—he was a magnificent heavyweight boxer—and his mess bill for drinks. I had seen several fine men trying to drown the War in whisky, but never a more good-humoured one than Kegworthy. There were no half-measures about him, however, and it was really getting rather serious. Anyhow the mess-waiter brought him another large one, and I left him to it.

On my way across the barrack square I saw someone coming through the gateway. He approached me. He was elderly, stoutish, with a pink face and a small white moustache; he wore a bowler hat and a smart blue overcoat. His small light blue eyes met mine and he smiled. He looked an extraordinarily kind old chap, I thought. We stood there, and after a moment or two he said 'Blarnett'. Not knowing what he meant, I remained silent. It sounded like some sort of Irish interjection. Observing my mystification, he amplified it slightly: 'I'm Blarnett', he remarked serenely. So I knew that much about him. His name was Blarnett. But how did he know who I was? But perhaps he didn't.

I have recorded this little incident in its entirety because it was typical of him. Mr Blarnett was a man who assumed that everyone knew who he was. It seldom occurred to him that many things in this world need prefatory explanation. And on this occasion he apparently took it for granted that the word Blarnett automatically informed me that he had seen me out hunting, had heard that I was very keen to come out again, that the hounds were meeting about four miles away to-morrow, that he had come to offer me a mount on one of his horses, and that he would call for me at the Barracks as punctual as the sun. The word Blarnett was, in fact, a key which unlocked for me the door into the County Limerick hunting world. All I had to do was to follow Mr Blarnett, and the *camaraderie* of the chase made the rest of it as easy as falling off a log, or falling off one of Mr Blarnett's horses (though these seldom 'put a foot wrong', which was just as well for their owner, who rode by balance and appeared to remain on the top of his horse through the agency of a continuous miracle, being a remarkably good bad rider).

He departed, having communicated all that was necessary, and nothing else. His final words were 'Mrs O'Donnell hopes you'll take tea with her after hunting.' I said I should be delighted. 'A grand woman, Mrs O'Donnell,' he remarked, and toddled away, leaving me to find out for myself who she was and where she lived. No doubt he unconsciously assumed that I knew. And somehow he made one take it all as a matter of course.

Returning to the ante-room I told Kegworthy how 'the old boy' had turned out to be a trump card; 'And now look here,' I added, 'I'd already got a hireling for to-morrow, and you've jolly well got to ride it.'

My suggestion seemed to cause him momentary annoyance, for he was, I regret to say, in that slightly 'sozzled' state when people are apt to be irrationally pugnacious. 'But, you bloody bastard, I've never been out hunting in my life. D'you want me to break by bloody neck?'

'Oh, I'm sorry, old chap, I'd no idea you were so nervous about horses.'

'What's that? Are *you* telling me I'm nervous? show me the something Irishman who says that and I'll knock his something head off.'

His competetive spirit having been stimulated, it was easy to persuade him that he would enjoy every minute of it, and it was obvious that a day in the country would do him no harm at all. I told him that I'd already hired a wild Irishman with a ramshackle Ford car to take me to the meet, so he could go in that. I assumed that Mr Blarnett and his horses would call at the Barracks, as he'd said nothing about any other arrangements. So the next morning I was waiting outside the gates in good time. After forty minutes I was still waiting and the situation looked serious when Kegworthy joined me—the Ford car being now just about due to arrive. Shortly afterwards it did arrive, and Mr Blarnett was in it, wearing a perfectly cut pink hunting coat, with a bunch of violets in his buttonhole. He looked vaguely delighted to see us, but said nothing, so we climbed in, and the car lurched wildly away to the meet, the driver grinning ecstatically round at us when he missed a donkey and cart by inches when swerving round a sharp corner. Mr Blarnett did not trouble himself to tell us how he came to be sharing Kegworthy's conveyance. With top hat firmly on his head and a white apron over his knees to keep his breeches from getting dirty, he sat there like a child that has been instructed to keep itself clean and tidy until it arrives at the party. And after all, what was there for him to explain? We were being bumped and jolted along a rough road at forty miles an hour, and this obviously implied that the horses had been sent on to the meet. We passed them just before we got there, and Mr Blarnett revealed their identity by leaning out of the car and shouting 'I have me flask' to the groom, who grinned and touched his hat. The flask, which had been brandished as ocular proof, was very large, and looked like a silver-stoppered truncheon.

It was a fine morning and there was quite a large crowd at the cross roads, where the hounds were clustering round the hunt servants on a strip of grass in front of an inn.

Having pulled up with a jerk which nearly shot us out of our seats, we alighted, and Mr Blarnett, looking rather as if he'd just emerged from a cold dip in the ocean, enquired 'Am I acquainted with your officer friend?' A formal introduction followed. 'My friend Kegworthy is riding one of Mike Shehan's horses. He's having his first day's hunting,' I explained, and then added, 'His first day's hunting in Ireland'; hoping thereby to give Kegworthy a fictitious advantage over his total lack of experience.

Mr Blarnett, in a confidential undertone, now asked, 'Will you take something before we start?' Powerless to intervene I followed them to the inn. Mr Blarnett's popularity became immediately apparent. Everyone greeted him like a long-lost brother, and I also became aware that he was universally known as 'The Mister'.

They all seemed overjoyed to see The Mister, though most of them had seen him out hunting three days the week before; and The Mister responded to their greetings with his usual smiling detachment. He took it for granted that everybody liked him, and seemed to attribute it to their good nature rather than to his own praiseworthiness.

But was it altogether advisable, I wondered, that he should confer such a large and ill-diluted glass of whisky on such a totally inexperienced man to hounds as Kegworthy? For the moment, however, his only wish seemed to be that the whole world should drink his health. And they did. And would have done so one again had time permitted. But the hounds were about to move off, and The Mister produced his purse with a lordly air, and the landlord kept the change, and we went out to find our horses.

Had I been by myself I should have been sitting on my hireling in a state of subdued excitement and eagerness, scrutinizing the hounds with a pseudo-knowing eye, and observing everyone around me with the detached interest of a visiting stranger. But I was with The Mister, and he made it all feel not quite serious and almost dreamlike. It couldn't have been the modicum of cherry brandy I'd sipped for politeness' sake which made the proceedings seem a sort of extravaganza of good-humoured absurdity.

There was The Mister, solemnly handing his immense flask to the groom, who inserted it in a leather receptacle attached to the saddle. And there was Kegworthy, untying the strings of The Mister's white apron; he looked happy and rather somnolent, with his cap on one side and his crop projecting from one of his trench boots.

Even The Mister's horse seemed in a trance-like condition, although the bustle and fluster of departure was in full swing around them. The Mister having hoisted himself into the saddle, I concentrated on launching Kegworthy into the unforeseeable. I had ridden the hireling before and knew it to be quiet and reliable. But before I had time to offer any advice or assistance, he had mounted heavily, caught the horse by the head, and was bumping full-trot down the road after the rest of the field. His only comment had been: 'Tell Mother I died bravely.'

'You'll be following to bring him home,' said The Mister to our motor-driver, who replied that sure to God it was the grandest hunt we'd be having from the Gorse. We then jogged sedately away.

'Will you be staying long in Limerick?' he asked. I told him that I might be ordered off to Egypt any day—perhaps to-morrow, perhaps not for a couple of weeks. This seemed to surprise him. 'To Egypt? Will you be fighting the Egyptians then?' No, it was the Turks, I told him. 'Ah, the Turks, bad luck to them! It crossed me mind when I said it that I had it wrong about the Egyptians.'

A quarter of a mile away the tail end of the field could be seen cantering up a green slope to the Gorse. It was a beautiful still morning and the air smelt of the earth.

''Ark!' exclaimed The Mister, pulling up suddenly. (Dropped aitches were with him a sure sign of cerebral excitement). From the far side of the covert came a longdrawn view-halloa, which effectively set The Mister in motion. 'Go on, boy, go on! Don't be waiting about for me. Holy Mother, you'll be getting no hunting with them Egyptians!' So I went off like a shot out of a gun, leaving him to ride the hunt in his own time. My horse was a grand mover; luckily the hounds turned toward me, and soon I was in the same field with them. Of the next forty minutes I can only say that it was all on grass and the banks weren't too formidable, and the pace just good enough to make it exciting. There was only one short check, and when they had marked their fox to ground I became aware that he had run a big ring and we were quite near the Gorse where we found him. I had forgotten all about Kegworthy, but he now reappeared, perspiring freely and considerably elated. 'How did you manage it?' I asked. He assured me that he'd shut his eyes and hung on to the back of the saddle at every bank and the horse had done the rest. The Mister was now in a glow of enthusiasm and quite garrulous. 'Sure that mare you're riding is worth five hundred guineas if she's worth a penny bun,' he ejaculated, and proceeded to drink the mare's health from that very large flask of his.

As I have already suggested, there was something mysterious about The Mister—a kind of innocence which made people love him and treat him as a perennial joke. But, so far, I knew next to nothing about him, since he took it for granted that one knew everything that he knew; and the numerous hunting people to whom he'd introduced me during a rather dull and uneventful afternoon's sport took everything about The Mister for granted; so on the whole very little definite information about anything had emerged.

'How the hell did he make his money?' asked Kegworthy, as we sat after dinner comparing our impressions of the day's sport and social experience. 'Men like The Mister get rid of their money quick enough, but they don't usually make any' he added.

'He certainly gives one the impression of being "self-made",' I remarked. 'Perhaps he won fifty thousand in a sweepstake. But if he'd done that he'd still be telling everyone about it, and would probably have given most of it away by now.'

'Perhaps he's in the hands of trustees,' suggested Kegworthy. I agreed that it might be so, and nominated Mrs O'Donnel as one of them. Of Mrs O'Donnell at any rate, we knew for certain that she had given us a 'high-tea' after hunting which had made dining in the mess seem almost unthinkable. It had been a banquet. Cold salmon and snipe and unsurpassable home-made bread and honey had indeed caused us to forget that there was a war on; while as for Mrs O'D herself, in five minutes she made me feel that I'd known her all my life and could rely on her assistance in any emergency. It may have been only her Irish exuberance, but it all seemed so natural and homely in that solid plainly-furnished dining-room where everything was for use and comfort more than for ornament.

The house was a large villa, about a mile from the barracks—just outside the town. There I sat, laughing and joking, and puffing my pipe, and feeling fond of the old Mister who had reached an advanced stage of cronydom with Kegworthy, while between them they diminished a decanter of whisky. And then Mrs O'Donnell asked me whether I played golf; but before I could reply the maid called her out of the room to the telephone, which enabled the word 'golf' to transport me from Ireland to Scotland and see myself cleaning my clubs in my room at the hydro, and deciding that the only thing to do was to go back to the War again. How serious that decision had been, and how blithely life was oliterating it until this visualized memory evoked by the mention of 'golf' had startled me into awareness of the oddity of my surroundings!

Every day that I went out with the Limerick Hounds was, presumably, my last; but I was able to make several farewell appearances, and I felt that each day was something to the good; these were happy times, and while they lasted I refused to contemplate my Egyptian future. Mentally, I became not unlike The Mister, whose motto—if he ever formulated anything so definite as a motto—was 'we may all of us be dead next week so let's make the best of this one'. He took all earthly experience as it came and allowed life to convey him over its obstacles in much the same way as his horses carried him over the Irish banks. His vague geniality seemed to embrace the whole human species. One felt that if Hindenburg arrived in Limerick The Mister would receive him without one tedious query as to his credentials. He would merely offer to mount him, and proudly produced him at the meet next morning. 'Let me introduce me friend Marshal Hindenbird,' he would say, riding serenely up to the Master. And if the Master demurred, The Mister would remark, 'Be reasonable, Master. Isn't the world round, and we all on it?'

He was a man who had few forethoughts and no afterthoughts, and I am afraid that this condition was too often artificially induced. He and Kegworthy had this in common; they both brimmed over with *bonhomie*, and (during the period when I knew them) neither could have told me much about the previous evening. In The Mister's case it didn't matter much; he was saddled with no responsibilities, and what he felt like next morning was neither here nor there. He looked surprisingly well on this regime, and continued to take the world into his confidence. (He was either solemnly sober or solemnly tipsy; his intermediate state was chatty, though his intermediate utterances weren't memorable.) But Kegworthy's convivialities were a serious handicap to his efficiency as an officer, though so far it had been 'overlooked'.

He did not make a second appearance in the saddle. But about a week after his début, when I was getting formal permission from the Assistant-Adjutant to go out hunting the next day, he suggested that I should take Kegworthy with me and get him, to put it candidly, sobered down. The meet was twenty-three miles away, which made it all the better for the purpose. So it was arranged. The Mister was mounting me, and we were to call for him with the erratic Ford car at Mrs O'Donnell's house (which was where he lived).

It was a pouring wet morning and blowing half a gale. Kegworthy, who said he was feeling like hell, was unwilling to start, but I assured him that the rain would soon blow over. Mrs O'Donnell came out on to her doorstep, and while we were waiting under the porch for The Mister, she asked me to try and bring him straight home after hunting. 'The O'Hallorans are coming to dinner—and of course we are expecting you and Mr Kegworthy to join us. But Mrs O'Halloran's a bit stiff and starched; and The Mister's such a terrible one for calling on his friends on the way back; and it isn't barley water they offer him.' At this moment The Mister came out, looking very festive in his scarlet coat and canary waistcoat. He was optimistic about the weather and I tried to feel hopeful that I should bring him and Kegworthy home 'the worse' for nothing stronger than water.

The maid now appeared carrying The Mister's hat box and flask; he was helped into an enormous overcoat with an astrakhan collar which Mrs O'Donnell turned up for him so that his countenance was almost completely concealed. He then put on an immense pair of fur gloves, pulled his voluminous tweed cap down over his nose, and gave Mrs O'Donnell a blandly humorous look which somehow suggested that he knew that whatever he did she couldn't be angry with him. And he was right, for he really was a most likeable man. 'Now Mister,' she said, 'bear it well in your mind that Mrs O'Halloran and her daughter are dining with us this evening.'

'Be easy about that,' he replied. 'Don't I know that Mrs O'Halloran is like Limerick itself? Would you think I'm one to overlook the importance of her?' With these words he plunged deliberately under the low hood of the car, settled himself down, and remained silent until we were about half-way to the meet. Kegworthy, hunched up in his corner, showed no sign of expecting his day in the country to be a success. But the driver was getting every ounce out of his engine, through the din of which he occasionally addressed some lively and topically-local comment to The Mister, who nodded philosophically from his astrakhan enclosure. As we proceeded, the road became rough and the surroundings hilly. And the weather, if possible, grew worse.

'What sort of country is it we're going to to-day?' I enquired of the driver.

'Sure it's the wildest place you ever set eyes on. There's rocks and crags where a jackass could get to ground and sleep easy,' he replied, adding, 'I'm thinking, Mr Blarnett, that the dogs'll do better to stay at home on such a day as this.'

The Mister opened one eye and remarked that it would sure be madness to go up on the hills in such weather. 'But me friend Tom Philipson will give us a bite to eat,' he added serenely, 'and you'll travel far before you find the like of the old brandy that he'll put in your glass.' He nudged Kegworthy with his elbow, and I inwardly hoped that Tom Philipson's hospitality wouldn't be too alcoholic.

For it was my solemn purpose that we should travel away from brandy rather than that it should be an object of pilgrimage. Tom Philipson, it transpired, was the owner of a big house; he also owned some of the surrounding country, the aspect of which fully justified its reputation for roughness and infertility. The village which was part of his property appeared to be an assortment of stone hovels in very bad repair.

I may as well say at once that when we arrived at Tom Philipson's the MFH had already decided that hunting was out of the question, and was about to go home. The hounds had already departed. Hospitality was all that awaited us, and after all there was nothing wrong with an early luncheon in a spacious and remote old Irish mansion. There was nothing wrong with Tom Philipson either. He was middle-aged, a famous character in that part of the world, and had something of the grand manner about him. My recollection of him is that he was extremely good company, and full of rich-flavoured Irish talk. What could have been more delightful than to sit in a dignified dining-room and listen to such a man, while the rain pelted against the windows and a wood fire glowed and blazed in the immense fireplace, and the fine old burnished silver shone reflectively on the mahogany table? I can imagine myself returning to the barracks after such an experience, my visit having been prolonged later into the afternoon while Tom Philipson showed me the treasures of his house. What charm it all had, ruminates my imagined self, remembering that evocative portrait of Tom Philipson's grandmother by Sir Thomas Lawrence, and the stories he'd told me about the conquest she made in Dublin and afterwards in London. Yes, I imagine myself soaking it all up and taking it all home with me to digest, rejoicing in my good fortune at having acquired such a pleasant period-example of an Irish country mansion, where one's host reticently enjoyed showing his heirlooms to an appreciative visitor. I should remember a series of dignified seldom-used rooms smelling of the past; and a creaking uneven passage with a window-seat at the end of it and a view of the wild green park beyond straggling spiral yews, and the evening clouds lit with the purplish bloom of rainy weather.

And then a door would be opened for me with a casual, 'I'm not a great reader, but the backs of old books are companionable things for a man who sits alone in the evenings'—and there would be—an unravished eighteenth and early nineteenth-century library, where obsolete Sermons and Travels in mellow leather bindings might be neighboured by uncut copies of the first issues of Swift and Goldsmith, and Jane Austen might be standing demurely on a top shelf in her original boards. And Tom Philipson would listen politely while one explained that his first editions of Smollett's novels were really in positively mint condition . . .

But this is all such stuff as dreams are made of. What authentically happened was that we had a hell of a good lunch and Tom Philipson told some devilish good stories, and The Mister was enchanted, and Kegworthy enjoyed every minute of it, and both of them imbibed large quantities of Madeira, Moselle, port wine and brandy and became very red in the face in consequence. This made me feel uneasy, especially as they seemed quite likely to sit there all the afternoon; the fact remained that at half-past three Kegworthy was lighting his second large cigar and Tom Philipson was pressing him to try some remarkable old Jamaica rum, though neither he nor the now semi-intoxicated Mister needed any 'pressing' at all. I felt a bit hazy in the head myself.

Our host, however, was a man who knew how to handle an inconclusive situation. His manner stiffened perceptibly when Kegworthy showed signs of becoming argumentative about Irish politics and also addressed him as 'old bean'. Daylight was diminishing through the tall windows and Tom Philipson strolled across to observe that the bad weather had abated, adding that our drive back to Limerick was a long one. This hint would have been lost on my companions, so I clinched it by asking for our motor. In the entrance hall, which bristled with the horned heads of sporting trophies, The Mister gazed wonderingly around him while he was being invested with his overcoat. 'Mother of God, it must have been a grand spectacle, Tom, when you were pursuing the wild antelope across the prairie with your gun,' he remarked, putting up a gloved hand to stroke the nose of a colossal elk. We then said grateful good-byes to the elk's owner, and our homeward journey was begun.

I say 'begun', because it wasn't merely a matter of being bundled through the gloom until we arrived at Mrs O'Donnell's door. About half-way home, The Mister—who had said nothing since his tribute to Tom Philipson's glory as a gunman—suddenly said to the driver, 'Stop at O'Grady's.'

Soon afterwards we drew up, and The Mister led the way into a comfortless little house, where Mr O'Grady made us welcome in a bleak front room, glaringly lit by a lamp which caused a strong smell of paraffin oil to be the keynote of the atmospheric conditions. There seemed no special reason why we were calling on O'Grady, but he handed each of us a tumbler containing three parts raw whisky to one part water. While I was wondering how on earth I could dispose of mine without drinking it, my companions swallowed the fiery fluid unblenchingly, and did not say 'No' to a second dose. O'Grady sustained the conversation with comments on what the hounds had been doing lately and what the foxes had been doing to his poultry. The Mister blinked at the lamp and made noises which somewhat suggested a meditiatve hen. When we got up to go, he remarked in confidential tones to O'Grady, 'I have yet to make up me mind about the little red horse that ye desire to sell me.' This, apparently, epitomized the object of our visit to O'Grady. My head ached, but the night air was refreshing, though I had some doubts as to its effect on my obviously 'half-seas-over' friends. Hope died in me when The Mister, after getting into the car, instructed the driver to 'stop at Finnigan's'.

I did not ask The Mister why he wanted to stop at Finnigan's, nor did I ask him not to. At the best of times he wasn't a man whose wishes one felt inclined to frustrate, and he was now alcoholically impervious to suggestion. He had it in mind that he wanted to stop at Finnigan's, and he had nothing else in mind, one concluded. The only information he volunteered was that Finnigan was an old friend of his. 'I knew him when I had but one coat to my back.' It would have been useless to remind him that his dinner-coat awaited him at Mrs O'Donnell's, and that his heavily-enveloped form had been by no means steady on its legs when he emerged from O'Grady's. There was nothing now that I could do except assist him out of the car and steer him through Finnigan's front door, which was open to all-comers, since it was neither more nor less than a village pub. In the bar-parlour about a dozen Irish characters were increasing the sale of malted spirits and jabbering with vehement voices. They welcomed The Mister like one of themselves, and his vague wave of a fur-gloved hand sufficed to signify 'whiskies all round' and a subsequent drinking of The Mister's health. 'Long life to ye, Mister Blarnett,' they chorused, and The Mister's reply was majestic. 'Long life to ye all, and may I never in me grandeur forget that I was born no better than any one of you and me money made in America.' His voice was husky, but the huskiness was not induced by emotion. The air was thick with bad tobacco smoke and I was longing to be back in Limerick, but there was something very touching in the sight of the tipsy old Mister. There he sat in his scarlet coat, nodding his white head and beaming hazily around him, every bit as glad to be among these humble people as he had been in Tom Philipson's fine house. More at home, perhaps, in his heart of hearts, and dimly aware of his youth and those hard times before he went to the States and—Heaven knows how—made, and failed to be swindled out of—his fortune. Kegworthy and I were completely out of the picture (I, because I felt shy, and Kegworthy because he was in a condition verging on stupor). Meanwhile Finnigan, elderly and foxy-faced, leant his elbows on the bar and held forth about the troubled state of the country. 'There'll be houses burnt and lives lost before the year's ended,' he said, 'and you officers, friends of Mr Blarnett's though you be, had better be out of Ireland than in it, if you set value on your skins.' A gruff murmur greeted this utterance, and I took a sip of my whisky, which half-choked me and tasted strong of smoke. But The Mister remained seraphically unperturbed. He rose unsteadily, was helped into his overcoat, and then muttered the following valediction: 'I'd be remaining among you a while longer, boys, but there's company expected at Mrs O'Donnell's, and it's my tuxedo I'll be wearing to-night and the pearl studs to my shirt.' Swaying slightly, he seemed to be collecting his thoughts for a final effort of speech; having done so, he delivered the following cryptic axiom: 'In politics and religion, be pleasant to both sides. Sure, we'll all be dead drunk on the Day of Judgment.' Table-thumpings and other sounds of approval accompanied him as he staggered to the door, having previously emptied all his loose silver into the hand of his old friend Finnigan. During the last stage of the journey he was warblesome, singing to himself in a tenor crooning that seemed to come from a long way off. I entered Mrs O'Donnell's door with one of them on each arm.

Explanations were unnecessary when she met us in the hall. A single glance showed her how the day's hunting had ended. I had brought them back, and they were both of them blind to the world.

This was unfortunate, and should have precluded their presence at the dinner-table. But Mrs O'Donnell had already got herself into a dark green bespangled evening dress and was deciding to be undaunted. I was about to suggest that I should take Kegworthy straight home, when she drew me aside and said in an urgent undertone, 'They've three-quarters of an hour in which to recover themselves. For the love of God make Kegworthy put his head in cold water, and I'll be getting The Mister up to his room.' Her large and competent presence created optimism, so I carried out her instructions and then deposited Kegworthy in the drawing-room. His manner was now muzzily morose, and I couldn't feel any confidence in him as a social asset. Mrs O'Donnell bustled back, and she and I kept up appearances gallantly until Mrs O'Halloran and her daughter were announced. Mrs O'Halloran was what one might call a semi-dowager; the first impression she made on me was one of almost frumpishly constrained dignity, and the impression remained unaltered throughout the evening. She moved in an aura of unhurrying chaperonage and one felt disapproval in the background of her mind. She began by looking very hard at my field boots, whereupon Mrs O'Donnel enlivened the situation with a fluent and even florid account of the day's adventures.

'Miles and miles they went in the wild weather, and the hounds not able to hunt—God be praised for that, for my heart was in my mouth when I thought of The Mister destroying himself over those bogs and boulders on the Mullagharier Mountains. And then what must Clancy's car do but break down twice on the way home and they five miles from anywhere.' Mrs O'Halloran signified her acceptance of the story by a stiff inclination of her head, which was surmounted by two large lacquered combs and an abbreviated plume dyed purple. She herself seemed to have travelled many miles that evening—from the end of the eighteenth century perhaps— drawn over rough roads at a footpace in some lumbering, rumbling family coach. This notion had just crossed my mind when The Mister made his appearance, which was impeccable except for the fact that he was carrying in one hand a glass of something which I assumed to be whisky.

By some Misterish miracle he had recovered his equilibrium—or leguilibrium—and was quite the grand seigneur in his deportment. His only social disadvantage was that he seemed incapable of articulate utterance. Whenever a remark was made he merely nodded like a mandarin. Kegworthy also was completely uncommunicative, but looked less amiable. We followed the ladies into the dining-room, and thus began a dinner which largely consisted of awful silences. At one end of the table sat The Mister; Mrs O'Halloran was to the right of him and Miss O'Halloran was to the left of him. Next to Miss O'Halloran sat me; Mrs O'Donnell, of course, faced The Mister, so Kegworthy's position may be conjectured. He was, beyond all conjecture, sitting beside Mrs O'Halloran.

Mrs O'Donnel and I did all the work. Kegworthy being a non-starter, she talked across him to Mrs O'Halloran, while I made heavy weather with Miss O'Halloran, who relied mainly on a nervous titter, while her mamma relied entirely on monosyllabic decorum. As the meal went on I became seriously handicapped by the fact that I got what is known as 'the giggles'. Every time I looked across at Mrs O'Halloran her heavily powdered face set me off again, and I rather think that Mrs O'Donnell became similarly affected. The Mister only addressed two remarks to Mrs O'Halloran. The first one referred to the European war. 'Tom Philipson was telling me to-day that we should be putting more pressure on Prussia.' Mrs O'Halloran glacially agreed, but it led to nothing further, as her attention was distracted by Kegworthy, who, in attacking a slab of stiff claret jelly, shot a large piece off his plate, chased it with his spoon, and finally put it in his mouth with his fingers. This gave me an excuse to laugh aloud, but Mrs O'Halloran didn't even smile. When the port had been round once The Mister raised his glass and said, with a vague air of something special being expected of him. 'If there's one man in Limerick I esteem, sure to God it's your husband. Long life to Mr O'Halloran.' At this, Kegworthy, who had been looking more morose than ever, made his only audible contribution to the festive occasion.

'Who the hell's O'Halloran?' he enquired. His intonation implied hostility. There was, naturally enough, a ghastly pause in the proceedings. Then Mrs O'Donnell arose and ushered her guests out of the room in good order.

There I sat, and for a long time neither of my companions moved. Closing my eyes, I thought about that dinner-party, and came to the conclusion that it had been funny.

When I opened them again I ascertained that both The Mister and Kegworthy were fast asleep. Nothing more remains to be told, except that soon afterwards I took Kegworthy home and put him to bed.

* * *

On my last day in Ireland I went out in soft sunshiny weather for a final half-day with the hounds. The meet was twelve miles off and I'd got to catch the 4.30 train to Dublin, so I had to keep a sharp eye on my watch. The Mister was mournful about my departure, and anathematized the Egyptians wholeheartedly, for he could't get rid of his notion that it was they who were requiring my services as a soldier. I felt a bit mournful myself as my eyes took in the country with its distant villages and gleams of water, its green fields and white cottages, and the hazy transparent hills on the horizon—sometimes silver-grey and sometimes that deep azure which I'd seen nowhere but in Ireland.

We had a scrambling hunt over a rough country, and I had all the fun I could find, but every stone wall I jumped felt like good-bye for ever to 'this happy breed of men, this little world', in other words the Limerick Hunt, which had restored my faith in my capacity to be heedlessly happy. How kind they were, those friendly fox-hunters, and how I hated leaving them.

At half-past two The Mister and I began to look for Clancy's car, which contained his groom and was to take us home. But the car was on the wrong side of a big covert, and while we were following it, it was following us. Much flustered, we at last succeeded in encountering it, and Clancy drove us back to Mrs O'Donnell's in a wild enthusiastic spurt.

Mrs O'Donnell had a woodcock ready for my tea, and I consumed it in record time. Then there was a mad rush to the station, where my baggage was awaiting me, plus a group of Fusilier friends. The Assistant-Adjutant was at his post, assuring the engine driver that he must on no account start without me, mail-train or no mail-train. With thirty seconds to spare I achieved my undesirable object, and the next thing I knew what that I was leaning out of the carriage window and waving good-bye to them all—waving good-bye to warm-hearted Mrs O'Donnel—waving good-bye to the dear old Mister.

LITTLE FUNKS

The Rising Tide
M. J. Farrell (Molly Keane)
1937

Nearly an hour with nothing to do. An hour feeling quite cold with rather a nasty taste in your mouth before Mummy came down, Mummy in her iron-dark habit and little tight pieces of hair like flat, netted coins under her velvet cap, Mummy, so brisk and hard and clean, picking up her white gloves and her whip in the hall and shouting for the terrier that was to go in the car with them, on the edge of being very angry if he had gone off rabbiting. But Diana had shut him in the car already so that he couldn't. They were glad she was hunting to-day. She often helped them when they were in trouble and never told if she saw them avoiding a stone wall.

Simon ran stiffly across the gravel, its little knobs frozen solid under his feet, to open the gate with a wreath of ice on its bars and latch. Crouching under rugs in the back of the car, he shared with Susan a period that was blank except for that slight, persistent feeling of nausea. They did not seem to belong to their own bodies at all. Those large hands in string gloves were strange people's hands. They crossed and uncrossed their legs clumsily as if they were wooden legs. They did not mind about each other, each feeling that the other was better equipped to contend with its beastly pony. Susan remembered that Simon's Dinty was much easier to sit on over a wall than her own Mouse, and Simon remembered that Susan was much more adhesive over any sort of fly fence than he was. Each felt that the other was less to be pitied and each longed for the end of the day with an ardour which saw such a month away at least.

They looked at the fields and the fences as they drove past them, seeing them with a curious relationship of fear and not fear. The fields were not ordinary fields and in summer. They were places you had to get out of, that you were inexorably carried over. That field now, with green plover waddling and pecking about on its dark, sheep-bitten turf, was a dreadfully unkind field with wire on its nice round banks and as cruel a coped stone wall across one side of it as a frightened child could face. The very young may be sick with cowardice about a fence but they are more afraid not to jump it than to jump it. Then there might be a wide, benignant field with an open gateway in a corner, or a ditch full of dark, cold water, but only a low bank in front of it, very heartening. It was not soft falls in water or bog that they dreaded, but that shameful, hurting, falling off and the moments before you fell, their agony seeming to endure in interminable uncertainty before you went with a sort of sob and the ground hit you from behind, strangely like a house falling on you, not you falling on a house.

Their ponies were waiting for them at the meet, looking hard and unkind and as if they would gallop and jump for weeks without ever being tired or ceasing to pull like bulls in those round, smooth snaffles. Cynthia liked the children's ponies to look fit and well and they were beautifully turned out, their tails pulled to the last hair and their manes plaited up. They eyed them for a moment with hatred from the car before they remembered to get out and fuss over them as keen, sporting children should.

'Thought we should hardly hunt coming along,' Richit said; his face looked red and blue and his eyes were as pale as a jackdaw's under the peak of his cap. You could not possibly have mistaken his mouth for the mouth of any one but a hunt servant.

'We'll hunt, all right,' Cynthia stood among the hounds, digging the heel of her boot into the grass at the side of the road. The smell of the hounds' bodies was like a warm, low cloud round her. She looked at the list of hounds Richit handed to her, and when he said, 'The north side of the fences will be like iron,' she did not answer.

'I shall have some lame hounds coming home to-night,' he said after a pause. The fact was, Richit was scarcely more anxious to hunt to-day than Simon and Susan. He hated his first horse and his piles had been giving him great trouble. Cynthia guessed about the horse though not about the piles. She went over to the public-house at the cross-roads and sent him out a double Irish whiskey. She and Diana drank a glass of disgusting port each.

'Isn't it filthy? Cynthia said, 'I suppose I'd better have another.'

The children visited a field before they mounted their ponies. When they had mounted they wished to visit the field again but hardly liked to. Their insides were most unsteady. Presently they were on the steep hill beside the covert, with that wall standing up very dark and tall at the foot of the hill. The covert was on the left-hand side of the field. They could only see the very edge of it. There was a steep lime-kiln, grey and white like the sky, and the gorse bushes appeared to be navy blue in the cold morning.

Their ponies fiddled about and tore up mouthfuls of grass and smelt other horses and screamed and then stood very still, galvanically still, with their heads up, gazing into the blue gorse bushes as though longing to see a fox. Once a hound came out under Dinty's tail and was kicked. Cynthia was on the other side of the covert and they hoped she did not hear the hideous noise it made. They were supposed to know most of the hounds and they wished they could remember the name of this one but they could not. A man they did not know said, 'Do the brute good.' He looked at them in a friendly way and said, 'She's all right, you hardly touched her. Cowardly, that's what it is. So am I.' They found this rather an embarrassing remark so did not answer. They did not have time really, for at that moment one of those hunting cries that are supposed to excite hounds and horsemen to a perfect fever pitch of determination and endeavour split the cold air with awful clarity. They gathered up their reins and looked wildly down towards the stone wall. Their ponies stood like trembling rocks about to hurl themselves over the edge of an abyss.

Then the strange man who had been looking up over the hill did a queer thing. He turned his horse round and galloped up the hill and away from the wall. Simon and Susan looked at each other. He couldn't be right. Foxes always went away at the bottom of the covert. The field always had to jump the wall. But still they whirled their ponies round and hurried up the hill after the cowardly stranger. He had jumped a little bank into the top corner of the covert, squeezed through a gorse-filled corner and was out in the field beyond. Screaming to each other to get out of the way, they followed.

From your point of view when you are a child a hunt is purely a question of obstacles and not falling off. It is a good hunt for Irish children if there are no high walls or pieces of timber and if you are not quite last in the chase, and if straggling hounds keep out of your pony's way, because in any case you can't stop. Susan and Simon were often borne along for miles with tears pouring down their faces, and every one said how much they were enjoying themselves and how well they went for children of their age. And it is the best sort of hunt of all if it is short, with a long dig at the end of it.

To-day that breathless moment of cowardice which had given them determination enough to turn their backs on the stone wall and follow the strange man out through the top of the covert put them in a surprisingly commanding position in the hunt, for any one who knew the covert was of the same opinion as they had been, as to the direction in which foxes usually left it. So for some time the stranger, the first whip and Simon and Susan clattered over the country in rather grand isolation with the hounds.

Susan's pony elected to follow the whip's horse. As his horse changed feet on the bank, Mouse took off and sprang up behind him, arriving in the next field just a second late and just mathematically without a collision. The first whip was an unimaginative boy and riding a steady and solid cob, he did not mind. But it was another matter for the stranger, who was riding a sketchy sort of hireling, to have Simon just missing the small of his back at every leap. He tried saying 'Not so close, old man,' and 'Take a pull, child,' but he soon saw that no admonition could have any effect, and at each mistake his hireling made he resigned himself to the worst and was mildly surprised not to find himself on the ground with Simon and his pony and the hireling all on top of him together.

In the end it was one of those tiresome, straggling hounds that caused all the trouble. The stranger, with misplaced consideration and *ésprit de chasse*, waited for it to scramble over a fence and the delay was just too long for Simon's pony. As the now rather weary hireling leaped, so did he, they met with a tremendous impact, and the hireling, without making the smallest effort to reassemble its forces, fell out on its head in the next field. Simon's pony staggered, recovered himself and jumped off the bank straight on top of the stranger whom he kicked in the head and clouted in the ribs before he galloped away in pursuit of Susan and the first whip. Simon, in the confusion and shock, had fallen off.

Cynthia was very upset about it, although pleased that Simon had been going well enough to knock David Colebrook off a fence and jump on him, and concuss him. She knew the stranger better by reputation than her children did or they might have faced the wall in preference to pursuing him through the country. As it was, he was put into the car and driven back to Rathglass and put to bed. The blinds were pulled down and his ribs were strapped up by the doctor.

The chidren were told they could only stay out to see one more covert drawn as they would have to hack home. Owing to their carelessness in nearly killing a famous jockey and spoiling Mummy's day hunting, there was not room for them in the car. They expressed suitable regret and then how they prayed that the covert might be blank. They prayed like anything. Their prayer was granted, too, because Richit was not very keen about hunting to-day either, so when they got back to a road they were able to turn their ponies' heads towards home almost before two o'clock.

That was a good day. They stopped at the pub and bought themselves ginger biscuits and ginger beer. Their insides felt marvellously steady and glowing again. It was not like one of those dreadful evenings when a court of inquiry was held over their failures as they sat in the back of the car and Cynthia shot questions at them over her shoulder all the way home: questions that always caught you out somewhere.

'Susan, how did your pony jump the wall near Lara Wood?'

Susan cast wildly about in her mind, how had she been so fortunate as to escape that wall?

'Jumped it well,' she might say.

'And didn't shift you?'

'No, I was all right.'

'And how did you get on, Simon?'

Simon said cautiously, 'I almost fell off.'

'But not quite? I see. Well, I think it's a pity you should tell lies as well as being little funks because I saw you both going through a gate.'

They felt ill with shame.

Then there were the Bad Scenting Days when she got behind them and beat their ponies over places when they stopped, knowing exactly where their riders' hearts were. And whether they fell off or did not fall off, they were certain they were going to, which is acute mental strain and agony.

Cynthia, too, minded dreadfully that they should be such pale, uncourageous children, these children of hers and Desmond's. Why could they not love hunting and dogs and ratting and badger digging and their ponies, as all right-minded children should, instead of having to be compelled and encouraged to take their parts in these sports and pleasures? The moments when she said to people, 'Simon? I think he's digging out a rat in the wood,' or, 'schooling his pony for the gymkhana,' or 'looking for a snipe's nest,' and all the time knew that he was playing the piano in the schoolroom or drawing one of those hideous, left-handed pictures, so unspeakably like Susan or Diana or the sewing-maid were really bitter moments for her. She did not love her children but she was determined not to be ashamed of them. You had to feel ashamed and embarrassed if your children did not take keenly to blood-sports, so they must be forced into them. It was right. It was only fair to them. You could not bring a boy up properly unless he rode and fished and shot. What sort of boy was he? What sort of friends would he have?

HOLIDAYS AT ALCONLEIGH

The Pursuit of Love
Nancy Mitford
1945

The next day we all went out hunting. The Radletts loved animals, they loved foxes, they risked dreadful beatings in order to unstop their earths, they read and cried and rejoiced over Reynard the Fox, in summer they got up at four to go and see the cubs playing in the pale-green light of the woods; nevertheless, more than anything in the world, they loved hunting. It was in their blood and bones and in my blood and bones, and nothing could eradicate it, though we knew it for a kind of original sin. For three hours that day I forgot everything except my body and my pony's body; the rushing, the scrambling, the splashing, struggling up the hills, sliding down them again, the tugging, the bucketing, the earth, and the sky. I forgot everything, I could hardly have told you my name. That must be the great hold that hunting has over people, especially stupid people; it enforces an absolute concentration, both mental and physical.

After three hours Josh took me home. I was never allowed to stay out long or I got tired and would be sick all night. Josh was out on Uncle Matthew's second horse; at about two o'clock they changed over, and he started home on the lathered, sweating first horse, taking me with him. I came out of my trance, and saw that the day, which had begun with brilliant sunshine, was now cold and dark, threatening rain.

'And where's her ladyship hunting this year?' said Josh, as we started on a ten-mile jog along the Merlinford road, a sort of hog's back, more cruelly exposed than any road I have ever known, without a scrap of shelter or windscreen the whole of its fifteen miles. Uncle Matthew would never allow motor-cars, either to take us to the meet or to fetch us home; he regarded this habit as despicably soft.

I knew that Josh meant my mother. He had been with my grandfather when she and her sisters were girls, and my mother was his heroine, he adored her.

'She's in Paris, Josh.'

'In Paris—what for?'

'I suppose she likes it.'

'Ho,' said Josh, furiously, and we rode for about half a mile in silence. The rain had begun, a thin cold rain, sweeping over the wide views on each side of the road; we trotted along, the weather in our faces. My back was not strong, and trotting on a side-saddle for any length of time was agony to me. I edged my pony on to the grass, and cantered for a bit, but I knew how much Josh disapproved of this, it was supposed to bring the horses back too hot; walking, on the other hand chilled them. It had to be jog, jog, back-breaking jog, all the way.

'It's my opinion,' said Josh at last, 'that her ladyship is wasted, downright wasted, every minute of her life that she's not on a 'oss.'

'She's a wonderful rider, isn't she?'

I had had all this before from Josh, many times, and could never have enough of it.

'There's no human being like her, that I've ever seen,' said Josh, hissing through his teeth. 'Hands like velvet, but strong like iron, and her seat—! Now look at you, jostling about on that saddle, first here, then there—we shall have a sore back to-night, that's one thing certain we shall.'

'Oh Josh—trotting. And I'm so tired.'

'Never saw her tired. I've seen 'er change 'osses after a ten-mile point, get on to a fresh young five-year-old what hadn't been out for a week—up like a bird—never know you had 'er foot in your hand, pick up the reins in a jiffy, catch up its head, and off and over a post and rails and bucking over the ridge and furrow, sitting like a rock. Now his lordship (he meant Uncle Matthew) he can ride, I don't say the contrary, but look how he sends his 'osses home, so darned tired they can't drink their gruel. He can ride all right, but he doesn't study his 'oss. I never knew your mother bring them home like this, she'd know when they'd had enough, and then heads for home and no looking back. Mind you, his lordship's a great big man, I don't say the contrary, rides every bit of sixteen stone, but he has great big 'osses and half kills them, and then who has to stop up with them all night? Me!'

The rain was pouring down by now. An icy trickle was feeling its way past my left shoulder, and my right boot was slowly filing with water, the pain in my back was like a knife. I felt that I couldn't bear another moment of this misery, and yet I knew I must bear another five miles, another forty minutes. Josh gave me scornful looks as my back bent more and more double; I could see that he was wondering how it was that I could be my mother's child.

'Miss Linda,' he said, 'takes after her ladyship something wonderful.'

At last, at last, we were off the Merlinford road, coming down the valley into Alconleigh village, turning up the hill to Alconleigh house, through the lodge gates, up the drive, and into the stable yard. I got stiffly down, gave the pony to one of Josh's stable boys, and stumped away, walking like an old man.

RUFUS

Wild Lone
Denys Watkins-Pitchford
1947

That afternoon, the fourteenth of November, Rufus had been lying in Clint Hill spinney. The night before he had killed a rabbit on the Brixworth road, that had been maimed by a passing car and could not get away. He had taken it into a field and eaten his fill, burying the rest close to a manure heap. Then he had gone off to Clint Hill to sleep off the effects of his meal. He was aware of the hounds in good time, but not before the whipper-in marked him away from the east corner. His meal had long been digested and he was in good trim, even though he limped slightly from his maimed foot. He went first to the railway, crossed it, and ran into Cottesbrook Park. Here, in the spinney, he tried an earth he knew well and found it stopped, so he turned right for Blueberry and with eight fields in hand, went into the thickets between the double mounds. There were two other foxes in Blueberry, but somehow or other hounds, when they came up, still held their original line, and when Rufus left the spinney they were on his heels only five fields away, and short fields at that.

Rufus ran to Robins' farm, and as no one was about, went into the yard and rolled in the manure heap. This was a dodge he had learnt in one of his previous runs, and it served to give him a breathing space. Hounds checked for five minutes at the foil. In that time he slipped away at an easy pace for Coldhangar and tried the earth under the rhododendrons . . . But that too was stopped.

Still with a good lead, he made for Maidwell Dales, and the scuttering moor-hens told of his passage through the reeds. Skirting Penny Plain and the lane where he encountered the gipsies, he went across to Hopping Hill. Here he was seen by a roadmender and a passing motorist, who stopped to see the fun. He crossed the road and ran up the brook towards Draughton. He began to feel weary so he lay up in the reeds of a little field pond. He waited for such a long time that a water-rat came out of the bank and sat on a little platform of withered sedges, nibbling a green shoot. Rufus, muddied and tired, watched it through his cunning slits, one ear still upright like a shark's fin. After a while it slipped off into the water and a ring under the farther bank told Rufus the rat had gone to earth. Then followed an uneventful pause, in which rooks cawed sleepily and a distant train went puffing up the valley.

About ten yards away, in the red-berried hedge, was a tall dead tree, struck and riven by lightning one summer night long years ago. To this tree a wood-pigeon came and sat for a long while on a dead splinter, puffed out into a grey ball. Then it began to crane its neck about and finally launched itself into space and came to a clappering landing on the margin of the little pond about five feet from where Rufus lay, hidden in the reeds. It waddled down to the water, after a good look round, and plunged its beak right in, not sipping like other birds, but drinking greedily with submerged bill. After taking its fill, it sat a moment, rather puffily and with raised crest, then flew heavily back to the tree, where it started to preen. All the while Rufus watched it, but his ears were alert to catch the faintest sound of pursuit.

On the dead bough, the pigeon turned and fanned its tail, working its soft broad bill round the root. Then it lifted its left wing and preened vigorously until a tiny speck of blue fluff floated down and lit with a gentle kiss on the weedy water.

Far away a song-thrush started to sing . . . 'Puwee, Puwee, Puwee. . . . Chip-uuuu, Chip-uuuu, Chip-uuuu' . . . and the pure notes sounded like a fairy flute. Redwings passed over, and some, arresting their flight, dived down with closed wings on to the dead tree. Up the hedge Rufus saw a rabbit hopping along, among some very pale green crab apples. It squeezed through the hedge and vanished. And still Rufus did not stir. Something told him he was being followed. . . .

On the other side of the little pond, its massive girth hidden in a welter of red berries of hips and haws, was a splendid oak tree. In this sheltered hollow, the frosts had miraculously spared the leaves and the foliage was still thick, almost green near the base. The upper part of the tree had turned a lovely amber colour here and there, but it would be some weeks yet before all its leave would fall. This tree seemed so splendidly sturdy and strong, so well grown and rich, and clusters of appetising acorns peeped from between the thick clumps of leaves. Over a generation it had grown in that spot, sown by a passing bird, dead now these many years. Season after season it had grown, pushing its way upwards through the tangling undergrowth, and much had happened in that time. In its early life the railway had come stealing up the valley, with the sound of shovels and picks at work, and later the first train, puffing and panting up the slope. Rooks were feeding on the acorns now, shaking the thick boughs as they feasted greedily, and several wood-pigeons had visited it in the early part of the afternoon.

The rooks were far too busy stuffing themselves to notice the advent of Rufus, and now he was lying well screened in the rusting reed spears by the water's edge. 'Caw, caw,' said the rooks, and now and then an acorn would come tumbling down, some falling with a loud plop into the pond and sending widening rings shaking to the weeds. Soon an aeroplane passed over, very high, and droning like a bee. Up there a man was sitting in a frail cockpit, removed from this world below, where a tired fox lay panting by a little pond and blue-shot rooks were feeding on the acorns. He did not even see the moving specks of red and black coming up to the gorse. Almost a disembodied spirit, the pilot flew on towards the east.

One by one the rooks left the oak tree and flew away, until there were only five left. These soon all left together with many caws, and glided down on a stubble field, three meadows away, where some partridges were moving, like brown slugs, over the stubbly ochre spikes.

Rufus, lying still in the reeds, noted all these things, even the aeroplane. He watched the latter come into a small square of sky that showed between the reed spaces, and pass resolutely across, like a steady flying gnat— indeed, he thought it was one. And then the pigeon on the dead tree ceased to preen. It was drawing itself up, and no longer sat bunched up, with its pink toes hidden by soft fluff. A wood-pigeon has sharp eyes, and can see a long way, nearly a mile, and now it was watching something very intently, away on the other side of the line. Its body seemed to become thinner and thinner, and then with one last look, it left the dead bough and flew away. For a second or two the dead branch rocked to and fro—one two, one two, one two—and then became static.

Rufus heard the pigeon take wing from the dead branch, and the redwings flew upwards and away on enviable wings into the soft grey sky. He heard, above his pumping heart, the hounds speaking to his trail and the clatter of the cavalcade as they crossed the metals. So he slipped out of the reeds and went up the ditch by the crab apples. He squeezed through the same place as the rabbit, and followed its trail until he reached a bramble brake. Clinging to the spined thicket were some rose-red leaves, and long yellow grass grew up between the raking branches. Rufus turned aside here, and went up the slope of a little hill, where some sheep were grazing. He was heading now for Scaldwell Wood, but the long climb from the valley had winded him, and he was feeling the effects of his maimed paw. No longer did he slip along at an easy lope, and his tongue was hanging.

Five fields away the hounds came up the ditch past the little pond. They had smelt the spot where Rufus had lain, and they went yelling up the ditch, scattering the rusty leaves. From the bramble brake the rabbit rushed, pursued for some yards by one of the young entry, who got the crack of a whip lash in his ear to teach him not to riot. Then they took the line at a fast pace up the hill, checking a little when they came to the sheep.

Meanwhile, Rufus, tiring still, crossed the Draughton road into Lamport Park. And then he did a cunning thing. He first made a dead line for Scaldwell spinney, and when within a hundred yards, he back trailed for about fifty, and scrambled up into the oak tree where he used to kennel. It was not long before the sounds of pursuit came to his ears. The hounds appeared across the park, materialising like magic out of the shrubs and coming at a great pace across the withered winter sward. They swirled round the tree in a torrent and carried on for Scaldwell

Wood. The Huntsman naturally thought he had gone there, though hounds began to falter a little on the outskirts of the spinney. Now the park was dotted with riders and a man dismounted close to the oak and tightened up the horse's girth. He could smell the sweaty horse and man beneath the tree. Then the man mounted again and walked slowly off to join some more riders that stood their restless mounts about fifty yards distant.

Rufus could hear the horn blowing its sad music in the wood, and hounds were now silent. He prayed that another fox might be there, but the spinney was deserted and hounds came filtering out of the tides, noses to ground, completely at fault. In a moment the hounds would be brought back and then the game would be up. Rufus took a furtive peep and saw the horsemen had their backs to him. They were talking, and one was smoking a cigarette, which showed he was not a good sportsman. Rufus slipped down a sloping branch and dropped to the ground as light as an autumn leaf. He was half-way across the park and nearly into a holly plantation, when a boy, standing on the wall that bordered the park, saw him and gave the halloa!

Very soon he heard the hound voices again, speaking to his trail, and a leaden weight seemed to drag upon his feet. Straining for air, for more air, his back began to arch, and from his lolling pink tongue little drops of saliva dripped off into the grass, and flecked his muddied coat. Everywhere eyes seemed to mark his passage, and to point the way he had fled. The lodge-keeper by the grey-lichened gates bearing their noble swans saw him crossing the park. He ran past the long, many-windowed house, with its family thoughts graven for ever on the weathered stone . . . 'In things transitory resteth no Glory' . . . and the windows were aflame with sunset, yellow and vivid, shining through the autumn trees. He crossed the winding drive, brushing lightly through the amber leaves that lay in great drifts under the breeches, and chaffinches flew up to the lower branches, white-barred wings showing vividly. They sat and 'pinked' at Rufus until he dived into the box bushes.

Hounds were gaining on him now, gaining, yes, gaining . . . When he crossed the main road they were only a few hundred yards behind, and horsemen were already coming out of the lodge gates and galloping along the turf at the side of the road. The schoolchildren were coming home and they saw Rufus cross. The air became shrill with their excited cries.

Below him the valley fell away to the brook and the yellow sunset was flashing in some flood water. Night was not so far distant, and already the pigeon hosts were streaming across to roost in Hieaway. Wearily Rufus turned along the ridge, and as he did so the last gleam of sunlight was shut out. There were a lot of bramblings and chaffinches feeding in the branch mast and they flew up in waves as he loped through them.

There stood Marly church; he could see it now, and the thick belt of trees that told of Wildwoods, and thither he ran, slower now and slower, so that the Huntsman viewed him. Down the valley now, where the going was easier, across the brook, where he stopped a moment to lap greedily and bathe his poor tired feet. Then on again up the gentle slope to the garden of Wildwoods. He saw the reek of a bonfire, and something made him turn for it; the pungent smoke might foil the hounds.

And that is where Pamela, watching from the long windows saw him—a hunted, beaten fox at his last gasp. She did not know (how could she?) that it was the selfsame fox that she had rescued from starvation in Coldhangar so long ago. Had she known, the fluttering farewell of the lime tree leaves might have had a more subtle significance. . . .

He went past the stables, slipped, unseen by the busy chauffeur, into the kitchen garden, and down through the cabbages into the field. Six fields away was Hieaway, and there was an earth that offered sanctuary. . . . If it was not stopped. But could he do it? It had been a seven-mile point and Rufus was almost done. Only a quarter of the field was up now, and the rest were jogging home. On! On! On! There had been a time before when those dark fir trees offered shelter and he had only just made it. But then he had to climb the hill; now it was on the same ridge.

Some cattle came blowing after him and actually stamped round him with tossing heads and rolling eyes. The smell of them might have checked the hounds, but he was viewed by the Huntsmen, and was as good as lost. He MUST make Hieaway . . . he MUST.

Four fields . . . three fields . . . two, one . . . and he was still ahead of the leading hound, though not twenty yards separated them in the last burst.

Rufus, his hard life and training standing him in good stead, made on final burst of speed. If this failed he was lost. His brush was raised and his back no longer arched; it was the last great effort. He gained the hedge with the jaws of Orator not a foot behind, and once through the binders of the thorns the hound was at a disadvantage. The lissom little prey could slip in between the thick underbrush. Rufus dragged himself up to the earth. It was open . . . the earth where he had been born.

He went down, slowly.

The little pine-needled hill was alive with hounds and men. Under the dark firs and sombre shadows the pink coats sang out in vivid spots of colour, and the white breeches of the dismounted men were the most vivid spots of all. A woodman in leather apron and a bill-hook in his hand came up over the mound.

'Aye, I seed 'im goo to groun' under this 'ere tree, I reckon 'e's the one-eared ole fox that's been plaguing us for weeks past.'

The Huntsman frowned. He would have liked to have left Rufus in peace, but like Pilate, he had to respect the people. If he was to leave this fox, the Hunt would get a bad name for letting them go free and that would mean foxes being shot. And yet . . . there was only a little time left, folly to start digging now. But hedge caffender was anxious and pleading, so the terrier was sent for, a sturdy little beast with a black saddle, and the pluck of Rufus himself.

The second whipper-in came up through the darkling trees with a couple of spades, and the terrier was pushed into the hole. He went down, excitedly, scrabbling the red earth. The second whipper-in lay with his ear to the ground, listening, but he could hear nothing. There was a hushed silence then, and the dark trees seemed to shut out most of the lingering light.

From the wood, riders began to move slowly away, talking and chattering excitedly, for it had been a great run. But a few still remained; some dismounted and stood by their tired horses.

All the birds in Hieaway were very silent, not a robin piped nor a wren scolded. Gravely watching the scene through half-closed eyes was the old owl in his big tree, who had first seen Rufus as a wee cub, playing with his fir-cones on the sandy bank.

Soon there was a rushing noise and a great cloud of wood-pigeons circled round. But they were afraid to come in to roost for they saw the floor of the wood alive with hounds and men. Some of the hounds sat down on their haunches, watching the earth, others wandered about the wood looking rather bored.

At the foot of the great pine sprawled the whipper-in. He had taken off his velvet hunting cap and his hair was wet with sweat. Now there was a muffled yapping deep below under the pine, and the sound of battle, thumps and snarls. In a short while the terrier came out slowly backwards, his stump of a tail tight between his legs and his face bloody. In vain did the whipper-in urge him to enter the earth again; for the first and last time in his life the terrier had met his match.

Then the men started to dig. The whipper-in took off his coat and the woodman did likewise, and they toiled under the pine root. Slowly it got darker and the last horseman trotted away from the wood.

'Well, try and get him out,' said the Huntsman. 'It's my belief you'll find him dead. I think the terrier has killed him.'

The whipper-in shook his head. 'I don't think so; look at his tail. I've never known him to put his tail down when he's killed a fox.'

'Well, do your best. You can't have much further to dig.'

The men went on digging until a great scar was cut across the root of the tree, and the whipper-in was almost hidden by the mount of red soil.

The Huntsman called the disappointed hounds, and they trailed away, one by one, into the shadows. Only the terrier remained, hind legs shivering, and growling quietly at unpleasant memories. Though he tried now and again to help the toiling man, he would not venture down into the hole.

Down by the gate a horse whinnied for the whipper-in, and champed grass between clinking bit. Carrion crows, like a cloud of evil spirits, circled the wood, cawing hoarsely, for they dared not come in to roost.

'Phew, I sweat!' The hedge caffender passed his brown knotted hand across his forehead and clumsily came out of the excavation. 'You 'ave a goo, mate. We'll 'ave 'im afore long, 'e can't be much furder in, the b—r.' But the spade gashed a great root and made a scar like blood upon it, so fierce had been the blow. 'Ah, that's why the tarrier couldn't get at 'im proper . . . We'll never get 'im outer this now.'

And sure enough, the mighty pine root was like a great hawser, barring the way to the digging men. The whipper-in tossed the spade out of the hole and it slithered a little way down the sand. He reached for his coat and put it on. He tried to brush some of the soil from his white breeches, for they were a sorry sight and would take hours to clean.

'Reckon we'll 'ave to let him be; Corfield'll catch it from the Master for this, 'e was told to stop this earth. . . . Anyway, 'e was a game 'un.' . . . They went off down the bank.

Now the carrions began to circle the wood again, cawing, cawing in the quiet. Then they all came in to roost, clumsily flapping in the topmost oak branches. Some low-flying pigeons came and went straight into the tangled shadow of the pine tops.

The wood had been raped of its peace and it would take some time to recover. In the burries and under the brambles the rabbits still cowered; birds were watchful in the thick bushes.

A lovely silence fell upon this sombre place. The huge pine stood, with the fresh scarred earth at its root, and the signs of ugly man all about. Hound droppings soiled the rusty leaves, and there was a torn Woodbine packet under the hollies. What a peace, this, after the bustle and turmoil of the last few hours!

The old owl flitted from his hollow tree and glided away, and a minute later his quavering cry floated up to the mound.

In the tops of the pines the night wind was crooning so softly—'Rush, rush, rush'— as though it would lull all its pitiful little woodland people to a never-ending sleep.

The first stars began to wink over the valley and one peeped down through the crevices of the dark interlacing branches.

And still, in the Hieaway firs . . . that sleepy surf of sound.

It is quiet now in the kennels save for the whimper of a sleeping hound or the rustle or straw on the benches as a dream-ridden leg thrusts spasmodically.

It is quiet also in the stables and in the dwellings of mankind. Strange this stilling of movement, this closing of eyes! Magical slumber, magical silences!

Such a short while ago all these actors in the past drama were afire with movement and life.

Where now the blackbirds that ran upon the lawn before the windows of Wildwoods, where the rooks, busy among the fruitful oak branches by the leaf-strewn pond?

Even the great cities are strangely muted and dimmed, the humming in the hive is low.

There is a waiting for the light, for the sun again. The birds and animals sleep as insects sleep in the chinks of a wintry tree, and even the astonishing brain of man comes under this magic spell, and reason yaws like a rudderless ship among the troubled seas of dreams.

The Hunstsman sleeps, on his back and snoring; the whipper-in is busy with fox phantoms, muttering to himself.

Buried deep within many walls the Master sleeps, and only a mouse is awake in his dressing-room, gnawing the woodwork under a wardrobe.

Old Bumpus, in flannel night-shirt, is playing a steady solo on the nosoon, an alarm clock to keep him monotonous company.

Under the cold sky and keen sweet airs the dark hump of Hieaway is still breathing; it seems that even the trees are dreaming.

Yet there is one that sleepeth not.

See! a shadow comes stealing from the skirts of the firs and goes, noiselessly, down into the valley fields, limping slightly with the old limp, one ear erect like a shark's fin.

OUT WITH THE COOLMORE HARRIERS

Major E. J. Tonson Rye
1950

I had come to Ireland to hunt. Jim Tennant, an old friend, had mounted me well, sport had been excellent, and I had made several friends among the local people.

Hacking home one evening, I met one of these, Jim Leary, a sporting old rascal, who knew the run of every fox and the position of every earth in the country.

'Wouldn't you come out for a day with the Harriers next Sunday, Major?' he asked. 'There'll be grand sport and plenty of lepping; 'tis better than the foxhounds.'

Inquiries elicited that the Harriers were a trencher-fed pack kept by some farmers and hunted by a priest.

'They're a nuisance,' said Jim. 'They seldom kill a fox, but they disturb the covers. However, everybody has a good time, and at least it shows a love of hunting.'

Two o'clock on Sunday afternoon found me clad in breeches and stockings at Carrig Bridge, where a large gathering was already assembled to meet the hounds.

The priest, mounted on a big, raking grey horse which looked as if it could gallop, stood surrounded by an imposing throng. The hounds, which arrived with their owners, were almost swamped in the crowd of traps, cyclists, and people on foot. They were the native Irish hounds, known as Kerry beagles, black and tan in colour, slower than their English cousins, but with a beautiful cry.

The mounted portion of the field rode horses that ranged from the cart mare clipped trace high, to shaggy and leggy three-year-olds, none of them hunters, but all of them able to hunt.

It was not long before Jim Leary discovered me.

'Is it on foot you are, Major?' he inqured. 'Yerra you had a right to bring a horse; it isn't much sport ye'll be seeing on yer feet. Wait a while now till I see what I can do.' He departed into the crowd, but a few minutes later I felt his hand pluck my sleeve.

'I have Tomeen Sullivan's mare got for you,' he croaked. There was a distinct smell of whisky on his breath. 'She's a grand mare to lep. He's away in Cork himself, but his boy, Bat, is after throwing a saddle on her.' His voice became more confidential. 'You wouldn't miss a ten-shilling note to the poor lad. His boots is broke this six months past, and Tomeen is that crabbed he wouldn't give him the price of a new pair.'

The conspiratorial atmosphere of the proceeding, and the roguish twinkle in his eye proved irresistible, and a few moments later I was in a small and dirty yard behind the largest public-house in the village.

A low corrugated iron shed ran along one side and from this emerged a red-headed untidy youth leading a narrow, long-tailed, chestnut mare up to about as much weight as would go by parcel post for sixpence. Close behind bounded a dog, a cross between a setter and a collie, and in colour adequately described by the Irish adjective 'foxy.'

'Get a hold of that fella, Bat,' warned Jim. 'The mistress is after shutting him up what way the hounds wouldn't catch him.'

It was too late. Excited by the noise and the crowd, the dog fled through the open door.

'No matter,' said Bat, with a shrug, 'he'll be back. That one won't go far from his dinner.'

Pressing ten shillings into Bat's hand, I mounted the chestnut and sidled out of the yard to follow the hunt. We clattered down a lane and cantered across two fields to the first cover, a vast expanse of brown, tussocky grass, interspersed with pools of stagnant water and dwarf furze bushes. The foot followers moved in line and encouraged the fox to break by their incessant chatter.

In a few minutes a hound spoke, and soon the whole pack were feathering on the line. They carried it over a stone wall, and then there was a deep burst of music. A shrill yell came from a man standing on a bank about five fields away. His arm showed which way the fox had gone, and in a second we were all riding hell-for-leather after the hounds.

The chestnut mare made up in spirit what she lacked in bone. In spite of my twelve stone six she rocketed like a pheasant over the first obstacle, a three-foot stone wall, and the speed at which she charged the solid stone-faced bank which followed brought my heart to my mouth.

Then came two grass banks, a rough patch of heather, a boggy field, and the first burst was over. The hounds had checked at the edge of a rocky, sedgy wilderness half a mile square—a jungle of gorse and thorn bushes which sloped down the side of a hill to a boggy stream.

Gone to ground, I thought, but a whimper came from the hidden depths below. 'Hark, hark!' roared his reverance, doubling his horn. Away on the farther side of the stream came a blood-curdling screech. Then babel broke forth as the hounds, converging from every quarter, flung themselves shrieking on the line.

We started to scramble and slither down a rough cattle track. The chestnut mare went straight up on her hind legs and dropped again with a bound into the middle of a gorse bush. Maddened by the prickles, and by the shouts of the men who thundered behind us, she bolted down the muddy track, cannoning into the broad quarters of his reverence's grey, which was making a sedate descent. She crashed through a thorn bush, cleared a boggy-looking pool, and rushed at the stream as if she would take it in her stride.

I did all in my power to steady her, but it was useless. The take-off was bad and I felt her sink down to her hocks as she rose at the ten feet of swirling water. For a second I saw the stream below, then a veil of water sprang up, blinding me. The mare's head disappeared, and I felt an icy shock as the water closed over me.

By some miracle I did not leave the saddle. The mare plunged wildly, striving to get her feet. She lurched against the opposite bank, and instinct prompted me to throw myself off. Water poured from me in streams but I still held the reins.

With the assistance of two foot-followers I led the mare down to a ford. A thin trickle of blood ran down the inside of her near foreleg and she was lame.

'Ah, sure 'tis only a prod from a thorn,' said my guide, in an effort to cheer me.

'Is it Tomeen Sullivan's mare you have?' he went on. 'Isn't it a quare thing the way he let you have the loan of her so aisy? It's planning to win the Ladies' Hacks class at the Cork Show he is. Sure, any other day of the week he wouldn't let the mare out of his sight. He's looking for great money for her from some English lady.'

This was indeed bad news. What on earth was I going to say to Mr Sullivan when I met him, or, worse still, what was Mr Sullivan going to say to me?

By this time I was back in the lane. Away in the distance came the sound of the horn. Then the wind brought the deep, melodious cry of the hounds. The fox must have turned.

We stopped and the men climbed on the bank. An excited exclamation drew my attention. 'Look at him over in the field below. Whist now but he's turning; get down off that bank what way you wouldn't head him.'

Through a gap I caught a glimpse of a reddish-brown form. Its appearance was unusual and it seemed to have no brush. As it scuttled on to the road I recognised Tomeen Sullivan's foxy dog, tail clamped tight between his legs.

It was going for home at full speed and the leading hounds were close behind. The pack crashed through the brambles on the bank and were down in the road hunting to view.

I saw the dog dart into the yard and the door slammed shut with the hounds not ten yards behind. At the same moment a large red-faced man leapt from a motor car and began to wave his arms and shout at the hounds. Tomeen Sullivan, I thought, home early from Cork.

Instinct told me that this would not be a suitable moment to make his acquaintance. Extracting a sodden note from my pocket, I pressed it into the hand of my guide. 'My car is here,' I said. 'Would you please take this horse home, and tell Mr Sullivan that I will be round to see him in a day or two.'

Jim Tennant arranged the meeting when things had returned to normal in the Sullivan household. Tomeen couldn't have been nicer, and graciously accepted my gifts and my apologies. The mare had recovered and was none the worse. I noticed that Bat was wearing a new pair of boots, but he seemed to sit down gingerly and avoided hard chairs. The foxy dog dozed by the fire, growling and whimpering in his sleep.

'Ah, the crayture,' sighed Mrs Sullivan. 'The hounds has him destroyed. 'Tisn't a day we'll be quickly forgetting, Major.'

THE HUNT TO SLIEVEMORE

A Long Way to Go
Marigold Armitage
1952

The rain drifted steadily and gently into our faces as we waited outside Kilgarvan; the soft, dilatory rain that seems to have no effect at all until, quite suddenly, you find you are soaked to the skin. It was warm, and already the more excitable amongst the horses were wreathed in clouds of steam.

'Rotten scenting day,' observed Colonel Wilbraham, planted like an enormous happy blancmange on his weight-carrying roan and already started on his sandwiches.

'If only you didn't eat all the time, Willy, you wouldn't be so fat,' observed his wife, plaintively and indisputably. She rode side-saddle in a correct and lady-like style, her reins held up delicately near her magnificent bosom, her scalloped hair twirled into a shining Chelsea bun; she swayed stiffly to the movements of her plain and amorous mare who had such a passion for her stable companion and followed him so closely and determinedly over every jump that disaster always seemed to be imminent between them.

'What is so wonderful', Roger had told me, 'is, when the Colonel and his good lady quarrel and try to ride away from each other in injured dignity and the horses refuse to go.'

'You've made it up?' Gillian had asked delightedly.

'I swear I haven't. Wait till you see. She once said to me, "The good dumb creatures set us an example."'

'You've made *that* up, Roger. I just don't believe you, that's all.'

'Wait till you see.'

The Colonel ate his sandwiches happily and talked in a bluff man-to-man way with old Heffernan, the owner of the covert, who was standing near him holding a thin greyhound which, half-crazy with rage and frustration, was making a good bid at strangling itself.

'There'd be a fox in there now,' said old Heffernan. 'Didn't I see him myself only yesterday, would be as big as a tiger; if they'd only get him out.'

'Feller ought to build us a *machan*, what? said the Colonel, delightedly slapping his thigh.

In Kilgarvan there was an almost dead silence, broken only from time to time by slightly peevish cries of encouragement from old George. Once a hound spoke dolefully and uncertainly and then decided against it. Kilgarvan was a large, straggling place, always badly stopped and very difficult to get a fox away from—but old Heffernan was a large cattle-dealer with a lot of land around Garnagarry and a fantastic quantity of money in roving cheques. So Kilgarvan remained the first draw from the best meet and Poodle and old Dicky gossiped in a far corner of the field with an odd Pytchley collar who had just flown over and smoked endless cigarettes and would have gone straight on to Speke by themselves only it would give old George apoplexy, but *really* darling, he *is* the quaintest old character, but such a sweet when he isn't being bloody, only he *will not* be teased and I must say I could rather admire him for it, couldn't you? Of this group were Jane and Mike, and Andrew was also in it, although not entirely of it, but all the same pretending that he was, hoping that Gillian and I wouldn't come up and spoil it and that, if we did, we wouldn't bring Aunt Emmy. For even the very nicest boy of eighteen may feel like this at times.

But poor Andrew was doomed to suffer hideously in quite a different way, for the little black horse had not, as Roger had promised, got his mind on getting to hounds, since hounds were obviously for the moment not gettable-to. His back was humped and he was waiting for an excuse to break loose. It was offered him when Mike's Grand Military lunatic suddenly jumped wildly sideways as a very tiny bird flew silently out of the hedge beside him.

The very next second Andrew was sitting on the muddy ground with his mouth slightly open and his bowler over one eye, while the little black horse careered round the field in a mad gaiety of misdirected energy.

'The young gentleman is gone,' remarked old Heffernan placidly.

'Loose horse,' bawled Colonel Wilbraham commandingly, although nobody could have failed to see it.

Unkindest cut of all, it was the shrill, excited trumpeting of Aunt Emmy's baby that lured the little black horse into stopping and sidling up and sniffing and finally being caught by Aunt Emmy, and it was Jane who cantered gaily across the field and could be seen to be laughing with Aunt Emmy before she brought him back to his crestfallen rider, who was unhappily having mud rubbed off his back by the delighted Poodle, who thought he was a sweet thing. Mike, a very generous man, told a comforting tale about how exactly the same thing had happened to him on a hell of a parade at Meerut and Andrew cheered up very slightly.

'Oh, the poor poppet,' said Gillian. 'The good it will do him, he'll be quite a pet now.'

She was safely and happily ensconced on the very confidential brown animal and was looking almost prim. Every fly-button seemed to be secure and I had refused to allow her to wear a diamond brooch in her stock.

('But it's all I've got, darling?'
'I'll lend you a lovely plain gold bar from Woolworth'.'
'You brute.')

Still no hopeful sounds came from Kilgarvan. A grinning hound, full of good-will, slipped out beside us, feathered in rather a hopeless was along the dry ditch, and went back again.

'That Reveller's a grand worker,' said Colonel Wilbraham, showing off slightly.

It was not only not Reveller, but a bitch, and I kept silent, hoping for more.

Suddenly and for no apparent reason, there went round the field one of those groundless rumours that always occur at a large covert and we all galloped mildly and rather aimlessly across the field we were in and through a gap and down a cart-track and then stopped and galloped back again.

'I bet you don't know why you're doing this,' said Gillian to me as we came barging through the gap for the second time.

'Certainly I don't. Neither does anybody else, however much they may pretend they do.'

The only two people who hadn't moved were Aunt Emmy and Roger. They still sat placidly in the same corner while their babies nervously snatched delicious mouthfuls of hedge. Roger grinned and waved at us derisively. He skipped the chestnut filly over to us and said:

'Anybody would think you were at Balaclava, you gallant things you.'

'I could slap you, sweet,' said Gillian. 'Just go away.'

Old George's horn now mournfully informed us from the far side that he had given up Kilgarvan and its fox as big as a tiger, and was going on to the famous Speke—a small, compact patch of gorse on the southerly slope of a sheltering hill, half a mile away across the fields, which had never been known not to yield a fox, even if only of normal appearance.

'If we go away down hill from Speke,' I said, 'poor Andrew won't stand a chance.'

'Never mind, he's as happy as a bee at the moment and his nervous system is set in reinforced concrete.'

We jogged off in a clattering, chattering cavalcade across the fields to Speke. A slight wind from the north was beginning to blow the rain away and here and there patches of a cold and washy blue showed between the grey, amorphous cloud. It was getting colder.

'Be a hell of a scent this evening,' said Mike cheerfully. 'Any time ground's hotter'n air you'll see 'em run like stink.'

Poodle said darling Mike, so optimistic always, she had thought it *quite* the other way round, Freddy had always said . . .

Any argument about what constitutes good scenting conditions is inconclusive and not infrequently heated, for somebody has always seen hounds running like stink in weather and over ground that somebody else has proclaimed to be utterly hopeless, might as well go home. Scent is as mysterious as God and causes almost as much controversy among its devotees.

'Oh do look at that terrible horse,' said Gillian suddenly.

Paddy Casey's lad had incautiously decided that a canter round might settle his sweating charge, who now swept past us suddenly as if powered by a jet engine, his head nearly on the ground and the lad perched on his withers, trying desperately to stop whilst looking as if he meant to go on—an art that can be seen at its highest on any Irish race course.

'The boy will be quinched,' said someone placidly. 'That's a horse wouldn't mind himself at all.'

Gillian gave a faint squeak and shut her eyes as this prophecy appeared likely to be fulfilled, for the horse was now approaching a narrow, straggly, bramble-topped bank and showed no sign of either abating his pace or allowing himself to be turned from his course. There was a bursting, crashing, catastrophic sound, and he disappeared from view. A few seconds later, undismayed, he and his rider could be seen continuing their career across the further field.

Colonel Wilbraham was hurt and puzzled.

'That's the horse that feller Casey wanted me to buy,' he said to me. 'Bit unneighbourly, what?'

'A bit,' I answered gravely.

Paddy Casey himself now appeared, hastening up alongside us to retrieve the situation. He always rode a thirty-year-old white mare who had long ceased to have any interest in anything except going home.

'I told the lad put him over something for you, Colonel. There's a horse now, would lep Aintree.'

'Sure, he'd lep into the Canal then,' a muffled voice was heard to exclaim behind us, 'for there's no one would turn that felly once he'd be off.'

'Oh, aren't they all divine,' said Gillian.

Paddy Casey glared reproachfully at her.

We jogged and chattered on across the grey-green fields and all around us, some not far away, some very far, blue, hazy, keeping with arrogant ease their incredible hold upon the heart, were the inevitable mountains that ring the middle of Ireland like the upturned edges of a saucer. One could go away from Kilgarvan, Speke, Kilquin, or any other covert in the West Tipperary country and there, in front of one, would be mountains— perhaps one far, faint peak showing dimly through trees; perhaps a familiar, mighty shoulder humping suddenly up out of the mild plains to make a landmark for lost foxhunters. They are all part of the magic; which, like all the good magic, is not easily definable—not to be dissected or labelled Black or White, or distilled successfully into railway posters or guide books. The land is no colour and all colours; drab and sad and achingly beautiful; and whichever it is changes while you try to look at it—for this reason nobody has ever yet painted it with truth; the land keeps its secret.

Everywhere is the haunting sense of nostalgia and poverty and sadness—of things begun and never finished, might have been, wasted, ruined, not every thought about. Even in the richest grazing lands, where the fattening bullocks move gravely about the fields like heavy princes, there still, are the broken-down, never-to-be-built-up walls; the black-thorn running riot on the rotting banks; the iron bedstead stuck in the gap; the un-openable gates, propped with stones, sagging on rusty hinges; the dusty, pot-holed little roads; the rush-choked ditches and the lame, straying donkeys. Here too, the Big Houses, the square Georgian boxes with their bland façades, their tall, flat windows, their cracked fanlights, their lovely and subtle simplicity, slide gently into ruin—until, as was happening so often at this time, they were rescued by the refugees, disappearing for long months behind a network of scaffolding and re-appeared rain-proof and centrally-heated and perhaps slightly reproving—for had anybody, after all, a right to rescue them; had anybody even bothered to enquire if they wanted to be rescued? rescued?

For I think that, perhaps, the closest one may come to analysing the spell of the land is to say that it owes much to the enormous, the subtle and speculative magic of the unsuccessful—and on the damp grey days, the cold blue mornings, the steamy gold evenings, the magic is there, triumphant and unvarying and rather frightening, and the lovely, lonely, ignoble land has you by the heart.

'What are you thinking of?' asked Gillian.

'The mountains.'

'Why does one like them so much?'

'I can't imagine.'

'But one does, madly.'

'Yes.'

'I was thinking about Jane and Little Daisy—see them together there, in front of the Wilbrahams—I was thinking how fantastic it is that they should both just be called the same thing—*Women*. There ought to be different names for them.'

'There are, sweet.'

'Don't be silly—I meant scientifically.'

Speke was blank; and so were the faces that turned away from it to begin the mile-long trek down the road to Drumanagh Glen. It was still getting colder, and people were beginning to turn up their coat collars and drop back to look for their cars and sustenance. At the bare and lonely cross-roads some easily-defeated spirits left for home. The Limerick visitors were quietly triumphant and the Pytchley one censorious. Nobody dared speak to old George.

'How about a drink?' asked Gillian. 'I see your sweet mother.'

The little green car was parked in a gateway up a side road and there was my mother and Richmond, Aunt Emmy, Roger, the babies and Poodle, who was telling my fascinated mother that what everybody was saying about old Dicky was *quite right* and, not only that, but *far worse*.

'Poor old man,' said my mother, 'if only he'd sack all those terrible servants, nobody would ever know anything.'

'I adore your mother,' said Gillian. 'And how I dislike that dreadful Poodle—she's too pneumatic and too blonde and altogether too fashionable—really, no one who hasn't been to bed with her has any social standing at all.'

'You're jealous.'

'Of course I am.'

She and Poodle greeted each other with delighted cries and Gillian was luckily able to keep her end up with a really hot and fresh piece of gossip, contained in a letter received only that morning (now lying amongst the break-fast litter at Knockmoree having been read and abandoned by Thomas Quin), about who had been seen by whom lunching with who at the quaint Brown's and talking *very earnestly*, 'do you think, darling, that that one is breaking up at long last for good and all?'

Gillian often told me sadly in cosier moments how she was always promising herself not to gossip and how she always broke her promises—it was something that was very much on her strange, tough, flexible, and often oddly troubled mind. So now she and the hated Poodle gossiped happily together and drank up what delicious whisky Roger had left, while Richmond leant against the bonnet of the little green car looking noble and courteous, until one of the babies trod heavily on his foot and remained on it. It is a very curious fact about horses—possibly part of their divine silliness that Gillian had noticed; possibly that something inimical in their attitude towards humans that has so often been complained of by those who don't love them—but a fact, certainly—that the most flippant and restless amongst them, having found an agonized human foot to stand on, becomes at once as immovable as a rock.

The baby gazed mildly over Richmond's shoulder, its mind apparently very far away; while its victim clawed unhappily at its chest and knee; while Poodle smartly smacked its quarters with her gloves; while my mother jumped up and down in front of its fixed gaze; while Roger pushed at its shoulder to throw it off its balance and I tried to pull its foot up by main force and Richmond snarled breathlessly:

'*Do* something, damn it—*take the bloody animal off my foot.*'

It was at this rather confused moment that hound voices suddenly rang together like a peal of bells from far down the road.

'Christ!' said Roger, and rocked the baby off Richmond's foot with a last despairing thrust. 'Listen!' We stood silent, our eyes popping.

A pause. Then one hound speaking.

'That really *is* Reveller.'

Then the triumphant chorus clamouring out again, shaking the cold air. Then the long, wild crying of the horn. The chills began in my spine, the thumping of the blood.

'Oh,' said Gillian faintly, 'I always feel like that woman in Somerville and Ross, who cried.'

Roger seized her ankle and put her up on to the brown animal, who looked suddenly less confidential.

'They must have picked up an outlier—they can't have got to Drumanagh. God help you now if they run away from you.'

The voices clamoured on. Nearer? Further? I was up on the grey, although I couldn't remember getting there.

'He's bound to come this way if they're between him and Drumanagh,' said Aunt Emmy, her eyes shining. 'The wind's right for it and even if it wasn't he'd try to get to Kilgarvan.'

The babies swung and wavered about, twittering and sweating and staring all ways at once. Poodle had bolted down the road to her horse. (Even at this enthralling moment Gillian found time to observe that she was the wrong shape for running in breeches.) Someone who had been going home, could be seen galloping back like mad across a far field, amongst jovially bucking bullocks.

Still the voices rang out, gay and confident.

'Wait, wait. Listen.'

'I *can't* breathe,' said Gillian, faintly.

'*Look!*'

The glowing, dramatic quality of Richmond's voice suited the moment. The fox stood a few yards away, in the middle of the road, staring at us.

'Is it—'

'*Sh-h-h-h-.*'

We froze.

Like a red blown leaf he slipped up the far bank and was gone.

'My God,' said Roger. 'If we'd headed him I believe old George would have strangled us all with his bare hands. Is he well away, Anthony?'

I moved the grey across the road and stood in my stirrups to see over the bank. My eyes searched the far field. Nothing. The wild spirit had vanished as he had come. Then suddenly, there was the flicker of red-brown again as he passed a gap.

'He's running the wall down to that bloody great ditch at the bottom. I'd say he's making for Kilgarvan all right, and going to cross the point-to-point course.'

The voices were faltering slightly.

'Holler, Roger. They'll have to bustle him to get through Kilgarvan.'

Roger jumped up on the bank, stuck a finger in his ear and produced a noise of ear-splitting intensity.

'My God!' said Richmond, struck to stone in the road.

Unable to follow the sequence of events, he found the world suddenly going made around him and was beginning to feel twitchy.

'It's all right,' said my mother comfortingly, patting his arm.'

Three fields away towards Drumanagh the sound reached old George who, already thinking of Kilgarvan, decided to take a chance on its authenticity. He lifted his lovely, deserving hounds and galloped straight to it.

They came pouring liquidly towards us over a wall and up the field, tense and eager and effortless.

'Oh,' said Gillian faintly, 'Oh, oh.'

I knew exactly what she meant for I was having great difficulty myself with my breathing—something odd seemed to have happened to my solar plexus.

'Where to, Roger?' old George was bawling as he galloped.

Roger was pointing.

'Straight down the wall—making for Kilgarvan.'

Hounds flowed around us—the babies were having hysterics—there was grunt and slither and curse—

'Ger-r on, you—*hold* up now'—as old George's wise horse came neatly down into the road and neatly and carefully up and out again over the bigger bank, and now old George was cheering them on to the line under the wall and they owned it at once in a crashing chorus and were off, and Gillian and her brown, who might be confidential, but knew when business was meant, were over and gone after them and I only just managed to keep the grey horse back by turning his head away, until Tommy Dwyer had gone by with one willing, embarrassed tail hound and then I was landing after him, the grey shaking his head and behind me the crash and clatter and growing thunder of hooves and Roger's faint shout of benediction:

'Oh, you lucky B—s.' For obviously, this was going to be altogether too much of a good thing for the babies.

On this day, at this time, over the piece of country, Mike's theory about good scenting conditions seemed to be right. Hounds were racing, flinging, driving forward like a dappled cloud. There they went, over the bloody great ditch, leaping, falling short, splashing, scrambling out and on without pausing to shake themselves. There went old George on his neat, wise horse, jumping cleverly, not an inch too far, not a second too soon, his ears cocked. Then Gillian, gloriously leading the field, going at it wildly. I knew that in the last second before the take-off, an expression of ecstatic agony on her face, she would shut her eyes and hang tightly on to a plait of mane, leaving the reins to flap loose, and I was glad that Jane's mare knew her business. Then Tommy Dwyer, still crying encouragement to the tail hound, now streaking just behind old George, a personification of silent, bitter determination to catch up with the pack. Then it was my turn and the grey's stride never seemed to vary, only the dark water, the rushes fleeted suddenly backwards and were going and he lowered his lean head as we met the steeply rising ground on the far side and his shoulder muscles worked like pistons beneath my knees. Now I was trying to control my wild excitement enough to think which would be the best line to take when we reached the top of the hill, where hounds were driving already over the low wall into the road. It was so long since I had hunted here I had difficulty in visualising the country. Once across the road there would be two or three fields, part of the point-to-point course, sloping gently towards Kilgarvan. But if they got him through the big covert would he swing right or left? On which flank of the pack should I station myself? And what the hell was the wind doing? It seemed to be blowing on my heated face from all directions at once. A snorting horse came up on my right hand, Father Carrigan tucked like a jockey behind its withers on a ragged racing saddle, his eyes gleaming wildly, his spectacles crooked on his nose, his bowler on the back of his head. I sighed inwardly with relief, for Father Carrigan knew the mind of every fox in the country.

'Follow me now, Anthony,' he shouted exultantly. 'Sure, I know this felly, he wouldn't mind how many miles he'd run. If he can't go down in Kilgarvan he'll go across the bog and make for the hills.'

Here he cursed his horse startling as it bungled the tiny walls into and out of the road, and streaked away down the big field, half-turned in his saddle to shout advice to me still over his black-clad shoulder.

'Bear right now, Anthony. Follow me. We must jump McCarthy's double where it's sound.'

McCarthy's double was the biggest bank in the country. Once I had gone over it on my feet when I was a boy and it was like climbing a minor Alp. I had sprung over the deep wet ditch, alighted about a quarter way up, hauled myself by grass-tuft and root and bramble on to the wide top where there was a beaten path amongst bushes and small trees, crept nervously half-way down the far side and then jumped unsuccessfully out over the six-foot stream and failed to clear it. I had got very wet and Nanny had lectured me.

In the middle of the field, cleared and reinforced, this bank was the official double of the point-to-point course—an enormous, smooth, green hummock, tempting you to jump it and carefully wired up to prevent just such goings-on. In some other places it was unsound, but Father Carrigan would know exactly where to have it. I took a pull and looked for Gillian. She was bearing away left, the silly piece, going down into Kilgarvan with old George and Tommy Dwyer, and she would certainly get lost and left and probably bogged. I yelled despairingly at her and waved furiously and at last she saw me, hesitated, pulled round and came galloping over to me.

'Follow me, you silly woman. Follow Father Carrigan.'

We fled together down the gentle slope.

'Jump this exactly where he does. Look—there he goes.'

'*Jump this?*'

'Just leave it to the mare.'

'Oh—it's too easy.'

'Of course it is. You go first. I'll push you off the top if you stick.'

'Oh God—why did I *ever* imagine I was an outdoor girl?'

She shut her eyes.

The mare knew exactly what to do and she did it very slowly and deliberately. She looked at the ditch and decided the bottom was sound and waded slowly into it. 'No heroics for me,' her behind expressed to my horse, who was dancing with impatience. She then reared herself straight up with a wallowing noise, like a sea-monster, and arrived at the top of the bank in two heaving bounds which slightly loosened Gillian, even though she had a different plait in each hand. They disappeared from my view and there was a series of sliding sounds and then a heavy thump. I could not see them, but I knew exactly what the mare had done. She had clambered carefully half-way down, just as I had done on my feet, and had then paused, waving her head and neck at the stream like an elephant testing something with its trunk and shifting her hind-legs carefully to see if she had a firm take-off, while Gillian crouched nervelessly in her saddle with popping eyes, swallowing. Then she had jumped out and over it, just far enough and no further.

'Are you out of the way?' I shouted.

A faint, worldless shriek of assent came back to me. Just as the grey started at it I was aware of Mike Harrington on his chestnut coming as if he was going into the last at Sandown and I thought, 'They'll both be killed without a doubt.' Then the grey was up and changing and over and out with a wonderful feeling of freedom and ease and effortless timing, so that for a second I saw myself on him, as Aunt Emmy did, 'tipping the double like a Punchestown horse' leading the field in the Hunt Cup—but only for a second.

Hounds were chiming away confidently down in Kilgarvan, and were obviously running hard through it. Father Carrigan had disappeared from my view but Gillian was galloping down the field in a determined manner that indicated she knew where he had gone. I set off after her, glancing uneasily back over my shoulder—for Mike was obviously going to be on the ground in a minute and supposing there was nobody else coming that way to pick them up? I wrestled unhappily with my conscience and the grey horse raked angrily at my uncertain hands and said 'For God's sake let's *go*.' And then Mike and his chestnut appeared behind us, apparently soaring down from the sky, and turned a complete somersault before they hit the ground.

I very much regret having to record that my sole feeling as I pulled my horse round, was one of fury. I was going to miss what looked like an excellent hunt because Mike chose to ride a crazy racehorse over a country where what was needed was a cross between a pony and a panther. As I trotted back to them the horse thrashed uncertainly to its feet, looked round vaguely, saw Gillian's mare and made off down the field at full gallop, inextricably entangled in its reins. But Mike remained on the ground. And then like an answer to prayer, something altogether too good to be true, O excellent, cosy, capable, self-sacrificing man, Dr Paddy Herlihy from Garnagarry came slipping down off the bank on Mick O'Connor's pony that drew a cart to the creamery when it wasn't hunting.

He pulled up and dismounted in sad resignation, his pug-like face puckered.

'Couldn't I see what would happen a field away? Not the thrack of a heel did the horse lay to it, only knocked back at it with his tail—was it hurdling, God help us, he thought he was at? And I to have my first hunt for a fortnight, with the 'flu that's about.'

I hovered helpfully, and he looked up at me, from where he was poking gently at Mike, and grinned.

'Get away on to them, then, you. What good that we'd both miss it? Sure, he's only winded and there's a dozen felly's about with dogs that can help me instead of confusing the hunt.'

With enormous relief and a certain amount of shame, I hustled the willing grey off down the field. At the bottom was a sticky gap jammed with thorny bushes. I jumped it and heard hounds very close and swung right through an open gateway and there were Gillian and Father Carrigan, that first-class reader of foxy minds, breathing heavily and trying to hold their shifting horses still, while fifty yards away hounds went streaming and singing across the field in front of us.

'Oh, oh,' said Gillian to me, with shining eyes, her stock under one ear and both leathers twisted where she had lost her irons over the double and jammed her feet back into them in a carefree manner.

'Didn't I tell you,' shouted Father Carrigan triumphantly. 'Sharp right he turned out to Kilgarvan and he's for the hills this minute.'

'Have you seen Brigadier Harrington's horse?' I asked him.

'I have, and he wouldn't let us lay a finger on him—he's gone in to McCarthy's yearlings below—sure, McCarthy'll catch him when he'd settle.'

'Have you seen Mike?' Gillian asked me.'

'I have, indeed, and the doctor from Garnagarry is with him now.'

'Oh, poor Mike—is he all right?'

'Not very.'

'Oh, Anthony, how can you be so heartless?'

'I feel like a character in Nimrod—the pace was too good to enquire. Come on, now.'

For old George had gone by, scrubbing his wise horse that wouldn't gallop unless the necessity was stark and Tommy Dwyer had gone by with a purple, intent face and as we set off again two or three toiling figures were coming up from Kilgarvan—I looked back and thought I saw Hubert and the roan mare, Jane Harrington and a couple of unidentifiable forms behind them.

'Where's Andrew?' I shouted to Gillian as we galloped along the rutty headland with Father Carrigan, all rebounding off each other from time to time in a not very controlled manner. Her answer which seemed to contain the words 'little brute' was lost to me in the confusion that ensued at the next gap, where Father Carrigan's horse, who was slightly leading as we came to it, resolutely refused to jump a timber rail jammed across it that could not have been much more than eighteen inches high, coming to a jarring halt with a swerve that sent its rider down its shoulder. Gillian always said afterwards that she had heaved him back into the saddle by his respectable black breeches, but all I can remember is Father Carrigan pulling out of our way with a despairing cry of 'Holy God!' and sending his now willing horse scrambling over the bank, which was about twelve feet high, very narrow, extremely slippery and crowned with jagged broken tree stumps.

I reflected, as I looked back at him, on what a pity it was that his horse and Mike's could not somehow manage to combine their respective talents.

We pounded on. The banks were becoming wide, low slipperry humps, with big ditches full of water—we were approaching the bog. Here we would cross it at its narrowest part—about a mile—and then if we were lucky find ourselves in an excellent part of the country; grazing ground with big, sound banks and small walls. 'The hills' which Father Carrigan had referred to was really *a* hill—Slievemore, the big blue shoulder rising out of the plain, with the dark, shifting cloud shadows fleeting across its bulk, and the low, ragged clouds themselves lying now across its peak in banks which the freshening wind was beginning to blow away.

'See where's he's making for,' I called to Gillian.

'If only I could breathe,' was her response, the brown mare plugging determinedly on beside me, her head low delighted with her breathless and light and unmasterful rider, and confident in her own power to get there, wherever it might be. Behind us came Father Carrigan, still bitterly lecturing his non-timber-jumper, and behind him, apparently, still no one else at all. We pulled to a walk to slide down an extremely steep, short slope, at the bottom of which we would jump a huddle of stones pretending to be a wall, and find ourselves on the bog-road.

'Are we leading the field?' gasped Gillian as we slithered down towards it.

'Pounded 'em.'

'Oh . . . *fascinating* . . . Do I look at all like Dick Christian?'

'Not really.'

'Oh . . . I so hoped I did . . . I've never done such a thing before.'

Hounds went fleeting like a blizzard across the bog, old George and Tommy Dwyer battering at a shameless gallop up the road after them.

'Oh,' said Gillian, as we landed together on to it, 'their poor glass legs will never stand it.'

I thought it more than probable. But there was nothing else to be done. There was goat-nibbled turf at the sides of the road, but there were deep, irregular ditches cut into it at frequent intervals, tiring and dangerous to horse and rider. Anyone who has tried to gallop a horse on a grass verge will know what a great penchant they have for the hard, high road in spite of their poor glass legs and how they will bend and lurch and pull sideways towards it, refusing to look where they are going until they get their way, and the unique sensation of galloping on a hard, clattering surface.

'Anyway, it's not slippery,' said Gillian hopefully, as we fled along, scattering stones, lurching in and out of ruts and making a noise like a hundred Crusaders charging in armour, 'but I couldn't feel guiltier, could you?'

Certainly I couldn't. Would the grey horse, I wondered, be lamed for life? But still the pace was too good to enquire. We must gallop or hounds would run away from us, so we galloped, guilty or not.

There was a broken-down cabin a little way on and from out of it slipped two lurchers, oblivious of shouted curses from within, to race, shrieking and nipping at the heels of old George's horse who, endeavouring to kick back at them as it galloped, very nearly came down. Old George's scream of execration and the pistol-cracks of his and Tommy Dwyer's thongs sent them howling and cowering into the ditch, from where they launched a further attack on us, while at the same time two apparently idiot children ran gaily out under our horses's feet. Their mother, incredibly tangled-looking and quite oblivious to their fate, hung over the half-door of their home and screamed harshly, hadn't she seen the fox himself and the dogs too ahead of us and they never stopping to draw breath?

Neither did we draw breath, not then or for some time after. It was a fearful moment. I shall never know exactly what the grey horse did, but he managed somehow not to lay the thrack of a heel on those undeserving brats—presumably he knocked back at them with his tail. Gillian's mare appeared to rise straight into the air in a sort of confused *fouetté*—her feet working on nothing. Then we were past.

'I can't look back,' chattered Gillian.

I did so, with dread. The children, undismayed, were just jumping gaily under Father Carrigan's horse—who became so unnerved and so muddled with its feet that it ended up wallowing in the ditch, with the lurchers in hysterics around it. Benediction flowed from the Father in an unending stream as they struggled out again. Gillian always swore that he had laid about the children with his whip, but I am ready to believe that this was artistic license on her part, for Father Carrigan, wild though he might be in appearance and behaviour, was the soul of kindness.

Now he came clattering on again behind us, talking angrily to himself and suddenly behind him again there was an eager hooting and, looking back, I saw my mother remorselessly driving the groaning little green car with Richmond hanging out of the window as if chasing gangsters in a rather bad film. On one step clung somebody in pink (Mike? Colonel Wilbraham? The Pytchley?) and on the other—could it be?—it surely must be the tangled and unmaternal figure from the cabin. Around the back wheels the indefatigable lurchers nipped and shrieked once again, and further back, running nobly but rather hopelessly, wreathed in smelly clouds from the exhaust came the abandoned children. And then, far, far, far behind, just coming down on to the road, four or six or so more conventional figures, correctly mounted and no doubt absolutely furious.

The grey cannoned heavily off Gillian's mare.

'Oh, do, *do* look where you're going, Anthony.'

'Oh, Lord,' I said, bending on the grey's neck.

'You're ill!' said Gillian, pallidly.

'No. But I've just seen Mama and Richmond with that terrible woman from the cabin.'

'Where? Where?'

'Not very far behind us.'

'I *can't* look. I daren't. If I start laughing now I'm finished.' She stared desperately ahead with a fixed face.

We were coming off the bog. The road was ceasing to have the appearance of a causeway and was tending to sink between thorn-crowned banks and become a boreen. We could hear hounds off on our left and bearing away.

'We must get out of here at the next jumpable place,' I said to Gillian.

Then we turned to a sharp, downhill corner and fell slap on to old George and Tommy Dwyer, who were penned up facing an enormous, enthralled horse who was drawing a cart that just fitted the boreen. A small boy gesticulated helplessly from where he was sitting on the near shaft.

'Back,' roared old George to him in a Jehovah voice. 'Back, damn it, *back!*'

The boy stood up obediently and leaned heavily on the reins with the whole weight of his meagre body. The horse opened its mouth very wide, stuck its neck straight out and advanced towards us with an eager, welcoming sound.

'Sweet Christ,' said old George hoarsely.

'Oh, *darling*,' said Gillian to me with tears in her eyes. '*Do* something. Make a hole in that.'

'That' was the high and healthy and thick growth of blackthorn that crowned the bank on our left. The bank itself was not very high, but it looked slippery and rotten and the take-off out of the boreen was appalling.

'And the grandest gate you ever saw only just down from us!' wailed Tommy Dwyer.

He backed his horse and turned and booted him into the bank. Both were game but the thorns made a quick, clean jump impossible and as the horse dwelt the bank gave way immediately under his floundering feet. For a long few seconds he thrashed like a stranded whale above us.

He was going to fall, but would he fall over or back into the lane? Tommy had slipped neatly off his back and was perched, like an anxious robin amongst the thorns, clutching the end of the reins. The horse gave one final desperate kick and disappeared from our view, sliding on his stomach. Tommy leapt after him into space. There was a hideaous squelching sound.

'They'll be into the boggy dyke beyond for sure,' the small boy remarked conversationally.

Old George gave him a brimstone look. Suddenly the boy's face became illuminated with an idea.

'Wait while I'd run down and get the slasher for you.'

He leapt up and disappeared down the boreen. The abandoned horse and cart moved further into the fearful mêlée.

'Tommy, are you clear, damn you?' bawled old George.

'Wait now, wait, sir.'

There were flounderings, and urging noises and then the encouraging cry 'Come on now sir, but sure 'tis a grave you have to lep, 'tis a fearful place altogether.'

Old George set his purple jaw and lepped. I hung desperately on to the cart horse who had a strong notion of lepping himself.

Old George and his horse went the same way as Tommy and his—with the difference that old George was not spry enough to nip off. They rolled together out of sight.

'He'll be killed,' said Gillian, faintly. 'Why do we like doing this?'

Crash. Flounder. Squelch. And then a slightly shaken bawl:

'Come on then, you two.'

I wrestled strongly with the cart horse.

'Listen, Gillian, don't have it. It's a bloody awful place. Give it up.'

I felt a sharp panic for her, she looked so small suddenly. Her lips folded obstinately. Apparently she was still feeling like Dick Christian. The brown mare cocked her ears and seemed to take a deep breath.

They had it, determinedly. Old George said afterwards that even at that flustering moment, with his hounds running away from him every second, with his own horse still on the ground trying to get its breath back, with the winded Tommy Dwyer's whole weight on him as he tried to put him up; even so he was struck to stone by the sight of Gillian's arrival. She came with her eyes shut. She had abandoned her reins alotgether and clung tightly with both hands to the pommel of her saddle. The mare made a wonderful effort, hit the edge of the 'grave' and tipped up. She ploughed on her head for a few yards and then righted herself, blowing mud triumphantly from her nostrils, with her bridle on the ground and her rider still in the saddle.

'I declare to my God', Tommy Dwyer was wont to say, in describing this feat afterwards, which he did very often, 'there's not a jock in the country, no not J. J. himself, would have stayed above the way Mrs

Lodwick did, and the mare walking on her head the way she might be in a circus.'

But now it was my turn and the grey's. The expression 'riding for a fall' is very easily used and has a dashing ring about it—actually to do such a thing, however, arouses a feeling of sick anticipation comparable only to that experienced at the moment when the dentist's hand reaches for the drill.

We were not only going to fall, I felt, but there was also nothing to prevent the cart and horse from falling on top of us, since the horse was obviously feeling ambitious and there was no one to curb his feelings once I had gone. I belaboured him rather hopelessly with my whip until he gave way sufficiently to allow us a little room. My heart and stomach had changed places as the grey heaved himself up into the thorny gap, with everything giving way at once under his clever feet. But I need not have worried. The grey had brains and he decided instantly that, with no firm take-off, any attempt to jump the boggy dyke beyond would end in failure. Instead he dropped lightly and neatly and deliberately down into it and heaved himself out again, light and neat still, and shook himself with a noise like thunder all over old George's horse, which at once got to its feet indignantly.

'By God, that's a clever horse of Emmy's,' said old George. 'My b— just lost his head.'

He was clasping Gillian's mare's naked face delicately to his chest by nose and ear while Tommy Dwyer endeavoured to pick up her bridle, much hampered by his horse who had decided that the bridle was alive, and was refusing to go near it. I jumped off and took his horse and old George's while they restored to Gillian a measure of control and then I put them both up, and by that time I was so breathless with fright and exhaustion that I really thought I should lose the hunt yet through sheer physical inability to get up and on the grey again. But Tommy Dwyer leant from his saddle and heaved nobly and I was aboard again and flying, for the grey had breathed himself nicely—there was agonizing mud in my right eye and I could not find my irons for the moment but ahead was good grass and sound banks—and behind a piteous, lonely beseeching scream. I looked back. The cart horse stood reared up with his forefeet on the bank, imploring us to return.

We fled on, through two delicious gateways without gates.

'Where's Father Carrigan?' Gillian shouted breathlessly.

Where indeed? I had forgotten him. I looked back. Nobody. He had been close behind us coming off the bog, and it was not like Father Carrigan to lose a good start. Nor had he, for as I looked forward again, across the country that was now beginning to rise slightly as we went towards Sleivemore, there was the familiar crouched dark back, slipping along at least two fields ahead of us all.

'How did he get there?'

God knows.'

'That damned priest,' growled old George, 'he's always ahead of me, blast his Papist soul.'

Old George was well known never to have entered a church since he had left Eton, but in the presence of Roman Catholicism his Protestantism was relentless and militant. He preferred, he said, his own type of damnation.

Old George's horse was tiring now; at the next bank he misjudged his distance and nearly fell back. Gillian's mare had a slight roll in her stride as we crossed the next field. I was frankly exhausted but the grey horse was going on as light as thistledown, his ears cocked still, still reaching for each jump eagerly, and I tried to sit as quiet as possible and not hinder him, even if I could not help him. There came a wall on to a cart-track, with stone-faced bank out of it. Old George's horse came to his knees over the wall, slithered and scuffled and heaved and stopped with his chest against the bank, his head hanging over it and his tail stretched out, quivering.

'He's beat,' said old George. 'The b—. He's old, like me.'

He ran his hand lovingly down the wet shoulder.

'Get on to them, Tommy, damn you. What the hell are you hanging about for?'

Tommy got on, with slither and slip and clatter, into a herd of young bullocks who wallowed excitedly with him down the field, ponderously playful.

'Get on, you two,' said old George. He had got off and was loosening his horse's girths, his head hidden under the saddle flap so that his voice was muffled.

He didn't want us to see his face. 'Oh, hell,' I thought, 'hell,' and got off the grey and plucked George's reins from his hand.

'Get up quick—he's a bottomless horse.'

Honour and glory for Aunt Emmy, anyway. Old George's face, taken from beneath the saddle flap, was even purpler than usual.

'I shouldn't do it to you, Anthony.'

'Don't be a fool.'

I pitched him up. My leathers were much too long—he crossed them over the pommel of the saddle and was gone, the grey jumping out big over the slight drop. Gillian looked woefully at me before she followed.

'Oh, darling, the *chivalry*. Roger need never speak about Round Tables again.'

Then she, too, was gone. There was the slap and thunder of their hooves and the bawling of the bullocks. Then silence, except for the heavy panting of old George's horse. Silence? Yes, silence. I strained my ears, but I could not hear hounds. And they had only been two or three fields ahead of us. A check? Had they over-run in this poached, bullock-foiled field? If so, there was hope for me yet. I turned the horse's head to the wind and earnestly exhorted him to breathe deeply which he did without hesitation. Then I heard Tommy Dwyer's voice not very far away raised in gentle encouragement to his hounds. Undoubtedly a check. And yet, what hope could there really be for me, since the fox was bound to be forward if he was making for Sleivemore? Or had he thought up something very tricky as he ran through the bullocks? I clambered to the top of the bank and looked about me. The field directly to the right of the one which the bullocks were in, ran increasingly boggily down to a narrow stream. Had he gone to cross it, the old customer, the cunning Charles James, running first in the middle of the bullocks and then turning sharply at a right angle off his point? If so, he would now be slipping at a right angle off his point? If so, he would now be slipping at ease along the far bank, looking for a suitable place to re-cross it and point again for the haven of Sleivemore. As I cogitated and still no hound spoke, the little green car came roaring indomitably towards me and lurched to a standstill with its curious load.

'Anthony,' said my mother serenly, peering out at me. 'That's not Emmy's horse.'

'I know,' I said.

'Then where *is* Emmy's horse?'

Before I could answer there was another diversion—a clapping and flapping and thudding and a loose horse landing over the wall into our midst, wild-eyed, mud on its saddle, a leather gone and broken reins. My heart leapt up as I beheld it to be Conor Molloy's horse. It slithered up to old George's horse and blew on it in a friendly 'Thank-goodness-I've-found-someone-at-last' manner. Old George's horse laid back its ears and bit the newcomer smartly on the shoulder just to show it its place.

'You hold this one,' said my mother sweetly to Richmond, pressing the broken rein into his hand with the air of someone distributing favours to the gentlemen at a charity ball. Richmond's hand closed, nervelessly, on it. He appeared to be speechless and was obviously strongly affected, but in what way I was not quite certain.

'Have the dogs the fox ate?' enquired the careless mother from the cabin.

'They have not, then,' I answered in the idiom.

'Where are they, Anthony? Oh, I forgot this is Colonel Bowser, he's staying with Poodle. [The Pytchley collar looked sharply defensive and fingered his stock.] And they're coming to have a drink with us tonight, that is, of course, if we can find her—or anyone—where *is* everyone, anyway?'

'All I know is that George has got Aunt Emmy's horse and he and Tommy and Gillian and Father Carrigan are over there—they seem to have checked and I think they probably over-ran it through those bullocks. I haven't seen anyone else at all, except as we came across the bog I thought perhaps I saw Jane and Poodle, a long way back.'

'Nearly everybody went to the left around Kilgarvan, that's what happened and they got thrown out and they haven't caught up yet.' She looked back over the wall. 'Here's somebody now.'

It was Caroline. The Araby little horse, black with sweat, landed neatly and jauntily beside us and tossed its head rudely at the other two. Caroline's smile was enchanting, her face creamy under the mud-splashes, her velvet eyes glowing.

'Thank heaven I found somebody at last—I do hate following hoof marks. Where are they? Why have you got my father's horse, Anthony?'

Oh, noble, pure and unselfish motive thus happily turned to glorious gain! I explained.

'How *very* kind of you. Listen, I'll tell you what you can do. Change bridles and get up on Conor's horse.'

'Oh, yes, Anthony,' said my mother. 'You mustn't miss it now.' She was already divesting George's horse of its bridle. 'Just take hold of an ear, would you, Mr Kerr. That's right, he won't try and move.'

But he did. For at that very instant the ringing, the clamour, broke again on the air and the triumphant twanging of old George's horn. My thumb was in Conor's horse's mouth as it mumbled angrily at the strange and frothy bit, refusing to take it.

'Oh, hurry, hurry,' wailed Caroline, in a frenzy. 'Oh, listen to them, the darlings—hurry, hurry.'

Old George's horse, breathed and rid of the weight and highly indignant at the strange turn of affairs, twitched his ear away from Richmond, jumped the bank with a grunt and was away, the saddle slowly sliding round under his belly as he went.

'I told you to hold his ear, Mr Kerr,' said my mother, mildly.

I twisted my thumb madly in Conor's horse's mouth, jammed in the bit, pulled the bridle with an effort over his ears—it was too tight for the poor brute—and left the throat-latch dangling as Poodle's boy-friend bent to give me a leg-up; a noble lift that nearly sent me clean over the big horse—the Pytchley back, I saw as he bent, was smeared with mud from collar to skirt.

I am very glad that there exists no photograph of myself jumping that bank on Conor's horse. I think my head was somewhere near his tail as we landed and I can remember seeing my hands raised in front of me as if in prayer. Then we were scudding away after Caroline and from somewhere not so very far ahead, once again unfaltering, the glorious voices came back to us.

I have no very clear recollection of the rest of that hunt. I realised at once that I had no hope of holding Conor's horse, who seemed to be as fresh as a daisy, and was taking delighted advantage of the mild half-moon snaffle that had replaced his own twisted one. He was big and awkward, green and hot, and his jumping was slapdash, to say the least of it. No thought of refusing ever entered his head, he went gaily and gallantly into his fences with ears cocked, but with no very clear-cut idea as to what he was going to do about them. He had great panache, but all his decisions were mad in mid-air. Twice he was nearly down—more times than I care to remember I was nearly off. I was riding without stirrups, since one is no good to anybody, and I was getting very tired. I gave him his head and prayed and once or twice adopted Gillian's expedient of shutting my eyes. We passed Caroline, who shouted something happily to me, we passed Father Carrigan, whose horse was reduced to a toiling jog, 'God help us, Anthony, what horse have you now?'

Half a field ahead Gillian's brown mare was doggedly cantering, rolling like the *Queen Mary* in a heavy sea, and ahead again, forging further, jumping cleanly still, the game grey horse carried old George to his hounds.

'By God,' I thought momentarily, 'I *will* win the Hunt Cup on him.'

The land was rising ever more steeply, the wide green fields, the sound banks giving way to rough, tussocky little enclosures, patchworked by little, crumbling walls. Sleivemore, enormous in the fading light, bulked silent and close above us, shutting out the pallid evening sky. We were coming on to its lower slopes. At the next wall Gillian's mare's heels waved in the air, she tipped up and crumpled amongst the tussocky grass. I landed near them.

'Oh, darling, *heavens*, what horse have you got now—did you see us fall?—do, *do* go on, quick. I'll just wait until this poor honey gets her breath—I see Father Carrigan coming—do, *do* go on.'

Now, as I went, I saw hounds again for the first time since we had crossed the bog, driving across a low ridge above and to the left of me. They had had a view, I thought, for the high screaming for blood had come into their voices. After them the grey horse slipped like a ghost. Conor's horse lowered his head to climb, picking his way on the rocky outcrop. We came up with Tommy Dwyer limping, leading his beaten horse, almost in tears.

'Sure, don't they deserve him, if hounds ever did? But he'll get into the rocks above and then he can run the whole inside of the hill—the bloody place is hollow—who'd ever think they'd bring him to here from Drumanagh?'

'Never mind, Tommy—it must be a twelve-mile point—you've given us all something to talk about.'

But Tommy was thinking of his hounds. Conor's horse slid and slithered.

'Best get off now, sir, 'tis a dreadful place for a tired horse.'

When I did so I went to my knees. My legs seemed to be made of cotton-wool, and my feet to have no connection with the rest of me. I was not quite sure where I was putting them and I staggered along drunkenly. Away in front, abruptly, the voices died. Then they clamoured again, but singly, brokenly, mournfully, informing us of frustration and a thirst unassuaged. Old George's horn told us the same and round the spine of the ridge we came upon them, a little above us, milling and crying around the great earth in the rocks, the grey horse standing amongst them, his head drooping at last, and old George's face glowing like a lantern through the deepening dusk.

'By God, they nearly had him, the darlings, they were running right into him—ten yards more, five even and he wouldn't have made it.'

'A good fox,' I said. 'A marvellous run, George. You've made history to-day. Congratulations.'

'And only the locals up,' said old George with immense satisfaction. 'Leave him, leave him now, my darlings. Count 'em, Tommy—I think they were all on.'

'Here comes one non-local,' I said, as Gillian came plodding up towards us, trailing Jane's mare, like a tired child dragging a balloon away from a party. Behind her came Caroline and Father Carrigan, both also on foot. Father Carrigan seemed to have caught old George's horse and was leading it by the thong of his whip looped round its throat. The old horse lifted his head and whinnied in a throaty murmur when he saw hounds.

We stood around idly, enveloped in an immense tiredness and content. Old George and Tommy were murmuring endearments to their lovely hounds as they counted them and pulled thorns out of sore pads.

There was a smell of sweating horses and the evening wind, and a star was out above Sleivemore. Old George put the horn to his lips for the last time and blew the long, heartrending 'Home'.

LIST OF SUBSCRIBERS

Mrs Christine Allen, MFH
O J R Allen
Mrs I Anstey Hebditch
Miss F L Archer
Kristine Arena
Julian Armytage
Ian Askew
Mrs J P Asquith

Col Glenn O Baker
Sir R Baker Wilbraham
H A S Bancroft
C D Barker
D I Barker
Miss A E Barlow
C G Barnett
T D Barry
C Bartholomew
Paul Bass
Lord Beaumont of Whitley
C E Beer
R A Bendall
F G Bendell
I J W Benson
John Beveridge, QC
Donald Bilham
Dr Bernard Black
P J W Black
James Blair
Hunter Bodkin
John Bodkin
James Borradaile
Mrs S Bourke
Colonel Mike Bowden
Zenon A Bowrey
Alasdair Boyd
Mr and Mrs Robin Boyd
Rupert Boyd
Dr O B Brears, OBE
Sophie Brem
Frank Brightman

Colonel J M Browell, MBE
Major Marcus Browell
Rosemary Brown
Mr and Mrs Andrew Brownlee
Sir A R J Buchanan-Jardine
Major W K Buckley
John S Burgess
William Stewart Burkland
A G Burne
Lieut A G Burns, RN
Dr Desmond Burrowes

E F Callaghan
N D Campbell
L R Campfield
Mr and Mrs Edward Cantillon
A R P Carden
P D Carrigan
Colonel J H (Pat) Carroll-Leahy, MC
Paul R Casavina, Jr, MFH
Mrs P A Cattell
Mrs E L Catto
Mrs E Cawkwell
George Cazenove
Lord Charles Cecil
Robert Chadwick
Francis Chamberlain
Lisa L Chamberlain
Michael Chichester
Mrs J B W Christie
Mrs M M C Clark
W Clunies-Ross
R F Coates
Mrs K A Coates
J H R Coe
Group Captain C J Collingwood
F L Collins
J P Colwill
Nicholas Comyn
E J Cooper

Mrs T K Cooper
Michael Corkery, QC
Stephen Costello
M H Couchman, JP, MA
Mrs M Coveney
Mrs F M K Cowper
Barry and Marie Cremin
Mrs Keith Cresswell
Lieut Colonel R N R Cross
William Curran

Dominic Daly
John Daly
Patrick J Daly
A W R Dangar, MFH
Clifford L Daniels
Ken Daunt
Ernest Dearing
Dennis Dee
Michael Dempsey, MFH
J H Dixon
Victor Dodd
Lady Douro
E A Dracup
P G Durrans

Peter Edwards
Gerald Ellison
D M Ely-Brown
Mrs E M R Etheridge
Mark Etherton
K Evans
L J C Evans

E S Faulkner
Dr J B Ferguson
S A Ferris
Anne, Countess of Feversham
R A J Finn
J S Fisher
Mrs T Fitch, MFH
J E Fleeman
R J Fleming
Mrs U R L Forinton
Mrs G D H Foster
N J Foster

Major J G Fountain
Dr R B Fountain

J T Gaisford St Lawrence
Margaret Gardiner
Major R H C Gates, MC
Mary Gaunt
Major A A Gibbs, MBE, TD
His Honour Stanley Gill
H R Gillespie
Richard A Gilman, MD
R J Glenday
Peter Goddard
John Godley
Capt Paul Goodlet
B A Gotto
Professor Edward Grant
A H B Grattan-Bellew
Lieut J Greener
Simon Greenwood
E Bracher Griffin
Mrs William Griffith
Gordon S Griffiths
David Guilding
P L Guy

A D A S Hall
Miss R Patricia Hall
Edward Hallinan
R S Hamilton
R M Hannam
Guy Hannen
Miss V E G Harper
David Harrington
Ronald Harrington
The Earl of Harrington
Mrs J A Harrold
Chris H Hay
Mrs D C Hayden
A C Heber-Percy
R J Hellier
Mrs A Hellyer
Mrs R C Henderson
R J Hepburn
Michael Hewison
T M Hickman

Patrick Brian Hicks
W B Hill
Lady Hirst
Rachel Hirst
M R Hoare
C J Hodgson
I S Hodgson-Jones
Ivan A Hoffe
C J Hollis
Sam van Holthe
Henry Hooker
Noel Horgan
Mrs Ian Horne
M A Houghton
G P C Howard
Mr and Mrs M J Howard
John Vivian Hughes
Brigadier K Hunt, OBE, MC
Mrs K Hunt

C Kenneth Irvine
Major General D E Isles, CB, OBE, DL

A R L Jervoise
Mr and Mrs R S Johns
Simon Johnson
The Revd J K Jones

Michael Leo Keane
Sir Richard Keane, Bt
Det Sgt C C Keating
A S A Kilpatrick
Christopher D King
Colonel Richard Kinsella-Bevan
David A Knight

Nicholas Lanham-Cook
Robert Law
The Hon H de B Lawson Johnston
Mrs G Leavy
D S W Lee
Dr J M Leith
John Limbocker, Jr, MFH
The Earl of Lindsay
Mrs Patricia D Lindsell

John Linsenmeyer
Brian Littlemore
J W Lockwood, MFH
G A Longbottom
Mrs J Longmore
Nicholas Luard
P M Luttman-Johnson

John Macfarlane
C L MacGregor
J H M Mackenzie
M J Mackinlay Macleod
Kenneth Macleod, DSC
Gerald MacSweeney
Conor Mahony
D C Mahony
Mrs Elizabeth Mahony
Katherine Mahony
Lucinda Mahony
MHC Mahony
Nicholas Mahony
Lady Mallalieu
Colin D Mann
R D Marshall
Andrew Martell
Charles Martyn-Hemphill
Roger Mason, LLB
P G B Maynard
John McCaig
Brian McGeough
Brigadier D S E McNeill
Michael Meacham
C J Mears
J D T Megginson
Peter Ault Meier
Ian B Michell-Young
Henry Seton Middleditch
A J B Mildmay-White
A P Millen
Mr and Mrs F K Mitchell
Dr James Molloy, MFH
Mrs S R Montagu
Arthur Montgomery
Lady Moore
W J N Moore
Olivia Mortensen

Daniel Moylan
E D Moylan
Edward Mullan
Miss Lindsay Mullan
A J Mulliner
S N Mulliner
Charles Murphy
Denis J Murphy
Frank J Murphy
Mrs R Murphy
Robert Musetti

David Nagle
Sir Philip Naylor-Leyland, Bt
Christopher Coles Newbury
Mrs M Newcomb
John Newenham
Mrs Worth Newenham
W P Worth Newenham
Brian Newton
Timothy Norton

Mrs Mervyn Orchard-Lisle
Lady Oswald
Anne O'Brien
Mrs Elaine O'Leary
Dermot J O'Meara
D J O'Meara
James M O'Neill
K P O'Reilly-Hyland

Henry Page
H M Parker
Mrs Sally Payne
Simon Peasley
Veronica and Simon Peck
Daphne Perrett
Geoffery Pieters
John Pieters
Colin M Plumbe
Peter Powell
Mrs R A Price
R A Price
Anthony Prince
Brion Purdey

J Quarmby

Michael F Race
P J Rankin
D R Read
Peter Read
Llewellyn Lloyd Rees
R S O Rees
W F Rendall
Clive Richards
H W Riddolls
Herbert J K Rieck
L Roberts
Mrs Susan Roberts, MFH
R F Roberts
D K Robertson
Mrs Hersey Robertson
A W Robinson, DFC
M R Robson
David Roche
H G C Roger
John Ronan
J F Rutherford
Declan Ryan
Kevin Ryan

R P A Sale
David Salt
Hugh Scott-Barrett
Dr Sarah Scott-Barrett
J Thomas Scrivener, MFH
J H Scrutton
Vernon Kenward Sharpington
Mary Sheahan
Sydney Sheard
Mark Sheardown
Clive Shenton, QC
N E C Sherwood
Miss M Shirley
J M Simmonds
D A L Skelton
John Kelynack Skinner
A J Skipp
Douglas A Sloan, MFH
Brian W Small
Mrs Diana Smallwood

Capt. Gordon Grenville Smith, MFH
N H Smith
J C S F Smithies
R C Smith-Ryland, MFH
Daniel Smyth
Mrs James Smyth
Dr H M Snow
Philip Snuggs
Mrs Sole
Thomas Somerville
J R Speid-Soote
Mrs P Spiller
C C E Stamford
Michael W Steele
Brigadier J W Stephens, DSO
Mrs Peggyanne Stevenson
James Stourton
Mrs R W Stratton
Mrs M E Summers
Philip Alexander Surtees
Captain Fergus Sutherland
Susan Swantek
Paul Sweeney
D R Symonds

C P C Taylor
H Thomson Jones
R W G Threlfall
B E Todd
Major E J Tonson Rye
Miss R Tonson Rye
I M Turner

Lieut Colonel D D Vigors
Captain & Mrs Anthony Villiers
Mrs A J V Villiers

Major M P Walker
Mrs Frankie Ward
The Marquis of Waterford
Ian R Watson
Mrs Jeanne Watts
R G Weaver
Norman Welch
Antonia Westendarp, MFH
Gordon S C Weston
J P G Weston
Donald Whiteley
Rev H D Wiard, MA
Gary L Wilkes, DVM
Adrienne Williams
A S R Williamson
Jim Willis
C N Wilmot-Smith
D J Wilson
Patricia Wilson
Audrey Wipper
Douglas J Wood
Thomas Edwin Woodhouse
Mrs David Wright

N W S Yonge

P J R Zisman

ACKNOWLEDGEMENTS

This book would not have been published without the help and advice of Sir Charles Pickthorn, Chairman of the R.S. Surtees Society. I am particularly grateful to him.

My sister Sophie Brem has been kind enough to take charge of all the organisation and administration in Ireland. There would have been chaos without her.

For help of various kinds I am indebted to Joanna Adair, Joseph Allen, Tessa Arnold, Gerald and Ros Ellison, Judy Jackson, Arthur Llewellyn, Colin MacGregor, Gerald MacSweeney, Tom Somerville, Jeremy Spede-Soote, James Stourton, Adrian Stroude, Eudo Tonson Rye, Valentine Villiers, Nicholas Westendarp and Geoff White.

George Sassoon has given permission for extracts from his father's works to be included in this book provided that the next time he turns up in Co. Cork someone will provide him with a mount to enjoy a 'nice little scramble over rough country' (be it horse, donkey, bicycle or whatever) with the Muskerry Hunt. Antonia Westendarp, MFH, has promised to provide whichever he prefers.

The following have given copyright permission for extracts from the works named: Quartet Books Limited for a passage from 'A Long Way to Go' by Marigold Armitage; Virago Press Ltd. for a passage from 'The Rising Tide' by M J Farrell (Molly Keane) copyright © M J Farrell 1937, Introduction copyright © Polly Devlin 1984, published by Virago Press Ltd.; The Society of Authors as the literary representative of the Estate of John Masefield for a passage from 'The Hawbucks' by John Masefield; for a passage from 'The Pursuit of Love' by Nancy Mitford, © the Estate of Nancy Mitford, permission granted by Peters, Fraser and Dunlop, author's agent; the Curtis Brown Group for two stories from 'Some Experiences of an Irish R.M.' by E Œ Somerville and Martin Ross; David Higham Associates for a passage from 'Wild Lone' by Denys Watkins-Pitchford, published by Eyre & Spottiswoode; and Major E J Tonson Rye for his own story 'Out with the Coolmore Harriers'.

While diligent efforts have been made, it has not been possible to identify the owners of all copyrights where such may exist. The Muskerry Hunt Club and the editor would welcome communications on this subject.

*Printed and bound
by
Smith Settle
Otley, West Yorkshire*

750 copies
have been made